The Mothman Prophecies

THE
MOTHMAN
PROPHECIES

JOHN A. KEEL

TOR®

A TOM DOHERTY ASSOCIATES BOOK
NEW YORK

THE MOTHMAN PROPHECIES

Copyright © 1975, 1991 by John A. Keel

www.themothmanlives.com

A Tor Book
Published by Tom Doherty Associates, LLC
175 Fifth Avenue
New York, NY 10010

www.tor.com

Tor® is a registered trademark of Tom Doherty Associates, LLC.

ISBN: 0-765-34197-2
Library of Congress Catalog Card Number: 91-73231

First Tor edition: February 2002

Printed in the United States of America

0 9 8 7 6 5 4

To Mary Hyre and the people of West Virginia.

"There was no mistake. The leathery wings, the little horns, the barbed tail—all were there. The most terrible of all legends had come to life, out of the unknown past. Yet now it stood smiling, in ebon majesty, with the sunlight gleaming upon its tremendous body, and with a human child resting trustfully on either arm."

—Arthur C. Clarke, *Childhood's End*, 1953.

Contents

THE
MOTHMAN
PROPHECIES

1:
Beelzebub Visits West Virginia

I.

Fingers of lightning tore holes in the black skies as an angry cloudburst drenched the surrealistic landscape. It was 3 A.M. on a cold, wet morning in late November 1967, and the little houses scattered along the dirt road winding through the hills of West Virginia were all dark. Some seemed unoccupied and in the final stages of decay. Others were unpainted, neglected, forlorn. The whole setting was like the opening scene of a Grade B horror film from the 1930s.

Along the road there came a stranger in a land where strangers were rare and suspect. He walked up to the door of a crumbling farmhouse and hammered. After a long moment a light blinked on somewhere in the house and a young woman appeared, drawing a cheap mail-order bathrobe tightly about her. She opened the door a crack and her sleep-swollen face winced with fear as she stared at the apparition on her doorstep. He was over six feet tall and dressed entirely in black. He wore a black suit, black tie, black hat, and black overcoat, with impractical black dress shoes covered with mud. His face, barely visible in the darkness, sported a neatly trimmed mustache and goatee. The flashes of lightning behind him added an eerie effect.

"May I use your phone?" He asked in a deep baritone, his voice lacking the familiar West Virginia accent. The girl gulped silently and backed away.

"My husband . . ." She mumbled. "Talk to my husband."

She closed the door quickly and backed away into the darkness. Minutes passed. Then she returned accompanied by a rugged young man hastily buckling his trousers in place. He, too, turned pale at the sight of the stranger.

"We ain't got a phone here," he grunted through the crack in the door just before he slammed it. The couple retreated murmuring to themselves and the tall stranger faded into the night.

Beards were a very rare sight in West Virginia in 1967. Men in formal suits and ties were even rarer in those back hills of the Ohio valley. And bearded, black-garbed strangers on foot in the rain had never been seen there before.

In the days that followed the young couple told their friends about the apparition. Obviously, they concluded, he had been a fearful omen of some sort. Perhaps he had been the devil himself!

Three weeks later these two people were dead, among the victims of the worst tragedy ever to strike that section of West Virginia. They were driving across the Silver Bridge, which spanned the Ohio River, when it suddenly collapsed.

Their friends remembered. They remembered the story of the bearded stranger in the night. It had, indeed, been a sinister omen. One that confirmed their religious beliefs and superstitions. So a new legend was born. Beelzebub had visited West Virginia on the eve of a terrible tragedy.

II.

Being a dedicated nonconformist is not easy these days. I grew my beard in 1966 while loafing for a week on the farm of my friend, zoologist Ivan T. Sanderson. I kept it until 1968 when hair became popular and half the young men in America suddenly began burying their identities in a great sea of facial hair. In those more innocent days only artists, writers, and college professors could get away with beards. People even seemed to expect it of us. Perhaps if crew cuts ever come back and beards disappear I will regrow my own. But today it would be sprinkled with gray. Too much gray, probably. Likewise, long hair was once the symbol of the superintellectual, the property of concert violinists and Einstein-type mathematicians—the ultimate squares, really.

I would prefer to believe that I did not look like the devil in my late beard. I certainly had no intention of launching new legends when my car ran off the road in West Virginia that November and I plodded from house to house searching for a telephone so I could call a tow truck. I had just come up from Atlanta, Georgia, where I had delivered a speech to a local UFO club. West Virginia was almost a second home to me in those days. I had visited the state five times, investigating a long series of very strange events, and had many friends there. One of them, Mrs. Mary Hyre, the star reporter of the Athens, Ohio, *Messenger,* was with me that night. We had been out talking to UFO witnesses, and earlier that evening we ourselves had watched a very strange light in the sky. Since there was a heavy, low cloud layer it could not have been a star. It maneuvered over the hills, its brilliant glow very familiar to both of us for we both had seen many such lights in the Ohio valley that year.

Mrs. Hyre waited in the car while I trudged through the mud and rain. We had been trying to climb a slippery hill to a spot where we had seen many unusual things in the past.

I found that the telephones in the houses closest to our location were not working, apparently knocked out by the storm. So I had to keep walking until I finally found a house with a working phone. The owner refused to open his door so we shouted back and forth. I gave him a phone number to call. He obliged and went back to bed. I never knew what he looked like.

My point, of course, is that Beelzebub was not wandering along the back roads of West Virginia that night. It was just a very tired John Keel busy catching a whale of a cold. But from the view of the people who lived on that road, something very unusual had happened. They had never before been roused in the middle of the night by a tall bearded stranger in black. They knew nothing about me or the reasons for my presence so they were forced to speculate. Even speculation was difficult. They could only place me in the frame of reference they knew best—the religious. Bearded men in city dress simply did not turn up on isolated back roads in the middle of the night. In fact, they didn't even turn up on the main streets of Ohio valley towns in broad daylight! So a perfectly normal event (normal, that is, to me) was placed in an entirely different context by the witnesses. The final proof of my supernatural origin came three weeks later when two of the people I had awakened were killed in the bridge tragedy. Some future investigator of the paranormal may wander into those hills someday, talk with these people, and write a whole chapter of a learned book on demonology repeating this piece of folklore. Other scholars will pick up and repeat his story in their books and articles. The presence of the devil in West Virginia in November 1967 will become a historical fact, backed by the testimony of several witnesses.

Those of us who somewhat sheepishly spend our time chasing dinosaurs, sea serpents, and little green men in space suits are painfully aware that things often are not what they seem; that sincere eyewitnesses can—and do—grossly misinterpret what they have seen; that many extraordinary events can have disappointingly mundane explanations. For every report I have published in my articles and books, I have shelved maybe fifty others because they had a possible explanation, or because I detected problematical details in the witness's story, which cast doubt on the validity of a paranormal explanation. On the other hand, I have come across many events which seemed perfectly normal in one context but which were actually most unusual when compared with similar events. That is, some apparent coincidences cease to be coincidental when you realize they have been repeated again and again in many parts of the world. Collect enough of these coincidences together and you have a whole tapestry of the paranormal.

As we progress, you will see that many seemingly straightforward accounts of monster sightings and UFO landings can be explained by irritatingly complex medical and psychological theories. In some cases, the theories will seem more unbelievable than the original events. Please bear in mind that the summaries published here are backed by years of study and experience. I am no longer particularly interested in the manifestations of the phenomenon. I am pursuing the source of the phenomenon itself. To do this, I have objectively divorced myself from all the popular frames of reference. I am not concerned with beliefs but with the cosmic mechanism which has generated and perpetuated those beliefs.

III.

There is an old house on a tree-lined street in New York's Greenwich Village which harbors a strange ghost. Hans Holzer and other ghost-chasers have included the house in their catalogs of haunted places. The phantom has been seen by several people in recent years. It is dressed in a long black cape and wears a wide-brimmed slouch hat pulled down over its eyes as it slinks from room to room. Self-styled parapsychologists have woven all kinds of fantasies around this apparition. Obviously a spy from the revolutionary war was caught and killed in the old house.

But wait. This ghost may not be a member of the restless dead at all. There were never any reports of hauntings there until about twenty years ago, after the house was vacated by a writer named Walter Gibson. He was, and is, an extraordinarily prolific author. For many years he churned out a full-length novel each month, and many of those novels were written in the house in Greenwich Village. All of them were centered around the spectacularly successful character Gibson created in the 1930s, that nemesis of evil known as The Shadow. If you have read any of The Shadow novels you know that he was fond of lurking in dark alleys dressed in a cape and broad-brimmed slouch hat.

Why would a Shadow-like apparition suddenly appear in an old house? Could it be some kind of residue from Walter Gibson's very powerful mind? We do know that some people can move objects, even bend spoons and keys, with the power of their minds alone. Mental telepathy is now a tested and verified phenomenon. And about 10 percent of the population have the ability to see above and beyond the narrow spectrum of visible light. They can see radiations and even objects invisible to the rest of us. A very large part of the UFO lore is, in fact, based upon the observations of such people. What seems normal to them seems abnormal, even ridiculous, to the rest of us. People who see ghosts or the wandering Shadow have these abilities. They are peering at forms that are always there, always present around us like radio waves, and when certain conditions exist they can see these things. The Tibetans believe that advanced human minds can manipulate these invisible energies into visible forms called *tulpas*, or thought projections. Did Walter

Gibson's intense concentration on his Shadow novels inadvertently bring a *tulpa* into existence?

Readers of occult literature know there are innumerable cases of ghosts haunting a particular site year after year, century after century, carrying out the same mindless activities endlessly. Build a house on such a site and the ghost will leave locked doors ajar as it marches through to carry out its programed activity. Could these ghosts really be *tulpas,* residues of powerful minds like the phantom in the broad-brimmed hat?

Next, consider this. UFO activity is concentrated in the same areas year after year. In the Ohio valley, they show a penchant for the ancient Indian mounds which stand throughout the area. Could some UFOs be mere *tulpas* created by a long forgotten people and doomed forever to senseless maneuvers in the night skies?

There are archaeological sites in the Mississippi valley which have been dated to 8,000 years ago . . . long before the Indians are supposed to have arrived. Some of the Indian mounds (there are hundreds of them scattered throughout North America) are laid out and constructed with the same kind of mathematical precision found in the pyramids of Egypt. While it is known that the Indians were still adding to some of the mounds in the south when the Europeans first arrived, other mounds seem to be considerably older. Some are built in the form of elephants. What did the builders use for a model? Others are in the shape of sea serpents. These forms can only be seen from the air. To plan and build such mountains of shaped earth required technical skills beyond the simple nomadic woods Indians.

Currently there is a revival in diffusionism, a popular scientific concept of the 1920s which asserted that many of the puzzling artifacts and ancient constructions found throughout the world were the products of a single world-wide culture. The cult of believers in Atlantis were the principal advocates of this idea, so sober scientists naturally turned away from it for a theory that is almost impossible to support. This was the notion that many inventions and ideas simply occurred simultaneously to widespread, isolated cultures.

The flying saucer entities have allegedly contacted many people in almost every country and have immodestly claimed credit for everything from the building of the pyramids to the sinking of Atlantis. Erich Von Däniken, a Swiss author, has popularized the concept that members of an extraterrestrial civilization did contact early earthlings, basing his theories on expansive misinterpretations—and in several instances, deliberate misrepresentations—of archaeological curiosities. Von Däniken seems to be totally ignorant of the work of European scholars such as Brinsley Trench, Paul Misraki, and W. Raymond Drake, who have examined the same curiosities very carefully in the past ten years and developed elaborate philosophical hypotheses about the intrusion and effect of alien beings on mankind since the beginning. Their concepts are wider in scope and significance, and far better documented than Von Däniken's simplistic efforts.

That unidentified flying objects have been present since the dawn of man is an undeniable fact. They are not only described repeatedly in the Bible, but were also the subject of cave paintings made thousands of years before the Bible was written. And a strange procession of weird entities and frightening creatures have been with us just as long. When you review the ancient references you are obliged to conclude that the presence of these objects and beings *is a normal condition for this planet.* These things, these other intelligencies or OINTs as Ivan Sanderson labeled them, either reside here but somehow remain concealed from us, or they do not exist at all and are actually special aberrations of the human mind—*tulpas,* hallucinations, psychological constructs, momentary materializations of energy from that dimension beyond the reach of our senses and even beyond the reaches of our scientific instruments. They are not from outer space. There is no need for them to be. They have always been here. Perhaps they were here long before we started bashing each other over the head with clubs. If so, they will undoubtedly still be here long after we have incinerated our cities, polluted all the waters, and rendered the very atmosphere unbreathable. Of course, their lives—if they have lives in the usual sense—will be much duller after we have gone. But if they wait around long enough another form of so-called intelligent life will crawl out from under a rock and they can begin their games again.

IV.

Back in the 1920s, Charles Fort, the first writer to explore inexplicable events, observed you can measure a circle by beginning anywhere. Paranormal phenomena are so widespread, so diversified, and so sporadic yet so persistent that separating and studying any single element is not only a waste of time but also will automatically lead to the development of belief. Once you have established a belief, the phenomenon adjusts its manifestations to support that belief and thereby escalate it. If you believe in the devil he will surely come striding down your road one rainy night and ask to use your phone. If you believe that flying saucers are astronauts from another planet they will begin landing and collecting rocks from your garden.

Many—most—of the manifestations accompanying the UFO phenomenon simply did not fit into the enthusiasts' concept of how a superior intelligence from another galaxy would behave. So the flying saucer clubs carefully ignored, even suppressed, the details of those manifestations for many years. When a black-suited man in a Cadillac turned up, he couldn't possibly be one of the endearing space people so he had to be a rotten, sneaky government agent. It was inconceivable to the hardcore UFO believers that the flying saucers could be a permanent part of our environment and that these men in black were residents of this planet associated with the UFOs.

But this is a fact; the "truth" the UFO fans have sought for so long. And as Daniel Webster put it, "There is nothing so powerful as truth, and often nothing so strange."

You can't learn the truth by chasing UFOs helter-skelter through the skies in planes. The air forces of several governments tried that for years. It is vain to hire astronomers. They are not trained in the kind of disciplines needed to investigate earthly phenomena, or even to interview earthly witnesses. Interviewing is an advanced art, the province of journalists and psychologists. One does not hire a parachutist to go spelunking in a cave or a balloonist to go diving for treasure. If you need a brain surgeon you don't hire a horticulturist who has spent his life trimming plants. Yet this is the approach our government has taken to the UFO phenomenon.

I realized the folly of trying to measure the circle from some distant point, so I picked a microcosm on the edge of the circle—a place where many strange manifestations were occurring simultaneously. And I hit the jackpot immediately, rather like the opening of an old Max Schulman novel: "Bang! Bang! Bang! Bang! Four shots ripped into my groin and I was off on the greatest adventure of my life."

2:
The Creep
Who Came in
from the Cold

I.

Friday, December 22, 1967, was bitter cold and the frayed
Christmas decorations strung across the main street of the
little West Virginian town of Point Pleasant seemed to hang
limply, sadly, as if to match the grim, ashen faces of the
townspeople who shuffled about their business, their eyes
averted from the gaping hole where the Silver Bridge had
stood only a week before. Now the seven-hundred-foot span
was gone. Clusters of workmen, police officers, and assorted
officials stood along the banks of the Ohio, watching silently
as divers continued to bob into the black waters. Occasionally ropes would jerk and a bloated, whitened body would be
hauled to the surface. It was not going to be a merry Christmas in Point Pleasant.

A few yards from the place where the bridge had been,
Mrs. Mary Hyre sat in her office revising a list of the missing
and the known dead. A stout woman in her early fifties, her
normally cheerful, alert face was blurred with fatigue. She

had had almost no sleep in the past seven days. After twenty years as the local stringer for the *Messenger*, recording all the births, marriages, and deaths in the little town, Mrs. Hyre suddenly found herself at the center of the universe. Camera teams from as far away as New York were perched outside her door. The swarms of newsmen who had descended on Point Pleasant to record the tragedy had quickly learned what everyone in the Ohio valley already knew. If you wanted to find out anything about the area and its people, the quickest way to do it was to "ask Mary Hyre."

For seven days now her office had been filled with strangers, relatives of the missing, and weary rescue workers. So she hardly looked up that afternoon when two men entered. They seemed almost like twins, she recalled later. Both were short and wore black overcoats. Their complexions were dark, somewhat Oriental, she thought.

"We hear there's been a lot of flying saucer activity around here," one of them remarked. She was taken aback. The bridge disaster had dominated everyone's thoughts for the last week. Flying saucers were the furthest thing from her mind at that moment.

"We have had quite a few sightings here," she responded, turning in her chair to pull open a filing cabinet. She hauled out a bulging folder filled with clippings of sighting reports and handed it to one of the men.

He flipped it open, gave the pile of clippings a cursory glance, and handed it back.

"Has anyone told you not to publish these reports?"

She shook her head as she shoved the folder back into the drawer.

"What would you do if someone did order you to stop writing about flying saucers?"

"I'd tell them to go to hell," she smiled wanly.

The two men glanced at each other. She went back to her lists and when she looked up again they were gone.

II.

Later that same afternoon another stranger walked into Mrs. Hyre's office. He was slightly built, about five feet seven inches tall, with black, piercing eyes and unruly black hair, as if he had had a brush cut and it was just growing back in. His complexion was even darker than that of the two previous visitors and he looked like a Korean or Oriental of some kind. His hands were especially unusual, she thought, with unduly long, tapering fingers. He wore a cheap-looking, ill-fitting black suit, slightly out of fashion, and his tie was knotted in an odd old-fashioned way. Strangely, he was not wearing an overcoat despite the fierce cold outside.

"My name is Jack Brown," he announced in a hesitant manner. "I'm a UFO researcher."

"Oh," Mary pushed aside the pile of papers on her desk and studied him. The day was ending and she was ready to go home and try to get some sleep at last.

After a brief, almost incoherent struggle to discuss UFO sightings Brown stammered, "What—would—what would you do—if someone ordered—ordered you to stop? To stop printing UFO stories?"

"Say, are you with those two men who were here earlier?" she asked, surprised to hear the same weird question twice in one day.

"No. No—I'm alone. I'm a friend of Gray—Gray Barker."

Gray Barker of Clarksburg was West Virginia's best-known UFO investigator. He had published a number of books on the subject and was a frequent visitor to Point Pleasant.

"Do you know John Keel?"

His face tightened. "I—I used to think—think the world of K—K—Keel. Then a few minutes ago I bought a—a magazine. He has an article in it. He says he's seen UFOs himself. He's—he's a liar."

"I *know* he's seen things," Mary flared. "I've been with him when he saw them!"

Brown smiled weakly at the success of his simple gambit.

"Could you—take me out—t—t—take me where you—you and K—K—Keel saw—saw things?"

"I'm not going to do anything except go home to bed," Mary declared flatly.

"Is K—K—Keel in P—P—Point Pleasant?"

"No. He lives in New York."

"I—I think he m—m—makes up all these stories."

"Look, I can give you the names of some of the people here who have seen things," Mary said wearily. "You can talk to them and decide for yourself. But I just can't escort you around."

"I'm a friend of G—G—Gray Barker," he repeated lamely.

Outside the office a massive crane creaked and rumbled, dragging a huge hunk of twisted steel out of the river.

III.

On April 22, 1897, an oblong machine with wings and lights "which appeared much brighter than electric lights" dropped out of the sky and landed on the farm near Rockland, Texas, owned by John M. Barclay. Barclay grabbed his rifle and headed for the machine. He was met by an ordinary-looking man who handed him a ten-dollar bill and asked him to buy some oil and tools for the aircraft.

"Who are you?" Barclay asked.

"Never mind about my name; call it Smith," the man answered.

The UFO lore is populated with mysterious visitors claiming inordinately common names like Smith, Jones, Kelly, Allen, and Brown. In 1897, they often claimed to come from known villages and cities and were even able to name prominent citizens in those places. But when reporters checked, they could find no record of the visitors and the named citizens disavowed any knowledge of them.

One of the proved hoaxes of 1897 (there were many hoaxes, largely the work of mischievous newspapermen) concerned an object which is supposed to have crashed into Judge Proctor's windmill in Aurora, Texas. The remains of a tiny pilot were supposedly found in the wreckage and buried in the local cemetery by the townspeople. The story was published in the *Dallas Evening News*. From time to time, Aurora was visited by self-styled investigators who sifted the dirt on the old Proctor farm and marched through the cemetery reading tombstones, always without finding anything.

The story was revived in 1972, and in 1973 a man identifying himself as Frank N. Kelley of Corpus Christi arrived in Aurora. He said he was a treasure hunter of long experience. He set to work with his metal detectors and instruments and quickly unearthed several fragments of metal near the windmill site. They appeared to be something like the skin of modern aircraft, he announced. He kept some of the pieces and turned the rest over to a reporter named Bill Case. Analysis showed the pieces were 98 percent aluminum.

Kelley's alleged discovery created a stampede to Aurora. UFO investigators descended from as far away as Illinois and battled for permission to dig up graves in the cemetery. The story received wide play in the national press in the summer of 1973.

When efforts were made to find Frank Kelley in Corpus Christi it was found that he had given a phony address and phone number, and that no one in treasure-hunting circles had ever heard of him. Mr. Kelley was apparently another one of the impressive but elusive hoaxsters who haunt the UFO field. The joke was pointless, expensive, and, sadly, very successful.

IV.

The moment I met Mrs. Hyre's niece Connie Carpenter in 1966, I knew she was telling the truth because her eyes were reddened, watery, and almost swollen shut. I had seen these symptoms many times in my treks around the country investigating UFO reports. Witnesses who were unlucky enough to have a close encounter with an unidentified flying object, usually a dazzlingly brilliant aerial light, are exposed to actinic rays . . . ultraviolet rays . . . which can cause "eyeburn," medically known as *klieg conjunctivitis.* These are the same kind of rays that tan your hide at the beach. If you lay in the bright sun without protecting your eyes you can get conjunctivitis. Whatever they are, UFOs radiate intense actinic rays. There are now thousands of cases in which the witnesses suffered eyeburns and temporary eye damage . . . even temporary blindness . . . after viewing a strange flying light in the night sky.

One of the more extreme cases of UFO blindness occurred on the night of Wednesday, October 3, 1973 in southeastern Missouri. Eddie Webb, forty-five, of Greenville, saw a luminous object in his rear-view mirror. He put his head out the window of his truck and looked back. There was a bright white flash. Webb threw his hands to his face, crying, "Oh, my God! I'm burned! I can't see!" One lens had fallen from his glasses and the frames were melted. His wife took over the wheel of their vehicle and drove him to a hospital. Fortunately, the damage was not permanent.

What puzzled me about Connie's case, however, was that she had not seen a splendid luminous flying saucer. She had seen a giant "winged man" in broad daylight.

According to her story, Connie, a shy, sensitive eighteen-year-old, was driving home from church at 10:30 A.M. on Sunday, November 27, 1966, when, as she passed the deserted greens of the Mason County Golf Course outside of New Haven, West Virginia, she suddenly saw a huge gray figure. It was shaped like a man, she said, but was much larger. It was at least seven feet tall and very broad. The thing that attracted her attention was not its size but its eyes. It had, she said, large, round, fiercely glowing red eyes that focused on her with hypnotic effect.

"It's a wonder I didn't run off the road and have a wreck," she commented later.

As she slowed, her eyes fixed on the apparition, a pair of wings unfolded from its back. They seemed to have a span of about ten feet. It was definitely not an ordinary bird but a man-shaped thing which rose slowly off the ground, straight up like a helicopter, silently. Its wings did not flap in flight. It headed straight toward Connie's car, its horrible eyes fixed to her face, then it swooped low over her head as she shoved the accelerator to the floorboards in utter hysteria.

Over one hundred people would see this bizarre creature that winter.

Connie's conjunctivitis lasted over two weeks, apparently caused by those glowing red eyes. At the time of my first visit to Point Pleasant in 1966 I did not relate the winged weirdo to flying saucers. Later events not only proved that a relationship existed, but that relationship also is a vital clue to the whole mystery.

V.

Max's Kansas City is a famous watering hole for New York's hip crowd. In the summer of 1967 an oddball character wandered into that restaurant noted for its oddball clientele. He was tall and awkward, dressed in an ill-fitting black suit that seemed out of style. His chin came to a sharp point and his eyes bulged slightly like "thyroid eyes." He sat down in a booth and gestured to the waitress with his long, tapering fingers.

"Something to eat," he mumbled. The waitress handed him a menu. He stared at it uncomprehendingly, apparently unable to read. "Food," he said almost pleadingly.

"How about a steak?" she offered.

"Good."

She brought him a steak with all the trimmings. He stared at it for a long moment and then picked up his knife and fork, glancing around at the other diners. It was obvious he did not know how to handle the implements! The waitress watched him as he fumbled helplessly. Finally she showed him how to cut the steak and spear it with the fork. He sawed away at the meat. Clearly he really was hungry.

"Where are you from?" She asked gently.

"Not from here."

"Where?"

"Another world."

Boy, another put-on artist, she thought to herself. The other waitresses gathered in a corner and watched him as he fumbled with his food, a stranger in a strange land.

VI.

A large white car with a faulty muffler wheezed and rattled up the back street in New Haven, West Virginia, where Connie Carpenter lived, and Jack Brown knocked at her door.

"I'm a—a friend of Mary Hyre's."

His strange demeanor and disjointed questions distressed her and disturbed her husband, Keith, and her brother Larry. It quickly became obvious that he was not particularly interested in Connie's sighting of the man-bird the year before. He seemed mainly concerned with Mrs. Hyre and my own relationship with her (we were professional friends, nothing more).

"What do you think—if—what would Mary Hyre do—

if someone told her to stop writing about UFOs?" he asked.

"She'd probably tell them to drop dead," Connie replied.

Most of his questions were stupid, even unintelligible. After a rambling conversation he drove off into the night in his noisy car. Connie called her aunt immediately, puzzled and upset by the visit. He was such a very odd man, she noted, and he wouldn't speak at all if you weren't looking directly into his dark, hypnotic eyes. Connie, Keith and Larry not only noticed his long-fingered hands, but there was also something very peculiar about his ears. They couldn't say exactly what. But there was something. . . .

VII.

"Did you ever hear of anyone—especially an air force officer —trying to *drink* Jello?" Mrs. Ralph Butler of Owatonna, Minnesota, asked. "Well, that's what he did. He acted like he had never seen any before. He picked up the bowl and tried to drink it. I had to show him how to eat it with a spoon."

Mrs. Butler was describing the man who had visited her in May 1967, following a flurry of UFO sightings in Owatonna. He said he was Major Richard French of the U.S. Air Force although he was dressed in civilian clothes and was driving a white Mustang. His neat gray suit and everything else he was wearing appeared to be brand-new. Even the soles of his shoes were unscuffed, unwalked upon. He was about five feet nine inches tall, with an olive complexion and a pointed face. His hair was dark and very long—too long for an air force officer, Mrs. Butler thought. Unlike Jack Brown, Major French was a fluent conversationalist and seemed perfectly normal until he complained about his stomach bothering him. When Mrs. Butler offered him the Jello she suspected for the first time that something was out of kilter.

Richard French was an imposter. One of the many wandering around the United States in 1967. For years these characters had caused acute paranoia among the flying saucer enthusiasts, convincing them that the air force was investigating them, silencing witnesses and indulging in all kinds of unsavory activities—including murder. When I first began collecting such reports I was naturally suspicious of the people making such reports. It all seemed like a massive put-on. But gradually it became apparent that the same minute details were turning up in widely separated cases, and none of these details had been published anywhere . . . not even in the little newsletters of the UFO cultists.

There was somebody out there, all right. A few, like Richard French, almost pulled off their capers without drawing attention to themselves. But in nearly every case there was always some small error, some slip of dress or behavior which the witnesses were usually willing to overlook but which stood out like signal flares to me. They often arrived in old model cars which were as shiny and well kept as brand-new vehicles. Sometimes they slipped up in their dress, wearing clothes that were out of fashion or, even more perturbing, would not come into fashion until years later. Those who posed as military officers obviously had no knowledge of military procedure or basic military jargon. If they had occasion to pull out a wallet or notebook, it would be brand-new . . . although most men carry beat-up old wallets and notebooks quickly gain a worn look. Finally, like the fairies of old, they often collected souvenirs from the witnesses . . . delightedly walking away with an old magazine, pen, or other small expendable object.

What troubled me most was the fact that these mystery men and women often matched the descriptions given to me by contactees who claimed to have seen a UFO land and had glimpsed, or conversed with, their pilots; pilots with either pointed features or Oriental countenances, dusky skin (not Negroid), and unusually long fingers.

VIII.

Linda Scarberry came home from the hospital on December 23, 1967, bringing with her Daniella Lia Scarberry, her brand-new daughter. She and her husband, Roger, lived in the basement apartment in the home of her parents, Mr. and Mrs. Parke McDaniel. It was a modest but comfortable home and, like Mary Hyre's office, had been a focal point for strangers ever since Linda, Roger, and another couple had seen the "Bird"—the preposterous winged man of Point Pleasant—the year before.

Now there was a steady flow of friends and neighbors stopping by to look at the new baby, one of the few joyous occasions that bleak December. When Jack Brown's noisy white car pulled into the McDaniel driveway he was welcomed as so many reporters, monster hunters, and UFO researchers had been before him. He announced himself as a friend of Mary Hyre, Gray Barker, and John Keel and entered the house hauling a large tape recorder which he set up on a kitchen table. It became immediately obvious that he was unfamiliar with the machine and didn't know how to thread or operate it.

The McDaniel family was used to reporters and tape recorders, and answering the same tiresome questions. But Brown's questions were not just tiresome. They were vague, detached, and unintelligent. He obviously knew nothing whatsoever about the complex subject of flying saucers, and he was totally disinterested in the legendary "Bird." His main interest seemed to be me—my present whereabouts and the nature of my relationship with Mrs. Hyre.

Not surprisingly, he asked the McDaniels how they thought Mary Hyre would react if someone ordered her to stop reporting flying saucer sightings.

Friends and neighbors dropped by all evening to view the new baby. Although the baby was the center of all attention, Brown totally ignored the child, not even bothering to show polite interest. When Tom C., a next door neighbor, was introduced Brown extended his thumb and two forefingers for a handshake. He said he was from Cambridge, Ohio, a small town just outside of Columbus, Ohio. Later a reporter for the Columbus, Ohio, *Dispatch* arrived and in the course of their casual conversation it became apparent that Brown had never heard of the *Dispatch*, one of the state's largest newspapers, and, in fact, did not even know where Cambridge was.

His general demeanor made everyone uncomfortable. His inability to converse intelligently and his hypnotic, piercing gaze bothered everyone. Despite the growing coolness, he lingered for five hours, leaving about 11 P.M. Early in the evening he denied knowing me personally. Later on he said he and I were good friends. He seemed surprised that I had not rushed back to Point Pleasant after the bridge disaster. Perhaps he expected to find me there.

Among other things, he said Gray Barker had told him that a UFO had been seen over the Silver Bridge just before it collapsed. Later when I spoke to Barker about this incident he denied emphatically knowing Brown or anyone matching his description. Gray had phoned me the night of the disaster and mentioned hearing a radio interview in which a witness reported seeing a flash of light just before the bridge went down. Afterward it became clear that this was a flash caused by snapping power cables strung along the bridge.

Jack Brown was never seen again. He did not turn up in other UFO flap areas. He just got into his white car and rattled off into the night, joining all the other Smiths, Joneses, Kelleys, and Frenches who seem to serve no purpose except to excite the latent paranoia of the UFO enthusiasts and keep one set of myths alive.

IX.

In room 4C922 of the Pentagon building in 1966 there was an L-shaped cubicle occupying about fifty square feet of area. A gray-haired, grim-visaged lieutenant colonel named Maston M. Jacks held forth there, sitting behind a cluttered desk and jangling phones. His job in those days was to handle reporters inquiring about the UFO situation. His opening line was a show-stopper.

"There's nothing to it, Mr. Keel. It's all a lot of hearsay."

On another desk there was a large red folder with the words *Top Secret* emblazoned in big black letters. While we talked, a secretary entered and put a newspaper clipping into the folder.

My first conversation with Lieutenant Colonel Jacks quickly turned into an argument. He parroted the well-known air force anti-UFO line and I explained gently that I had seen some of the damned things myself. At one point he pulled himself up and glared at me.

"Are you calling an officer in the U.S. Air Force a liar?"

Later on the phone rang and from his inflection it was obvious he was talking to a superior officer. I discreetly strolled to the far end of the room and stared out the tiny, prisonlike window. He mumbled something about some movie film and then in a very low voice he added, "I'll have to call you back. There's somebody here in my office that I've got to stop."

After he hung up we resumed our argument. He had clearly gone through this many times before. It was all an act. His moods changed abruptly from rage to politeness to chumminess. Finally he escorted me down the hall to a library and dumped me.

Jacks told me several times that the air force did not have any kind of a UFO photo file. A year later, however, a science writer named Lloyd Mallan was given over one hundred pictures from that nonexistent file. Jacks also informed me that no UFO reports were stored in the Pentagon. They were all at Wright-Patterson Air Force Base in Ohio. I didn't visit Wright-Patterson but Mort Young of the now-defunct New York *Journal-American* did. I asked Mort to write his experience for this book.

"Records of UFO reports, I was told at the Pentagon, are all kept at Wright-Patterson Air Force Base in Dayton, Ohio," Mort explains.

> So I went to Dayton. There I was told that UFO reports are filed at the Pentagon, and I could have seen them in Washington. I later learned that not only are UFO reports filed at the Pentagon and at Project Blue Book headquarters in Dayton, but are also forwarded to at least two other addresses where, presumably, they are also filed. One might hope that at these other places, the files are in better order than at Blue Book, where individual sightings are incomplete. Files I asked for were either handed to me with pages missing, entire parts missing, or the file itself was missing: the air force having "no information" on the sighting in question. Some files were in disreputable state: page upon page jammed into brown folders. The information that was there would have to be sorted chronologically, at least, before one could sit down, read it through and come out the wiser. I would rather try to explain a UFO than make sense out of an air force UFO report.

Some of the allegations of the UFO believers had merit. The air force was struggling to keep the issues confused. They did lie, and on occasion they lied outrageously, to reporters. Photographs sent to them by well-meaning citizens often disappeared forever into the maw at Wright-Patterson.

But from my own investigations I could not honestly accuse them of having a wing of Oriental officers whose assignment was to squelch witnesses. Other writers such as

Lloyd Mallan were reaching similar conclusions. By 1967, Lieutenant Colonel Jacks had retired and been replaced by Lt. Col. George P. Freeman. Freeman was a kinder, more tactful soul and gave our reports serious consideration. On February 15, 1967, a confidential letter went out from the Pentagon to all commands.

> Information has reached headquarters USAF that persons claiming to represent the air force or other defense establishments have contacted citizens who have sighted unidentified flying objects. In one reported case, an individual in civilian clothes, who represented himself as a member of NORAD, demanded and received photos belonging to a private citizen. In another, a person in an air force uniform approached local police and other citizens who had sighted a UFO, assembled them in a schoolroom and told them that they did not see what they thought they saw and that they should not talk to anyone about the sighting. All military and civilian personnel and particularly information officers and UFO investigating officers who hear of such reports should immediately notify their local OSI [Office of Special Investigations] offices.
>
> (Signed)
> Hewitt T. Wheless, Lt. Gen. USAF
> Asst. Vice Chief of Staff

Project Blue Book was formally shut down in December 1969. But the "Men in Black" have not retired. They were busy again in the wake of the October 1973 UFO wave. And in January 1974 they even appeared in Sweden, using the same tactics that were so effective here. Even the gasoline shortage failed to deter those black Cadillacs from their mysterious rounds.

3:

The Flutter of Black Wings

I.

Another kind of Man in Black haunted Brooklyn, New York, in 1877–80. He had wings and performed aerial acrobatics over the heads of the crowds of sunbathers at Coney Island. A Mr. W. H. Smith first reported these strange flights in a letter to the *New York Sun*, September 18, 1877. The creature was not a bird, but "a winged human form."

This flying man became a local sensation and, according to the *New York Times*, September 12, 1880, "many reputable persons" saw him as he was "engaged in flying toward New Jersey." He maneuvered at an altitude of about one thousand feet, sporting "bat's wings" and making swimminglike movements. Witnesses claimed to have seen his face clearly. He "wore a cruel and determined expression." The entire figure was black, standing out sharply against the clear blue sky. Since he wasn't towing an advertising sign behind him, and since the primitive gliders of experimenters during that period rarely traveled far, and then usually downhill, the incidents are without explanation.

Leonardo da Vinci studied the flights of birds in the fifteenth century and tried to build a man-powered ornithopter without success. Thousands of other basement inventors have worked on the idea since, constructing canvas wings that were moved by the muscles of the optimistic pilots. Most of these weird-looking machines became instant junk on their first test flights. And several overconfident types went crashing to their deaths when they leaped off cliffs and high buildings in their homemade wings. It was not until May 2, 1962, that a man really succeeded in flying under his own power. Mr. John C. Wimpenny flew 993 yards at an altitude of five feet in a contraption with rigid wings and a pedal-driven propeller at Hatfield, Hertfordshire, in England.

The principle of the ornithopter—propulsion through the birdlike movement of wings—has been known for centuries but no one has been able to make it work. No human, that is. Machines flying through the air with moving wings have frequently been sighted during UFO waves. But the UFO enthusiasts tend to ignore any reports which describe things other than disks or cigar-shaped objects.

In 1905 "a titanic white bird" fluttered around California. One witness, J. A. Jackson, "a well-known resident of Silshee," was paying a visit to his outhouse at 1:30 A.M. on August 2 when he saw a brilliant light in the sky. It seemed to be attached to a seventy-foot "airship" with wings. "The mysterious machine appeared to be propelled by the wings alone and rose and fell as the wings flapped like a gigantic bird," the Brawley, California, *News* reported, August 4, 1905. Others in the area reported seeing the same thing.

Winged beings are an essential part of the folklore of every culture. From the times of Babylonia and the Pharaohs, sculptors were preoccupied with putting wings on lions and unidentifiable beasts. Although the angels of biblical times were never described as being winged, painters and sculptors have always persisted in giving them feathered appendages. (Actually, the old-time angels appeared like ordinary human beings. They even had supper with Lot.) When demons overran the planet during the Dark Ages they were also recorded as monstrous entities with bats' wings.

Remote areas of the world are still said to be inhabited by harpies and winged humans. On July 11, 1908, the famous Russian traveler V. K. Arsenyev was trekking along the Gobilli River when he had this encounter:*

> . . . I saw the mark on the path that was very similar to a man's footprint. My dog Alpha bristled up, snarled and then something rushed about nearby trampling among the bushes. However, it didn't go away, but stopped nearby, standing stock-still. We had been standing like that for some minutes . . . then I stooped, picked up a stone and threw it towards the unknown animal. Then something happened that was quite unexpected: I heard the beating of wings. Something large and dark emerged from the fog and flew over the river. A moment later it disappeared into the dense mist. My dog, badly frightened, pressed itself to my feet.
>
> After supper I told the Udehe-men about this incident. They broke into a vivid story about a man who could fly in the air. Hunters often saw his tracks, tracks that appeared suddenly and vanished suddenly, in such a way that they could only be possible if the "man" alighted on the ground, then took off again into the air.

In Mexico there are stories of the *ikals*, tiny black men endowed with the power of flight who live in caves and kidnap humans. In India the giant bird known as the

Yuri B. Petrenko, "Forerunner of the Flying 'Lady' of Vietnam?" *Flying Saucer Review*, vol. 19, no. 2 (March-April 1973): 29–30.

Garuda is an important part of the mythology. The gods Vishnu and Krishna traveled around the heavens on the back of a great Garuda. North American Indians have extensive legends about the Thunderbird, a huge bird said to carry off children and old people. It was accompanied by loud noises, hums, buzzes and, apparently, rumbles from the infrasonic and ultrasonic levels. Known as *Piasa* to the Indians of the Dakotas, it was supposed to have terrifying red eyes and a long tail.

We are dealing with three types of phenomena in these cases. The first is the winged man; the second is a giant bird, so huge it is a biological impossibility; third, we have a monstrous demon with red eyes, bat's wings, and a body closely human in form. All three are probably interrelated.

Research is still fragmentary but there is journalistic evidence that the winged man of 1880 was not confined to Coney Island. His activities there were just a publicity gambit, attracting the notice of the staid *New York Times* and thus attaining a measure of respectability so that when anyone anywhere else saw him they had a frame of reference.

According to the Louisville, Kentucky, *Courier-Journal*, July 29, 1880, the winged man was busy in that area. Two men, C. A. Youngman and Bob Flexner, reported seeing "a man surrounded by machinery which he seemed to be working with his hands." He had wings or fans on his back which he was flapping rather desperately to keep aloft. The startled men watched him flutter unsteadily out of view.

But he would be back.

II.

A year before the first flying saucer "scare" erupted in the state of Washington in 1947, a group of sixteen people in San Diego, California, witnessed a strange phenomenon. They were gathered on a rooftop to watch a meteor shower on the night of October 9, 1946, when a bluish-white winged object appeared in the sky. It looked like an extremely long airplane carrying two reddish lights and it left a luminous contrail.

"The strange object was certainly no airplane," one witness told Harold T. Wilkins.[1] "The wings, which moved, were too wide for any bird. Indeed, they were rather like the wings of a butterfly. The whole object emitted a red glow."

The object was especially conspicuous as it crossed the face of the moon. Some of the witnesses thought it resembled a gigantic bat.

Astronomers have also reported similar objects. In *Popular Astronomy*, 1912, Dr. F. B. Harris stated: "In the evening of January 27, 1912, I saw an intensely black object, like a crow, poised upon the moon. I estimated it at 250 miles long by 50 miles wide. I cannot but think that a very interesting phenomenon happened."

In that crazy year 1880, an Italian astronomer named Ricco, of the observatory at Palermo, Sicily, was studying the sun at 8 A.M., November 30, when he saw "winged bodies in two long parallel lines slowly traveling, apparently across the disk of the sun. They looked like large birds or cranes."

Cranes on the sun? Crows 250 miles long on the moon? Black-garbed men swimming through the skies over Coney Island? Ornithopters over Kentucky and San Diego?

On December 30, 1946, Ella Young, an American writer, saw one of our bats at dusk near Morrow Bay, California. "On the golden sky it looked very black," she reported. "It came forward head on, and had a batlike appearance, owing to the curvature of its wings. I am not sure if there were motions at the extreme tip of the wings; but the strange machine seemed to stand still for several minutes, and its

[1] Harold T. Wilkins, *Flying Saucers on the Attack* (New York: Citadel Press, 1954), chapter III.

form was very distinct. Suddenly, it either lowered itself toward the horizon, or the bank of cloud-mist made an upward movement—maybe, both movements occurred—for the machine passed behind the cloud and did not reappear. Immediately afterward, a great flush of color spread over the sea."

May through August 1947 saw the first modern UFO wave in the United States. Odd lights, glistening circular machines, and reddish flying cigars captured the American imagination. Tiffany Thayer, the eccentric novelist and founder of the Fortean Society, named after Charles Fort, chortled over the air force explanations in the society's journal, *Doubt.* Obviously the government was determined to cover up the true facts in this new situation. Mystics and cranks quickly appeared, explaining the phenomenon as the work of people from outer space. The press gave the sensation a two-week run, then went back to the intricacies of the cold war. No one, not even the beady-eyed Forteans, paid much attention to the giant birds and machines with flapping wings that returned to our skies in 1948.

Early in January 1948, Mrs. Bernard Zaikowski reported seeing a "sizzing and whizzing" man with silver wings maneuvering about 200 feet above her barn in Chehalis, Washington. The air force scoffed. Four months later, two laundry workers in Longview, Washington, about forty miles south of Chehalis, claimed to see a trio of "birdmen" circling the city at an altitude of 250 feet.

"When they first came into sight, I thought they looked like gulls, but as they got closer I could make out that they weren't gulls and I knew they were men," Mrs. Viola Johnson told reporters. "I could see plainly that they were men. . . . They wore dark, drab flying suits. I couldn't make out their arms but I could see their legs dangling down and they kept moving their heads like they were looking around. I couldn't tell if they had goggles on but their heads looked like they had helmets on. I couldn't see their faces."

That happened on April 9, 1948. That same day, a couple in Caledonia, Illinois, reported seeing "a monster bird ... bigger than an airplane." Researchers Jerome Clark and Loren Coleman dug into Illinois newspapers and discovered that state had an epidemic of funny birds in 1948.[2]

That January James Trares, twelve, excitedly exclaimed to his mother, "There's a bird outside as big as a B–29!" They lived in Glendale, Illinois. In April, a huge bird was reported in Alton, Caledonia, Overland, Richmond Heights, and Freeport, all in Illinois. Walter Siegmund, a retired army colonel, saw it on April 4.

"I thought there was something wrong with my eyesight," he said, "but it was definitely a bird and not a glider or jet plane. . . . From the movements of the object and its size, I figured it could only be a bird of tremendous size."

Three people in Overland, Illinois, viewed the creature on April 10. At first they thought it was an airplane, then it began to flap its wings.

By late April the Garuda was buzzing the city of St. Louis. Dr. Kristine Dolezal saw it on the twenty-sixth. A group of instructors at the Mississippi School of Aeronautics observed "an awfully big bird" at 1,200 feet the next day. A salesman named Harry Bradford complained, "I've seen it three times in the last four days and that's too much tomfoolery for a man of fifty to take."

"I thought people who reported seeing the thing were 'bugs' until I looked into the sky last night," Charles Dunn, an inspector for U.S. Steel, declared on April 30. "It was flapping its wings and moving quite fast at about 3,000 feet altitude and it appeared to be illuminated by a dull glow. It looked about the size of a Piper Cub plane but there was no engine sound and it was not a plane. I could hardly believe my eyes."

Although the plane-sized bird was seen sporadically dur-

[2]Jerome Clark and Loren Coleman, "Winged Weirdies," *Fate*, March 1972.

ing the next decade, the flying saucers stole the limelight. The air force and the amateur investigators chose to pursue the more exciting Martians and Venusians.

But the figure of a man with "wings like a bat," dressed in tight-fitting black clothes and surrounded by an eerie glow startled three people in Houston, Texas, on June 18, 1953.

"I could see him plain and could see he had big wings folded at his shoulders," Mrs. Hilda Walker said. He was about six and a half feet tall and was perched on the limb of a pecan tree. His halo of light slowly faded out and he vanished. "Immediately afterward," Mrs. Walker continued, "we heard a loud swoosh over the housetops across the street. It was like the white flash of a torpedo-shaped object."

"I may be nuts, but I saw it, whatever it was," Howard Phillips, another witness, declared.

The next big year for our phantom fliers was 1961. Residents along Florida's Tamiami Trail began seeing what one woman described as "a big vulture . . . with a wingspread of about fifty-five feet. Isn't that sorta unusual?" In May 1961, a New York pilot was buzzed by "a damned big bird, bigger than an eagle. For a moment I doubted my sanity because it looked more like a pterodactyl out of the prehistoric past." The thing had swooped at his plane as he cruised up the Hudson River valley.

Far away, in the Ohio River valley, another startled pair had an even more breathtaking experience. A woman prominent in civic affairs in Point Pleasant, West Virginia, was driving on Route 2 along the Ohio River with her elderly father. As they passed through a sector on the edge of a park known as the Chief Cornstalk Hunting Grounds, a tall man-like figure suddenly appeared on the road in front of them.

"I slowed down," she told me years later, "and as we got closer we could see that it was much larger than a man. A big gray figure. It stood in the middle of the road. Then a pair of wings unfolded from its back and they practically filled the whole road. It almost looked like a small airplane. Then it took off straight up . . . disappearing out of sight in seconds. We were both terrified. I stepped on the gas and raced out of there.

"We talked it over and decided not to tell anybody about it. Who would believe us anyway?"

Dr. Jacques Vallee, French statistician and computer expert, was given access to the air force's UFO files and he came across a curious report from an air force colonel who was driving alone along a road in Illinois one night (no date is given) when he became aware of something flying above his car. It was, he said, a huge bird the size of a small airplane. It flapped its wings and soared away.

There are shaggy bird stories by the pound. A businessman in Arlington, Virginia, wrote to me recently, describing an experience he and three friends had in the winter of 1968–69. They were at a farm near Haymarket when they heard a strange rushing sound near a small lake. Intrigued, they set out with flashlights and a couple of dogs to investigate. Suddenly the dogs howled, turned tail, and ran. There, standing by a tree was a huge dark shadow between eight and twelve feet tall. The quartet scurried back to their car, turned on their lights, and swung toward the shadow. "All we saw," he reported, "was this huge thing with large red-orange eyeballs and winglike arms. We couldn't get out of there fast enough."

We even have a naked woman with wings in our collection. The case was investigated by Don Worley, an experienced student of the unknown, who interviewed the witness in depth. "He is a reliable observer," Worley notes, "and he swears that this event is well beyond the capacity of his imagination."

Earl Morrison, the witness, was serving as a private, first class in the marine corps in Vietnam in the summer of 1969. He and two buddies were sitting on top of a bunker near Da Nang on a warm summer evening.

All of a sudden—I don't know why—we all three looked out there in the sky and we saw this figure coming toward us," he told Mr. Worley. "It had a kind of glow and we couldn't make out what it was at first. It started coming toward us, real slowly. All of a sudden we saw what looked like wings, like a bat's, only it was gigantic compared to what a regular bat would be. After it got close enough so we could see what it was, it looked like a woman. A naked woman. She was black. Her skin was black, her body was black, the wings were black, everything was black. But it glowed. It glowed in the night—kind of a greenish cast to it.

There was a glow on her and around her. Everything glowed. Looked like she glowed and threw off a radiance. We saw her arms toward the wings and they looked like regular molded arms, each with a hand, and fingers and everything, but they had skin from the wings going over them. And when she flapped her wings, there was no noise at first. It looked like her arms didn't have any bones in them, because they were limber just like a bat.

She started going over us, and we still didn't hear anything. She was right above us, and when she got over the top of our heads she was maybe six or seven feet up.

We couldn't do anything. We didn't know what to do. We just froze. We just watched what was going over because we couldn't believe our eyes. . . . So we watched her go straight over the top of us, and still she didn't make any noise flapping her wings. She blotted out the moon once—that's how close she was to us . . . As we watched her—she got about ten feet or so away from us—we started hearing her wings flap. And it sounded, you know, like regular wings flapping. And she just started flying off and we watched her for quite a while. The total time when we first saw her and could almost define her until we lost sight of her and were unable to define her was between three or four minutes.[3]

Vietnam had a big UFO wave in 1968–69, which included an epidemic of phantom helicopters. On several occasions the military forces on both sides fired at the objects without effect.

Pfc. Morrison's account stands as one of the best close-up sightings of a winged entity.

IV.

A bright "star" appeared over the trees of Sandling Park, Hythe, in Kent, England, on the night of November 16, 1963, and so began one of the classics in ufology. Four teen-agers were strolling along a country road near the park, going home from a dance, when the movements of the "star" caught their eyes. It dipped out of the sky and headed straight for them, finally dropping down behind some nearby trees.

John Flaxton, seventeen, said he suddenly felt very cold, and a sense of overpowering fear engulfed the group. They started to run. The light, now a golden oval-shaped object, reappeared from behind the trees and seemed to move along with them from a distance of about two hundred feet. When they stopped, the light stopped. Then it was lost from sight behind the trees. The four youngsters slowed down, catching their breath.

Suddenly a tall, dark figure emerged from the woods and waddled toward them. It was completely black and had no discernible head. Mervyn Hutchinson, eighteen, described it as looking like a human-sized bat, with big bat wings on its back. All four took off as fast as they could go.

More strange lights were seen in Sandling Woods in the days that followed. Investigators found three giant footprints, an inch deep, two feet long, and nine inches across. Three weeks later a group of people, including two newspaper reporters, visited the site and found the whole forest illuminated by a strange pulsating light. They watched it from a distance for half an hour, afraid to go closer.[4]

These great Garudas and winged beings are closely associated with luminous phenomena. They tend to appear in areas where UFOs have been active and, like UFOs, they tend to linger for days or even weeks in the same specific area. The big luminous bird of the Illinois-St. Louis region in 1948 was visiting an area of the Mississippi valley that would see continuous UFO and hairy monster activity thereafter.

In many instances the witnesses have clearly seen the objects in the process of materialization or dematerialization. A glow is observed first, usually a reddish glow marking the emergence of the object from the invisible band of the spectrum into infrared and then into the narrow band of visible light. Or, if the object is passing through the visible band to the higher frequencies it is cyan (bluish-green) before it fades into blue (hard to see at night) and then enters the ultraviolet range. The chills experienced by John Flaxton and his group were probably caused by microwaves above the infrared (which produces heat), just as the very cold atmosphere accompanying ghosts is a radiation effect.

The absence of any overpowering odor, either sickly sweet like violets or roses or nauseous like hydrogen sulfide, in these bird and batman cases puzzles me, however. This could indicate some subtle difference in the basic structure of these creatures; a difference in the energy components or molecular structure.

People are still seeing flying freaks. On May 21, 1973, a group of men in a woods near Kristianstad, Sweden, reported an incredibly huge black bird which passed within one hundred feet of them. One witness had a camera with a telephoto lens and attempted to take a picture, but his film jammed. Camera malfunctions are remarkably common

[4]Charles Bowen, ed., *The Humanoids* (London: Neville Spearman, 1969).

among would-be UFO photographers, and even those who try to take pictures of the serpent at Loch Ness. It almost seems as if some outside force fouls up cameras when monsters and UFOs are around.

4:
Take the Train

I.

"From Bad.Axe to Bethesda the happy news comes in," wrote an anonymous "Talk of the Town" contributor in *The New Yorker*, April 9, 1966. "Flying saucers! . . . We read the official explanations with sheer delight, marveling at their stupendous inadequacy. Marsh gas, indeed! . . . Our theory is that flying saucers are not of this earth. The beings who control them are attempting to make contact with man in the gentlest possible fashion. . . ."

Dr. Isaac Asimov, dean of science writers, commented: "I am told, though, that so many people have seen objects that looked like spaceships that 'there must be something in it'. . . . Maybe there is, but think of all the people in the history of the world who have seen ghosts and spirits and angels. It's not what you see that is suspect, but how you interpret what you see."

At a scientific convention held in Baltimore in 1966, Dr. Edward C. Walsh, executive secretary of the National

Aeronautics and Space Council, remarked: "So many airline pilots report seeing them, that's why I take the train."

Wherever you were in the year 1966, you must have heard about the coming of the flying saucers. The news media beat the story into a froth of ennui. The newsstands were glutted with one-shot UFO magazines and quickie paperbacks rehashing the reported sightings from previous flap years. Everywhere great crowds of people gathered on hilltops, in swamps and cemeteries, and around reservoirs and gravel pits, their eyes turned heavenward. Saucer-hunting became a national sport, rallying to the excited cry, "There goes one!"

That year I stood on hilltops and beaches with those crowds, watching funny lights bob around in the night. But an uneasiness was overtaking me; a dark suspicion that Dr. Asimov's tongue-in-cheek observation may have contained more truth than even he knew.

The Year of the Garuda was at hand. A dark force was closing over a little town I had never even heard of: Point Pleasant, West Virginia. In a matter of months I would be arriving there like some black-suited exorcist, lugging my tattered briefcase, waving the golden cross of science. My life would become intertwined with the lives of the people of the Ohio valley.

In March 1966, a shapely housewife, whom I will call Mrs. Kelly because she asked that her name be withheld, was waiting in her car for her children near the Point Pleasant school when she saw an unbelievable apparition low in the sky. It looked like a glistening metal disk and was hovering directly above the school playground. A doorlike aperture was open at its rim and there was a man standing outside. He was not standing *in* the doorway, he was standing outside the object in midair! He wore a silvery skin-tight costume and had very long silvery hair. He was looking down into the schoolyard intently. She watched him for a long moment until her children bounded up to the car. When she looked again, the man and object were gone. She decided not to tell anyone about this strange vision, attaching religious significance to it.

That summer, Mrs. Mary Hyre was driving along the Ohio side of the river when a sudden glint in the sky attracted her attention. "At first I thought it was a plane," she recalled. "Then I got a better look at it. It was perfectly round. I couldn't make out what it was but I didn't give it any thought at the time."

Another round object chose to hover above Tiny's restaurant just outside Point Pleasant that summer, where it was seen by a number of customers including the wife of a local police officer. Tiny's stands on the corner of the street where the McDaniels live. The McDaniel family would later serve as the focus for many of the strange manifestations.

Not one person bothered to report a UFO sighting to the law or press in Point Pleasant, although there were many such sightings all summer long.

People in distant Salt Lake City, Utah, weren't so squeamish, however. When a bird "about as big as a Piper Cub airplane" circled that Mormon community on July 18, 1966, some people ran for cover while others ran for their telephones.

Shortly after 2 P.M. on September 1, Mrs. James Ikart of Scott, Mississippi, grabbed her phone to call the *Delta Democrat Times* (Greenville). She and her neighbors were watching a whitish man-shaped flying object. "It got down pretty low and then would go up," Mrs. Ikart said. "I never saw anything like it."

John Hursh, a local meteorologist, whipped out Standard Explanation No. 425. "It's apparently somebody's research balloon that's gotten away," he announced.

Whatever it was, it bounced around Scott most of the afternoon.

II.

Three thousand years ago a small group of brilliant men investigated *and solved* the mystery of unidentified flying objects. Since then a great many others have approached the same mystery from different perspectives and solved it over and over again. Unfortunately, their staggering solutions were obfuscated by intellectual extrapolations and the ponderous terminology of philosophy and theology. Few modern UFO enthusiasts have the educational background to understand such literature. They choose, as an alternative, to deal with the phenomenon on a materialistic level, assuming that the presence of unlikely objects and entities in our atmosphere is evidence of some extraterrestrial civilization.

Xenophanes, one of the first great philosophers (sixth century B.C.), observed that the Ethiopians thought their gods were black and snub-nosed like themselves. Today many of us no longer believe in direct visits with our God, so we have shaped a new mythology based upon the belief in spacemen carved in our own image. When the ancients sighted giant, shambling bipeds covered with hair, their eyes blazing like fierce coals, they assumed they were confronting demons. Early investigators eventually concluded that such demons did not really exist, even though they often left footprints behind and caused physical damage. They coined the word *khimaira* (chimera) to describe them. Others noted that the eerie aerial lights changed colors up and down the visual spectrum and the word specter was born. Several times each year tall, hairy creatures with red eyes are still seen throughout the United States and, in fact, throughout the world. Like many forms of chimeras, they are usually accompanied by the smell of rotten eggs—hydrogen sulfide. The "fire and brimstone" of the ancients. The same odor frequently surrounds the fabled flying saucers and their space-suited pilots.

Seeing a spaceman disembark from a flying saucer is no

more remarkable than seeing an angel descend in a luminous cloud (and angels are still reported hundreds of times each year). The report of a nine-foot-tall humanoid strolling down the main street of Buffalo Mills, Pennsylvania, on August 19, 1973, was no more outlandish than the dinosaurs who appear from time to time to terrify witnesses and baffle police posses. In 1969 there were dinosaur reports in Texas. In 1970 the police in Italy scoured a mountain range after several witnesses reported seeing a saurian.

To the regret of the true believers, the majority of the witnesses to chimerical events were alone at the time of their experience. While the amateur investigators tend to concentrate on the very subjective descriptions of the observers, I probed deeper and studied the witnesses themselves. Many, I found, suffered certain medical symptoms such as temporary amnesia, severe headaches, muscular spasms, excessive thirst and other effects, all of which have been observed throughout history in religious miracles (the appearances of religious apparitions), demonology, occult phenomena, and contacts with fairies. All of these manifestations clearly share a common source or cause.

While chimeras can come in all sizes and shapes, ranging from twenty-foot giants to animated tin cans only a few inches in height, the most fascinating type is one who has appeared in almost every country on earth. In other ages he was regarded as the devil incarnate. He dressed in black and rode a black horse. Later he arrived in black horsedrawn carriages, even in hearses. Today he steps out of flying saucers in remote farm fields. He is built exactly like us, stands from five feet six inches to six feet tall, looks very human but has high cheekbones, unusually long fingers, and an Oriental cast to his features. His complexion is olive or reddish. He speaks every language, sometimes mechanically as if he is reciting a memorized speech, sometimes fluently. He has trouble breathing, often wheezing and gasping between words. Like our dinosaurs and hairy bipeds, he often leaves a few footprints behind . . . footprints which suddenly end as if he had vanished into thin air.

I have been chasing these critters for twenty-five years and have traveled from Tibet, the land of the Abominable Snowman, to West Virginia, home of the strangest unknown "Bird." In the course of all these adventures and frenetic activities I have come to reject outright the popular extraterrestrial hypothesis.

My long and very expensive excursions into the borderland where the real and unreal merge have failed to produce any evidence of any kind to support the idea that we are entertaining shy strangers from some other galaxy. Rather, I have come to realize that we have been observing complex forces which have always been an essential part of our immediate environment. Instead of thinking in terms of extraterrestrials, I have adopted the concept of ultraterrestrials—beings and forces which coexist with us but are on another time frame; that is, they operate outside the limits of our space-time continuum yet have the ability to cross over into our reality. This other world is not a place, however, as Mars or Andromeda are places, but is a state of energy.

The UFO phenomenon itself is only one trivial fragment of a much larger phenomenon. It can be divided into two main parts. The first and most important part consists of the mysterious aerial lights which appear to have an intelligence of their own. They have been observed throughout history. Often they project powerful searchlight-like beams toward the ground. Persons caught in these beams undergo remarkable changes of personality. Their IQ skyrockets, they change their jobs, divorce their wives, and in any number of well-documented instances they suddenly rise above their previously mediocre lives and become outstanding statesmen, scientists, poets and writers, even soldiers. In religious lore, being belted by one of these light beams causes "mystical illumination." When Saul, a Jewish tentmaker, was zapped by one of these beams on the road to Damascus it blinded him for three days and he was converted to Christianity on the spot and became St. Paul.

The second part of the phenomenon consists of the cover or camouflage for the first part, the "meandering nocturnal lights" as the air force has labeled them. If these lights appeared in cycles, year after year, century after century without any accompanying explanatory manifestations they would cause much greater fear and concern. But explanatory manifestations *have* accompanied them always, and these manifestations have always been adjusted to the psychology and beliefs of each particular period in time. The flying saucer/extraterrestrial visitants are not real in the sense that a 747 airliner is real. They are transmogrifications of energy under the control of some unknown extradimensional intelligence. This intelligence controls important events by manipulating specific human beings through the phenomenon of mystical illumination. Our religions are based upon our longtime awareness of this intelligence and our struggle to reduce it to humanly acceptable terms.

The ancient Ethiopians viewed their gods as black, snubnosed entities. The Greeks and Romans populated their mountaintops with longhaired, handsome gods and goddesses. The Indians of South America worshiped bearded gods who traveled the night skies in luminous discs of light, as did the ancient Egyptians. But religious views were modified in the nineteenth century with the coming of the Industrial Age. The lights were still there but a new frame of reference was needed to cover their activities.

Somebody somewhere does not want us to understand the true nature of this phenomenon and its true purpose. For years the UFO enthusiasts believed the U.S. Air Force was the culprit and that government agents were tapping the phones of teen-agers and little old ladies, tampering with their mail, and following them around in black Cadillacs. I wish the answer was that simple.

We have been victimized by this phenomenon, not just

since 1947 but since ever! It is the foundation of all our religious and occult beliefs, of our philosophies, and our cultures. The ancient Chinese marked out the routes of the lights in the sky (LITS) and called them "dragon tracks" because, apparently, fearsome dragons appeared along with the mysterious lights. In a later age, these became fairy lights and were associated with the little people who actually plagued whole generations not only in Europe but also in North America . . . for the American Indians were telling stories about the little people long before the Europeans arrived here.

During the witchcraft craze of a few hundred years ago, people really thought they saw witches flying through the air . . . with lanterns hanging from the front of their brooms. The vampire legends of middle Europe are almost identical to the modern UFO lore. As late as the nineteenth century the devil existed as a physical personage to many people.

If you saw a strange light in the sky in 1475 you *knew* it had to be a witch on a broom because you had heard of others who had seen witches on brooms skirting the tree-tops. Now in 1975 you might decide it is attached to a spacecraft from some other planet. This conclusion is not a qualified deduction on your part. It is the result of years of propaganda and even brainwashing. If you are under thirty, you grew up on a diet of comic books, motion pictures, and television programs which educated you to believe in the extraterrestrial hypothesis. A small knot of nuts has talked to you year after year on interview programs, telling you how the sinister air force has been keeping the truth about flying saucers from the public; that truth being that UFOs are the product of a superior intelligence with an advanced technology, and that the flying saucers have come to save us from ourselves. The gods of ancient Greece are among us again, in a new guise but still handing out the old line. Believe.

Belief is the enemy.

The people of the Middle Ages were as convinced of the

reality of the little people and their underground palaces as you might be of an extraterrestrial civilization with gleaming cities of glass on some far-off planet. One hundred years from now the phenomenon may be playing some new game with us. The whole interplanetary bag may be forgotten. But those lights—and that damnable procession of strange critters and nine-foot humanoids—will still be marching in our midst. Isolated individuals on lonely back roads will still be getting caught in sudden beams of energy from the sky, then shuck their families, quit their jobs, and rocket into notoriety or plunge into the hell of insanity and bankruptcy.

III.

"While driving toward New Cumberland, we saw a light hovering near a hillside," John Vujnovic, an attorney from Weirton, West Virginia, said, describing his experience on the evening of October 7, 1966. "The light started coming toward the car and I guess my son was frightened and I slowed the car so that we were a good distance behind the object.

"The object had an outer circular light that glowed, but there was no sound at all. I stopped the car for a better look and the thing started coming down over the highway. I think it was about four hundred feet in the air."

Mr. Vujnovic was driving south on State Route 66 from Chester, West Virginia, to Weirton in the northernmost tip of the state. His was one of the first important sightings in West Virginia that October . . . a month that would produce sensational incidents all up and down the eastern seaboard.

"At one time, it looked as if there were windows in the craft and after it got past we could see a revolving light. The outer glow of the light made a fast-flickering type of light as the object was hovering."

It eventually disappeared as Mr. Vujnovic went on his way.

In the weeks that followed, the lights and some dark objects of awesome size were seen from one end of the state to another. In Sistersville, a town mentioned in the 1897 "airship" reports, local UFO fans organized an informal warning system, calling each other on party lines to announce curtly, "UFO—northeast," etc. The town's newspaper did not bother to publish a single report.

Every night at approximately 8 P.M. one of these brilliant flashing lights would cruise majestically over the Ohio River, traversing Point Pleasant from north to south. Those who bothered to notice it at all assumed it was an airplane.

Mrs. Kelly, the lady who had seen the longhaired man standing in the sky seven months earlier, lived in a house on the edge of a deep gully. She and her children were seeing blinding globes of light traveling close to the ground along that gully nightly. And her telephone was behaving strangely, ringing when there was no one on the line, and sometimes emitting beeps like Morse code.

Early in November, an elderly man walked into Mary Hyre's newspaper office. "I've just got to tell somebody," he began nervously. The story he unfolded seemed totally unbelievable to Mrs. Hyre, who knew nothing of UFOs at the time, but she knew the man and was impressed by his sincerity.

On November 2, 1966, he said, he and another workman were driving home to Point Pleasant from their job near Marietta, Ohio, on Interstate 77. As they neared Parkersburg, West Virginia, an elongated object appeared low in the sky and descended directly in front of them. They stopped their car and a man emerged from the object and walked over to them. He looked like a normal man and was grinning broadly. He wore a black coat and kept his arms folded with his hands out of sight under his armpits. The witness rolled his window down and there was a very brief conversation. The stranger asked the pair who they were, where they were from, where they were

were going, and what time was it? Then he strolled back to the dark cylinder and it rose quickly into the chill, drizzling sky.

The two men had a strong emotional reaction to the seemingly pointless encounter. They debated whether they should tell anybody, deciding against it. But the Point Pleasant resident found himself suffering from insomnia. And when he finally slept he had strange nightmares. He started to hit the bottle, something very unusual for him.

Mrs. Hyre listened to his story, nonplused, and made a few notes. A day or so later the man's son called on her and asked her not to print the story. Several weeks later she repeated the story to me and we called the man on her office phone. He verified the details and then said, "Look, don't use my name. I don't want to get involved in this thing. That scientist fella told me—"

"What scientist?" I asked.

"A couple of weeks after this thing happened, a scientist from Ohio came to see us. He told us it would be better if we forgot the whole thing."

"How did he hear about it? How did he find you?"

"Damned if I know."

"Did he identify himself?"

"Sure . . . but I can't remember his name. But he seemed to know what he was talking about."

I couldn't get much else out of him. I would have ignored the whole story except for one jarring fact. The same thing had happened that same night on the same road to another West Virginian. Unlike the two Point Pleasant residents, he had gone to the police with his story. A press conference was held and he was catapulted into the never-never land of the UFO contactees, the center of one of the biggest UFO stories of 1966.

5:
The Cold Who Came Down in the Rain

I.

Woodrow Derenberger is a tall, husky man with close-cropped sandy hair, twinkling blue-gray eyes, and an honest open face. In 1966 he was in his early fifties but looked considerably younger. His life had been normal to the point of being mundane—a long succession of modest jobs, hard times, constant movement from one rented house to another pursuing no particular ambition. Surviving. Feeding and clothing his attractive young wife and two children. Now he was working as a salesman for an appliance company and living in a simple two-story farmhouse in Mineral Wells, West Virginia. It was a good time in his life.

At 7 P.M. on November 2, 1966, he was heading home in his panel truck after a long, hard day on the road. The weather was sour, chill, and rainy. As he drove up a long hill outside of Parkersburg on Interstate 77 a sudden crash sounded in the back of his truck. He snapped on his interior lights and looked back. A sewing machine had fallen off the top of a stereo, but there didn't seem to be any real damage. A car swept up behind him and passed him. Another vehicle seemed to be following it. He eased his foot on the accelerator. He had been speeding slightly and thought it might be a police car. The vehicle, a black blob in the dark, drew alongside him, cut in front, and slowed.

Woody Derenberger gaped in amazement at the thing. It wasn't an automobile but was shaped like "an old-fashioned kerosene lamp chimney, flaring at both ends, narrowing down to a small neck and then enlarging in a great bulge in the center." It was a charcoal gray. He slammed on his brakes as the object turned crossways, blocking the road, stopping only eight or ten feet from it. A door slid open on the side of the thing and a man stepped out.

"I didn't hear an audible voice," Woody said later. "I just had a feeling . . . like I knew what this man was thinking. He wanted me to roll down my window."

The stranger was about five feet ten inches tall with long, dark hair combed straight back. His skin was heavily tanned. Grinning broadly, his arms crossed and his hands tucked under his armpits, he walked to the panel truck. He was wearing a dark topcoat. Underneath it Woody could see some kind of garment made of glistening greenish material almost metallic in appearance.

Do not be afraid. The grinning man did not speak aloud. Woody sensed the words.

We mean you no harm. I come from a country much less powerful than yours.

He asked for Woody's name. Woody told him.

My name is Cold. I sleep, breathe, and bleed even as you do.

Mr. Cold nodded toward the lights of Parkersburg in the distance and asked what kind of a place it was. Woody tried to explain it was a center for businesses and homes—a city. In his world, Cold explained, such places were called "gatherings."

While this telepathic conversation was taking place, the chimney-shaped object ascended and hovered some forty or fifty feet above the road. Other cars came along the road and passed them.

Cold told Woody to report the encounter to the authorities, promising to come forward at a later date to confirm it. After a few minutes of aimless generalities, Cold announced he would meet Woody again soon. The object descended, the door opened, Cold entered it, and it rose quickly and silently into the night.

When he got home, Derenberger was in a very disraught state. His wife urged him to call the Parkersburg police. They seemed to accept his story without question and asked if he needed a doctor.

The next day he was questioned at length by the city and state police. The story appeared in the local press and on radio and television. People who had driven that same route the night before came forward to confirm that they had seen a man speaking to the driver of a panel truck stopped on the highway. Mrs. Frank Huggins and her two children had reportedly stopped their own car and watched the object soar low over the highway minutes after Woody watched it depart. Another young man said the object had frightened him out of his wits when it hovered over his car and flashed a powerful, blinding light on him.

Woodrow Derenberger became a supercelebrity. Crowds of people gathered at his farm every night, hoping to glimpse a spaceship. His phone rang day and night. He switched to an unlisted number but within a short time the calls began again. Crank calls, threatening him if he didn't "shut up." Calls that consisted of nothing except eerie electronic sounds and codelike beeps.

Mr. Cold kept his promise. He returned.

II.

The Indians must have known something about West
Virginia. They avoided it. Before the Europeans arrived
with their glass beads, firewater, and gunpowder, the Indian
nations had spread out and divided up the North American
continent. Modern anthropologists have worked out maps
of the Indian occupancy of pre-Columbian America according to the languages spoken.[1] The Shawnee and Cherokee
occupied the areas to the south and southwest. The Mona-
can settled to the east, and the Erie and Conestoga claimed
the areas north of West Virginia. Even the inhospitable
deserts of the Far West were divided and occupied. There
is only one spot on the map labeled "Uninhabited": West
Virginia.

Why? The West Virginia area is fertile, heavily wooded,
rich in game. Why did the Indians avoid it? Was it filled
with hairy monsters and frightful apparitions way back
when?

Across the river in Ohio, industrious Indians—or someone—built the great mounds and left us a rich heritage of
Indian culture and lore. The absence of an Indian tradition
in West Virginia is troublesome for the researcher. It creates
an uncomfortable vacuum. There are strange ancient ruins
in the state, circular stone monuments which prove that
someone had settled the region once. Since the Indians
didn't build such monuments, and since we don't even have
any lore to fall back on, we have only mystery.

Chief Cornstalk and his Shawnees fought a battle there
in the 1760s and Cornstalk is supposed to have put a curse
on the area before he fell. But what happened there before?
Did someone else live there?

The Cherokees have a tradition, according to Benjamin

[1] *American Indian Linguistic Families and Tribes*, a map issued by C. S. Ham-
mond & Co., New York.

Smith Barton's *New Views of the Origins of the Tribes and Nations of America* (1798), that when they migrated to Tennessee they found the region inhabited by a weird race of white people who lived in houses and were apparently quite civilized. They had one problem: their eyes were very large and sensitive to light. They could only see at night. The fierce Indians ran these "mooneyed people" out. Did they move to West Virginia to escape their tormentors? There are still rumors of an oddball group of albino people in the back hills of Kentucky and Tennessee. But there are also myths and rumors of mysterious people living in the hills of New Jersey forty miles from Manhattan.

III.

The day before Woodrow Derenberger's unexpected meeting with Mr. Cold in the rain, a national guardsman was working outside the national guard armory on the edge of Point Pleasant when he saw a figure perched on the limb of a tree beyond the high fence. At first he thought it looked like a man in a brown suit. It was as large as a man, but after he studied it for awhile he decided it was some kind of bird. The biggest bird he had ever seen. He went to call some friends and when they came the bird was gone.

IV.

On November 4, Derenberger was riding with a co-worker on Route 7 outside Parkersburg when he felt a tingling sensation in his forehead. Then thoughts from Mr. Cold began to spring full-blown into his mind. Cold explained that he was from the planet of Lanulos which was in the "galaxy of Ganymede." Lanulos, he said, was very like the earth, with flora, fauna, and seasons. He was married to a lady named Kimi and had two sons. Folks on Lanulos had a life expectancy of 125–175 earth years. Naturally there was no war, poverty, hunger, or misery on Lanulos.

When the transmission was completed, Cold urged Woody to brace himself because withdrawal would be painful. Woody felt a sharp pain in his temple and nearly passed out.

Two weeks later, though Woody wasn't aware of it at the time, two salesmen visited Mineral Wells and went from house to house with their wares. They weren't very interested in making sales. At one house they offered bibles. At another, hardware. At a third they were "Mormon missionaries from Salem, Oregon" (a UFO wave was taking place in Salem at that time). One man was tall, blond, and looked like a Scandinavian. His partner was short and slight, with pointed features and a dark olive complexion. They asked questions about Woody and were particularly interested in opinions on the validity of his alleged contact.

V.

"Old Bandit's gone," the six-year-old boy said sadly. "Mister, do you think you can bring him back?"

Gray Barker shifted his large frame uneasily. The boy's father, Newell Partridge, ordered the child off to bed.

"It's all so weird," Partridge complained. "I just can't figure it out."

Barker smiled understandingly. Ever since he had investigated the Flatwoods monster back in 1952, he had been listening to weird stories. A pioneer ufologist, Gray had made many outstanding contributions to the subject. He had also managed to make himself a somewhat controversial character in a field riddled with controversies and characters. The die-hard fanatics who dominated sauceriana during the early years were a humorless lot and Gray's mischievous wit baffled and enraged them. At times it baffled me, too. This towering bear of a man was very hard to "read." But his investigations were always thorough and uncompromising.

Now he was sitting in the home of Newell Partridge near Salem, West Virginia, talking about an errant television set and a missing dog. On the evening of November 14, 1966, Bandit, a big, muscular German shepherd, had dashed into the darkness and vanished.

"It was about 10:30 that night, and suddenly the TV blanked out," Partridge said. "A real fine herringbone pattern appeared on the tube, and at the same time the set started a loud whining noise, winding up to a high pitch, peaking and breaking off, as if you were on a musical scale and you went as high as you could and came back down and repeated it. . . . It sounded like a generator winding up. It reminded me of a hand field generator that one might use for portable radio transmission in an emergency."

Outside on the porch, Bandit began wailing. Partridge picked up a flashlight and went outside to investigate.

"The dog was sitting on the end of the porch, howling down toward the hay barn in the bottom," Partridge continued. "I shined the light in that direction, and it picked up two red circles, or eyes, which looked like bicycle reflectors. Still there was something about those eyes that is difficult to explain. When I was a kid I night-hunted all the time, and I certainly know what animal eyes look like—such as coon, dog and cat eyes in the dark. These were much larger for one thing. It's a good length of a football field to that hay barn. Probably around 150 yards; still those eyes showed up huge, for that distance."

As soon as the flashlight picked out the "eyes" Bandit snarled and ran toward them. A "cold chill" swept over the man and he felt a wave of fear which kept him from following the dog.

That night he slept with a loaded gun beside his bed.

The next day he went looking for the dog.

"I walked out to the barn, looking for tracks. Here and there I could see Bandit's paw prints. These were rather easy to find, for he was a heavy dog, and the area was muddy."

At the approximate position of the "eyes" he found a large number of dog tracks.

"Those tracks were going in a circle, as if the dog had been chasing his tail," Partridge explained, "though he never did that. And that was that. I couldn't see them go off anywhere, though I did see a series of fresh tracks which apparently led from the porch to the spot where he ran in circles. There were no other tracks of any kind."

Bandit simply vanished into thin air.

"I think that the hardest thing to explain is the feeling involved . . . except to say it was an eerie feeling. I have never had this sort of feeling before. It was as if you knew something was wrong, but couldn't place just what it was."

Sudden fear. Eerie feelings. Something unnatural was stalking the hills of West Virginia that November. The fear would become contagious. Those frightening red eyes would settle in Point Pleasant, while Mr. Cold and his crew of cosmic zanies would spread their propaganda in Mineral Wells, forsaking their flying lantern chimney for a black Volkswagen.

6:
Mothman!

I.

High explosives were manufactured in Point Pleasant during
World War II. Seven miles outside of town part of the
2,500-acre McClintic Wildlife Station, an animal preserve
and bird sanctuary, was ripped up. Miles of underground
tunnels were dug, linking camouflaged buildings and factories. One hundred "igloos" were scattered across the fields
and woods—huge concrete domes with heavy steel doors
where the finished explosives could be safely stored. Dirt and
grass covered the domes so from the air the whole area had
a harmless, pastoral appearance. A few scattered buildings
linked by unimproved dirt roads with no suggestion of all the
activity going on below ground. It looked like nothing more
than what it was supposed to be, a haven for birds and
animals in the Ohio River valley.

After the war most of the explosives were carted away.
The factories were dismantled. The entrances and exits of
the tunnels were plugged with thick concrete slabs. Some of

the igloos were given to the Mason County government as possible storage vaults. They still stand empty. Others were sold to the Trojan-U.S. Powder Co. and the LFC Chemical Co. Some were leased to American Cyanamid.

The years washed away the camouflage and now the igloos stand out starkly on the landscape, row upon row of white mounds with deer and rabbits running between them. The old factory buildings are broken shells. The big generator plant near the entrance to the area still stands, its boilers rusting, its windows gone, water dripping shyly across its floor while the wind rattles the high steel catwalks and pigeons flutter in its rafters.

Local teen-agers use the decaying dirt roads for drag strips, and further back, where the woods thicken, lovers park in the deep shadows during the summer mating season. While the TNT area had witnessed many biological events over the years, it had no reputation as a haunted place. The local police cruised through it every evening, occasionally flashing their lights into a darkened car. Everyone raised in the area knows every corner of the place. Sportsmen clubs have built an archery range and picnic area there.

At 11:30 P.M. on the night of November 15, 1966, two young couples from Point Pleasant, Mr. and Mrs. Roger Scarberry and Mr. and Mrs. Steve Mallette, were driving through the TNT area in the Scarberrys' 1957 Chevvy. They were looking for friends but no one seemed to be out that night. All of the twisting back roads were deserted. The few homes scattered among the igloos were dark.

Roger, then a strapping blond eighteen-year-old, was driving. They aimlessly made the circuit of the roads around the igloos, returning to the old generator plant near the unlocked gate. As they pulled alongside the plant, Linda Scarberry gasped. They all looked into the blackness and saw two bright red circles. They were about two inches in diameter and six inches apart. Roger slammed on his brakes.

"What is it?" Mary Mallette, a strikingly attractive brunette, cried from the back seat.

The lights bobbed away from the building and the startled foursome saw they were attached to some huge animal.

"It was shaped like a man, but bigger," Roger said later. "Maybe six and a half or seven feet tall. And it had big wings folded against its back."

"But it was those eyes that got us," Linda declared. "It had two big eyes like automobile reflectors."

"They were hypnotic," Roger continued. "For a minute we could only stare at it. I couldn't take my eyes off it."

It was grayish in color and walked on sturdy manlike legs. It turned slowly and shuffled toward the door of the generator plant which was ajar and hanging off its hinges.

"Let's get out of here!" Steve yelled.

Roger stepped on the gas and they shot through the gates, spun onto the exit road, and headed for Route 62. Suddenly they saw it, or another one like it, standing on a small hill near the road. As they hurtled past it, it spread its batlike wings and took off straight up into the air.

"My God! It's following us!" The couple in the back seat cried. Roger swung onto 62 on two wheels.

"We were doing one hundred miles an hour," Roger said, "and that bird kept right up with us. It wasn't even flapping its wings."

"I could hear it making a sound," Mrs. Mallette added. "It squeaked like a big mouse."

"It followed us right to the city limits," Roger went on. "Funny thing, we noticed a dead dog by the side of the road there. A big dog. But when we came back a few minutes later, the dog was gone."

Panic-stricken, the red eyes still burning in their minds,

they went directly to the Mason County courthouse, charged into the sheriff's office, and blurted out their story to Deputy Millard Halstead.

"I've known these kids all their lives," Halstead told me later. "They'd never been in any trouble and they were really scared that night. I took them seriously."

He hopped into a patrol car and followed Roger's car back to the TNT area. At the edge of town they looked for the dog's body. It was gone.

Back at the power plant there was no sign of the red-eyed specter. Halstead switched on his police radio and a very loud signal blasted out of the speaker, drowning out the voice of the police dispatcher in Point Pleasant.

It was a loud garble, like a record or tape recording being played at very high speed.

Deputy Halstead, an experienced cop, looked taken aback but said nothing. He switched the radio off quickly and peered uncomfortably into the darkness, reluctant to really search the old building. But he was convinced.

The next morning Sheriff George Johnson called a press conference. Local reporters interviewed the four witnesses. Mrs. Mary Hyre sent the story out on the AP wire and that evening the "Bird" was the chief topic at supper tables throughout the Ohio valley. Some anonymous copy editor gave it a name, spun off from the Batman comic character who was then the subject of a popular TV series. He tagged the creature Mothman.

II.

November 16, 1966. Three years to the day since John Flaxton and his companions had seen the ambling winged monster in Kent, England. Long lines of cars circled the TNT area slowly. Men bristling with guns surrounded the old power plant, poking into every bush. There wasn't much to do in Point Pleasant, a town of six thousand people, twenty-two churches, and no barrooms, so Mothman was almost a welcome addition.

A large red light moved around in the sky directly above the TNT area that night but few of the monster-hunters paid any attention to it.* One carload of people was watching it, however. Mr. and Mrs. Raymond Wamsley and Mrs. Marcella Bennett and her baby daughter, Teena, studied it, puzzled.

"It wasn't an airplane. We couldn't figure out what it was," Mrs. Bennett said.

She and the Wamsleys were probably the only people in the crowd who were not looking for the red-eyed creature. They were on their way to visit the Ralph Thomases who lived in a neat bungalow back among the igloos. Mr. Thomas was the superintendent of the Trojan-U.S. operations there. His wife, Virginia, was a slender, gentle woman blessed—or cursed—with second sight. She had accurately predicted numerous accidents and local events over the years. She was careful not to seek attention and only her friends knew of her remarkable abilities. Deeply religious, she went to church almost every evening and on this night both she and her husband were out. The Wamsleys and Mrs. Bennett found only three of the Thomas children, Rickie, Connie, and Vickie, at home. After exchanging a few words with the youngsters, they headed back to their car. Off in the distance they could hear some trigger-happy hero firing a rifle around the power plant.

Suddenly a figure stirred in the darkness behind the parked car.

"It seemed as if it had been lying down," Mrs. Bennett told me. "It rose up slowly from the ground. A big gray

---

*In one of my notebooks covering this period I find the following notation: "Nov. 16th-UPI man from Charleston saw low-flying object over TNT area— made humming sound—flashing red light. Some girls with him. They watched object for several minutes."

thing. Bigger than a man, with terrible glowing red eyes."

Mrs. Bennett uttered a little cry, so horrified she dropped the small baby in her arms. The child began to cry, more insulted than hurt, but her mother couldn't move to pick her up again. She stood transfixed, hypnotized by the blazing red circles on the top of the towering, headless creature. Its great wings unfolded slowly behind its back. Raymond Wamsley grabbed the paralyzed woman and the child and they all ran back into the house, slammed the door, and bolted it. There was a sound on the porch and the two red eyes peered in through a window. The women and children became hysterical while Wamsley frantically phoned the police. It was 9 P.M. Hundreds of people, many of them armed to the teeth, were less than a mile away and would not know about the episode until they read it in the local papers the following evening.

By the time the police reached the house the creature was gone. But for Mrs. Bennett this was just the beginning of a long and frightening series of adventures.

III.

Woodrow Derenberger was living in bedlam. A group of local UFO enthusiasts representing the Washington-based National Investigations Committee on Aerial Phenomena (NICAP), largely a lobby urging congressional UFO investigations, visited or phoned him daily, raising his ire by ordering him not to talk to anyone else about his experiences.

His farm looked like the TNT area. Every night streams of cars would park all over the property he was renting and people would sit quietly in the dark. Watching. Waiting. Some brought guns and hiked into the nearby hills to sit behind trees. Widespread rumors said the UFOs planned to come back and land on the farm. Some of Woody's visitors were determined to bag themselves a spaceman.

In the midst of all the chaos, a black Volkswagen drove up, parked, and a tanned man in a neat black suit got out. He and Woody walked casually to the edge of the porch and talked. After a few minutes, the man got back into his VW and drove off. The great hunters continued to sit in the bitter cold behind their trees, their eyes anxiously searching the skies.

According to Derenberger, he had been suffering from a stomach ailment for some time. Mr. Cold gave him a vial of medicine, he claimed, which cured his problem instantly. Cold now had a first name—Indrid.

IV.

Across the Ohio River, almost directly opposite the TNT area, a music teacher, Mrs. Roy Grose, was wakened by the barking of her dog at 4:45 A.M. on the morning of November 17, 1966. It was unusual for her little pet to bark late at night, so she got up to investigate. The moon was out and was very bright, she recalled. She looked out the kitchen window and saw an enormous object hovering at treetop level in a field on the other side of Route 7. It was circular, the size of a small house, and brilliantly illuminated. It seemed to be divided into sections glowing with dazzlingly bright red and green lights.

"I was stunned," she said. Before she could wake up her husband, the object made a zig-zag motion and suddenly disappeared. She did not mention the sighting to anyone outside her immediate family until weeks later.

That afternoon a seventeen-year-old boy was driving down Route 7, not far from Mrs. Grose's home in Cheshire, Ohio, when a huge bird suddenly dove at his car and pursued him for a mile or so.

On the eighteenth two firemen from Point Pleasant, Paul Yoder and Benjamin Enochs, were in the TNT area when they encountered a giant bird with big red eyes. "It was definitely a bird," they stated flatly. "But it was huge. We'd never seen anything like it."

Everyone was now seeing Mothman or the "Bird," or so it seemed. Sightings were reported in Mason, Lincoln, Logan, Kanawha, and Nicholas counties. People were traveling for hundreds of miles to sit in the cold TNT area all night, hoping to glimpse the creature. Those who were unlucky enough to see it vowed they never wanted to see it again. It evoked unspeakable terrors. Like flying saucers, it delighted in chasing cars . . . a very unbirdlike habit, and it seemed to have a penchant for scaring females who were menstruating, another UFO/hairy monster peculiarity.

Five teen-agers driving along Campbells Creek on the night of November 20 got the shock of their lives when their headlights bounced off a man-size birdlike creature standing beside a rock quarry. It turned and scurried into the woods. "Nobody believes us because we're teen-agers," Brenda Jones of Point Lick complained. "But it was real scary."

An elderly businessman in Point Pleasant found Mothman standing on his front lawn. He stepped outside to see why his dog was barking and confronted a six- or seven-foot tall gray apparition with flaming eyes. He stood transfixed for several minutes, unaware of the passage of time. Suddenly the creature flew off and he staggered back into his house. He was so pale and shaken his wife thought he was having a heart attack.

V.

While the people of West Virginia were being overrun with Garudas, the rest of the country was being engulfed in wingless flying objects. A great wave began that Halloween and continued through November. On November 22 a family from Wildwood Crest, New Jersey, near the tip of thinly populated Cape May, crossed the thin line that separates our reality from something else.

At 7:45 P.M. the Edward Christiansen family, seven people, were driving southward along the Garden State Parkway, just north of Mayville, when a bright red, green, and white object plummeted from the sky and disappeared directly in front of them. They thought an airplane had crashed until they were parallel to Burleigh, New Jersey. Then they saw a large glowing sphere just above the treetops a few miles to the front and right. Thinking it was a fire from the crashed plane, they pulled over to the side of the parkway and stopped (an illegal maneuver).

All of the witnesses got out of the car to watch. Traffic was light but several cars did speed past them. As they watched, the object began to move and they realized it was not a fire but was some kind of flying sphere. It executed a sharp turn and came toward the witnesses, passing directly over their heads. It was completely silent. As it approached their position, three powerful "headlights" became visible on the front of the object. These lights appeared to be elongated and passed from the top of the craft to the underside. The object disappeared northward and the witnesses experienced a strong emotional reaction. Mrs. Arline Christiansen and her sister Gwendoline Martino became hysterical, alarming their four children. Two of the youngsters began to cry. They all returned to the car and drove home to Wildwood Crest.

Edward Christiansen, forty, a hard-nosed businessman, refused to believe in flying saucers and tried to assure the women that there had to be a natural explanation. His sister-in-law Gwendoline decided to call the local air force base at Palmero. She spoke to an officer there and he seemed quite interested in her story and asked several questions. An hour later the family received a long-distance phone call from another air force base (none of them could remember the name of the base or the names of the officers when I interviewed them several months later). Each one of them was interviewed at great length by "three or four officers." They were told that their conversation was being taped, and the questions followed a pattern which suggested the officers were filling out detailed forms on the other end of the line. However, all of them were disappointed to find the air force would not give them any information or answer their own questions.

Something extraordinary seems to have happened that night. Instead of simply filing a report through normal channels, the officer at the Palmero base may have called Wright-Patterson in Ohio immediately. Officers from Project Blue Book then called the Christiansens for additional details. However, it is puzzling that "three or four different officers" would participate in the questioning. Incidently, these witnesses are above average in income and intelligence and their overall reliability is unquestioned.

Later that evening as Mrs. Martino, who was spending the night at the Christiansens, was preparing for bed she suddenly heard a loud radio signal . . . a series of dots and dashes. She knew her brother-in-law had a portable CB (Citizen's Band) radio and she assumed he had accidentally left it turned on. He and his wife were already in bed and asleep but she didn't understand the radio and didn't want to tamper with it. She continued to hear the signals as she entered their bedroom and awakened them. *They were unable to hear the signals* . . . and the radio was turned off and in its case.

The signals faded and Mrs. Martino went to bed baffled. A beautiful, lithe divorcee, Mrs. Martino had not had any unusual psychic experiences before.

VI.

Roger and Linda Scarberry were living in a house trailer at the time of their Mothman sighting. In the week that followed they were suddenly plagued by strange sounds around the trailer late at night. Beeps and loud garbled noises like a speeded-up phonograph record. They could not locate the source of the sounds outside or inside the trailer. Worried and frightened, they finally moved out of the trailer and settled in the basement apartment in the home of Linda's parents, Parke and Mabel McDaniel.

VII.

On November 24, four people, two adults and two children, were driving past the TNT area when they saw a giant flying creature with red eyes. Their report added to the growing chaos. Now thousands of people were pouring into the old munitions site nightly, some traveling from hundreds of miles away. Television crews and newsmen from other states hovered around the old generator plant, hoping to glimpse the monster. Some visitors divided their time between the TNT area and Woodrow Derenberger's farm in Mineral Wells.

Mothman was not to be outsmarted, however. He staged his appearances with clever showmanship, popping up in unexpected places in front of witnesses who had previously been skeptical.

At 7:15 A.M. on November 25, a young shoe salesman named Thomas Ury was driving along Route 62 just north of the TNT area when he noticed a tall, gray manlike figure standing in a field by the road. "Suddenly it spread a pair of wings," Ury said, "and took off straight up, like a helicopter.

"It veered over my convertible and began going in circles three telephone poles high."

He stepped on the gas as the creature zoomed down over his vehicle. "It kept flying right over my car even though I was doing about seventy-five."

Mr. Ury sped into Point Pleasant and went straight to the sheriff's office thoroughly panicked. "I never saw anything like it," he confided to Mrs. Hyre later. "I was so scared I just couldn't go to work that day. This thing had a wingspan every bit of ten feet. It could be a bird, but I certainly never saw one like it. I was afraid it was going to come down right on top of me."

The old familiar symptom, unreasonable terror, took hold of him. "I've never had that feeling before. A weird kind of fear," he said. "That fear gripped you and held you. Somehow, the best way to explain it would be to say that the whole thing just wasn't right. I know that may not make sense, but that's the only way I can put into words what I felt."

That same week some very freakish birds appeared in Ohio and Pennsylvania, far north of Point Pleasant. George Wolfe, Jr., twenty-three, of Beaver Falls, Pennsylvania, was out hunting when he came across a "seven-foot-tall bird that looked something like an ostrich" in a cornfield.

"I could see it dodging in and out among the trees," he said. "It didn't leap over the brush like a deer would do, but just zig-zagged through the trees, in a strange sidewise motion.

"I was so startled I didn't take a shot at it. It had a long neck and a round body with a plumed tail that reached high above its body.

"It was a grayish color and looked about seven feet tall. It was about fifty feet from me when it stood up and began to run. My dog ran after it, but when Old Ringo caught up with it, he let out a howl. He ran back to me with his tail between his legs and he was howling and whimpering."

In Lowell, Ohio, about seventy miles north of Point Pleasant, Marvin Shock and his family watched a group of gigantic birds for about two hours on November 26. "They looked about as big as a man would look moving around in the trees," Shock reported. "When we started walking toward them for a closer look—we were about one hundred yards from them—they took off and flew up the ridge."

Shock, his two children, and Ewing Tilton, a neighbor, watched the creatures from a distance. They were from four to five feet tall and had a wingspread of at least ten feet. There was "a reddish cast" to their heads, but the witnesses did not see the famous glowing red eyes.

"They had dark brown backs with some light flecks," Ewing Tilton noted. "Their breasts were gray and they had five-or-six-inch bills, straight, not curved like those of hawks or vultures."

These reports indicate that some very unusual birds were in the general region at the time of the Mothman fracas, even though a systematic search of ornithological literature has failed to identify the creatures seen by Wolfe, Shock, and Ewing. One Ohio college professor insisted it was a rare sandhill crane, so I carried a picture of the sandhill crane in my briefcase and not a single witness recognized it or thought it resembled what he or she had seen.

Altogether, more than one hundred adults would see this winged impossibility in 1966–67. Those who got a close look at it all agreed on the basic points. It was gray, apparently featherless, as large—or larger—than a big man, had a wingspread of about ten feet, took off straight up like a helicopter, and did not flap its wings in flight. Its face was a puzzle. No one could describe it. The two red eyes dominated it. (In a majority of the reports of angels, demons, and saucer spacemen the faces are also either covered in some manner or are nonexistent.)

The "ostrich" in Pennsylvania and the big birds in Ohio did not seem to fit into the picture. If they were real birds of some kind, where did they go? Why weren't they seen again?

On the evening of November 26, a housewife in St. Albans, a suburb of Charleston, West Virginia, found Mothman standing on her front lawn. Mrs. Ruth Foster was one of the very few witnesses who claimed to see a face on the creature.

"It was standing on the lawn beside the porch," Mrs. Foster said. "It was tall with big red eyes that popped out of its face. My husband is six feet one and this bird looked about the same height or a little shorter, maybe.

"It had a funny little face. I didn't see any beak. All I saw were those big red poppy eyes. I screamed and ran back into the house. My brother-in-law went out to look, but it was gone."

The next morning the winged phantom pursued young Connie Carpenter near the Mason, West Virginia, golf course (Chapter Two). That evening, it encored in St. Albans. Sheila Cain, thirteen, and her younger sister were walking home from the store when they saw an enormous "something" standing next to a local junk yard.*

"It was gray and white with big red eyes," Sheila reported, "and it must have been seven feet tall—taller than a man. I screamed and we ran home. It flew up in the air and followed us part of the way."

Aerodynamically, Mothman was ill-suited for flight. A creature larger than a big man, and therefore weighing in excess of two hundred pounds, would require more than a ten-foot wingspan to get aloft. And large birds take off by running along the ground and flapping their wings franti-

---

*Monsters, UFOs, and apparitions have an interesting affinity for garbage dumps and junk yards. Even the famous miracle at Lourdes, France, in 1858, took place at the local garbage dump.

cally. My favorite, the gooney bird of the Pacific, runs back and forth desperately trying to build up airspeed and then, more often than not, falls flat on his face.

Mothman, with his helicopterlike takeoffs, was impossible.

I was in Washington, D.C., that November, harassing the air force in my black suit, when I spoke to Gray Barker on the phone. Despite the furor then taking place in West Virginia, I had not heard or read a thing about the "Bird's" arrival.

When Gray brought the matter up, I thought he was joking. A red-eyed bird with a ten-foot wingspan who loved to chase speeding automobiles seemed utterly ridiculous. Now if it had been a ten-foot tall hair-covered monster with a terrible smell I might have taken it seriously.

But Gray convinced me it was no joke. I looked Point Pleasant up on the map . . . it was about eight hundred miles from New York . . . oiled my fourteen-foot monster traps, got into my car, and headed for the Ohio valley.

7:

The Night
of the
Bleeding Ear

I.

Gwendoline Martino was back in her apartment in Cherry
Hill, New Jersey, early in December 1966, packing her
things for a trip to Europe. Her unlisted phone rang. A
female voice with a slight foreign accent came on the line.

"Hello, Gwen?"

"Yes, this is Gwen . . . "

"Gwen Stevens?"

"No, this is Gwen Martino."

"You're not Gwen Stevens?"

"No . . . you've got the wrong Gwen."

This same woman called back again on two successive
nights. The conversation was always the same. Mrs. Martino
was mildly irritated that the woman would call her three
times in a row but she thought nothing of it until I met her
a few months later and asked my routine questions about
unusual phone calls.

Because of the woman's accent, it is possible she was
asking for "Jen Stevens." Mrs. Martino had never heard of

anyone named either Gwen or Jen Stevens. But at that time a woman named Jennifer ("Jen") Stevens was very active in UFO research in the Albany-Schenectady area of New York State. Mrs. Stevens experienced a wide range of problems with her unlisted phone and a personal tragedy which seemed to be related to her UFO investigations.

In February 1968, Mrs. Stevens reported the following:

> [One] night when my husband, Peter, and I returned home we found Jenny, our fifteen-year-old daughter, in a highly nervous state. She said the phone had been ringing all evening. She would answer it and hear nothing at the other end but heavy breathing. When her boyfriend called they were interrupted several times by high-pitched beeping noises and were also cut off twice. The next day the calls continued. Sometimes there would be mechanical sounds, and others, the high-pitched whining, beeping sound that sent sharp pains through the mastoid bones. Our number is unlisted so I knew no one could have gotten it out of the phone book or through the operator. We had long since screened all calls through another number in order to avoid cranks. I called the telephone company and they gave our line a complete check with NO findings. The service man offered his personal opinion that the line "could have been tapped."

Several days after our telephone problems began, my husband, who is a building contractor, was in a large downtown Schenectady store inspecting some work and dropped into the snack bar for a cup of coffee. A few moments after he seated himself, a tall, tan, "saturnine"-looking man, whom my husband had never seen before, sat down next to him and started a conversation. He began with, "There have been people watching the sky every night down by the river in Scotia." Since Peter was one of "those people," he was shocked . . . but kept cool and said, "I beg your pardon?"

The man proceeded to talk about UFOs. Peter tried to draw him out and asked his name, and so on. All his questions were either parried or avoided. My husband was beginning to feel a bit uncomfortable when the stranger finally excused himself after noting, "People who look for UFOs should be very, very careful."

At my request, Peter Stevens made two sketches of the "saturnine"-looking man. They sent me one copy and kept the other. A few weeks later their home was broken into and thoroughly ransacked. But nothing was stolen . . . *except their copy of the sketch.*[1]

Two months later Peter Stevens, a young man in his thirties, died very suddenly. Anguished, Jen abandoned UFO research. I never learned the full circumstances of his death. She would tell me only that it was "related" to the UFO business in some way.

I have shown Peter Stevens's drawing to numerous Men-in-Black witnesses over the years and the usual response is, "It looks close enough to be a brother."

Today "heavy breathers" plague telephone subscribers from coast to coast and are usually assumed to be sex nuts. When I received many such calls in 1967–68 I recorded some of them and studied the tapes. The sound is more mechanical or electronic than human and is probably caused by the introduction of a modulated current into the telephone line. This phenomenon is not isolated to the cities. People in remote towns with a population of only twenty-five or so also get these calls. The heavy breathing of the sex nut who (supposedly) masturbates while he listens to a female voice on the line contains certain recordable vocal characteristics which are totally absent in the heavy breathing calls I taped. Played at a slower speed, the recorded "breathing" was an evenly spaced series of pulses resembling the swishing sound of a phonograph when the needle reaches the end of the record and does not reject. Heavy breathing would not be so uniform.

[1]No one ever tried to steal my copy. It was subsequently published in a special issue of *Flying Saucer Review*, June 1969.

II.

Mr. Kevin Dee and his NICAP subcommittee urged Woodrow Derenberger to submit to a psychiatric and medical examination. In early December Woody voluntarily entered St. Joseph's Hospital in Parkersburg and underwent hours of tests administered by Dr. Morgan (I have changed his name here for reasons that will become obvious later on), a leading local psychiatrist, and Peter Volardi, an EEG technician. In his final report, Dr. Morgan stated:

> There was no evidences of abnormalities at all. Subsequently, a report and interpretation was obtained from Baltimore, and the report indicated no abnormalities at all and was a perfectly normal electroencephalogram. There was no evidence of organic brain damage or of seizure disorders. We were particularly concerned about epilepsy and there was no evidence of this. The record was a normal record with no indication of any central nervous system pathology at all. There was no evidence of any psychiatric disorders. I submitted a report to the Pittsburgh Subcommittee of NICAP, of the psychiatric exa·nination of Mr. Derenberger in which I stated that I could find no evidence of mental disorder. There was no indication of any lower pathology. I found Mr. Derenberger to be normal.

The NICAP investigators sent the medical records on to the Washington office of the organization, along with detailed reports on Woody's encounter and his personal background. Typically, the NICAP newsletter later devoted a couple of paragraphs to the Derenberger case, denouncing it as a hoax, misspelling Woody's name, and referring to Cold as "Kuld." Woody had spelled the name C-o-l-d from the outset and it was spelled that way throughout the subcommittee's documents. How NICAP arrived at the K-u-l-d spelling is a mystery in itself.

III.

"Look at that crazy character coming in downwind in that plane," Eddie Adkins commented. He and four other men were standing on the field of the Gallipolis, Ohio, airport, just across the river from Point Pleasant on Sunday, December 4, 1966.

At 3 P.M. that afternoon a large winged form came cruising majestically along the Ohio River, just behind the airport. The pilots later estimated that it was about three hundred feet in the air and was traveling about seventy miles an hour. As it drew closer they realized it was not a plane but was some kind of enormous bird with an unusually long neck. It seemed to be turning its head from side to side as if it were taking in the scenery. The wings were not flapping.

"My God! It's something prehistoric!" one of the men cried.

Everett Wedge grabbed his camera and sprinted to his small plane. But by the time he was airborne the giant creature had vanished somewhere down river.

Three days later, on December 7, I arrived in Point Pleasant for the first time. I found a sleepy little town, clean, well-managed, prosperous. The Ohio valley is a busy industrial area and the river is lined with chemical factories and thriving businesses. It is a far cry from the dreary coal mining towns of Appalachia further east. The neat, modern homes of the valley boasted more than their share of color television sets and late model cars. The people are not hillbillies but, for the most part, are skilled technicians employed in the many factories; well-educated, well-paid Americans leading quiet, average lives. Although there was a hotel in Point Pleasant I chose to cross the Silver Bridge and take a room in one of the many modern motels on the Ohio side of the river.

My first stop was the Mason County courthouse and a chat with Deputy Halstead, a soft-spoken, serious man with a receding hairline and just a trace of the curse of all small-town policemen—the potbelly.

"There's something to it," he assured me. "The people who have seen this Bird were all mighty scared. They saw something. I don't know what. Some say it's just a crane."

I asked him if there had been any flying saucer reports in the area.

"No, we haven't had any of that. Just the 'Bird.' That's enough!"

He told me how to find the McDaniel home and I drove out to do the thing I hated most—knock on the door of a total stranger, introduce myself as a hotshot writer from New York, and invade the privacy of people already weary from the publicity, reporters, and self-styled investigators. Mabel McDaniel came to the door, an attractive woman not at all like the frail, drawn sparrowlike women I so often met up in the hills of Appalachia. It was early evening and within an hour Mabel had made a series of phone calls and the little house was filled with people. Roger and Linda, Steve and Mary Mallette, and Connie Carpenter and her fiance Keith, and Mrs. Mary Hyre all arrived. My first reaction to Mrs. Hyre was negative. Every town has a local busybody and I pegged her as that, erroneously it turned out.

Connie's eyes were red and swollen, as I have already noted, but she was the only one who had experienced this telltale reaction. She seemed to be an emotionally fragile girl, but down-to-earth. Roger and Steve, lifelong buddies, talked with great enthusiasm about their great adventure. But I had learned long ago that young men usually tend to color their experiences with rich imagination and heroic posturing. However, there were no false heroics here. They had been genuinely frightened out of their wits and were not ashamed to admit it.

Later Mary Hyre told me she had heard them recount the episode dozens of times to innumerable reporters and investigators. "None of them have ever changed it or added a word," she noted.

Since they had viewed the creature only briefly and in the dark, their descriptions were understandably lacking in significant detail. Even Connie, who had seen the creature in broad daylight, could not describe the thing beyond the fact that it was gray, huge, and flew. Its face, she said, was "science-fiction-like." The glowing red eyes had made the biggest impression on her, as they had on the others. And the overriding sense of unreasonable fear was the main reaction. There had been no smells in the areas of the sightings. No footprints or droppings or other tangible evidence.

After taping their individual stories, we decided to go out to the TNT area so I could have my first look at the site. At about 9 P.M. we drove to the old ammunition dump. The police had now locked the old gate leading to the power plant, but it was no problem to squeeze through the fence. The night was dark and overcast and the rickety building was just a huge, black lump on the landscape. We gathered outside the main entrance. The crowds who had swarmed there weeks earlier had given up so we were alone . . . ten people. I carried my powerful six-cell flashlight. To me, this was just another broken, deserted building in a remote spot. I was used to prowling around such places alone in the dark, but I was troubled by the fear that now seemed to be gripping our little expedition. Their nervousness was real. Only Connie and Keith volunteered to enter the building with me. The others clustered outside.

The three of us went into the ruin. Connie was joking and in good spirits. Keith was sober and quiet. The interior of the building was filled with debris and silence except for the soft sound of dripping water. Large rusting boilers stood on the ground floor. I peered into them with my flashlight. Mothman wasn't hiding there. I climbed the steel ladders and strolled the catwalks. Even the pigeons seemed to have deserted the place.

Satisfied that the building was empty, we started for the exit. I preceded the other two with my flashlight. As she stepped through the door which led into the smaller chamber where the main exit was located, Connie glanced over her shoulder and let out a horrified gasp.

"Those eyes!" She screamed. "He's there!"

She dissolved into total hysteria, crying uncontrollably. The brave, cheerful girl of a moment ago was now a blubbering wreck. Keith and I rushed her outside.

"I saw those eyes—two big red eyes—by the wall in the back," she managed to choke out.

While everyone gathered around her and tried to calm her, I turned and rushed back into the building. The wall at the far end of the boiler room was blank. There was nothing there that could have reflected the light from my flashlight. Again I searched the building from top to bottom and found nothing.

When I got back outside I found a police officer, Deputy Alva Sullivan, had joined our group. Like the others, he had been reluctant to enter the building and help me with my search. They were all looking through a fence facing a field that went behind the power plant.

"We thought we saw something back of the plant," Mary Hyre explained. "A tall figure running. Was it you?"

"No . . . I never left the building."

"What was that noise while you were in there?" Mabel McDaniel asked.

"What noise?"

"It was metallic and hollow. A loud noise. Like a piece of metal had fallen all the way down from the top or something."

Everyone had heard the sound . . . except me. And I hadn't done anything to make such a noise.

Keith led Connie, still crying, to their car.

"Please, let's get out of here," she begged.

"I'm bleeding," Mary Mallette suddenly exclaimed, cupping her hand to her ear. I flashed my light into her ear. A small trickle of blood was oozing out.

"Did you hear anything else?" I asked. Everyone shook his head.

"No, but it doesn't feel right here, does it?" Mary Hyre observed. "It feels oppressive . . . heavy."

I had to agree with her. Something did seem to be out of whack. Steve Mallette led his wife away. Now we had two hysterical women on our hands!

"Did you really see somebody back there?" I asked Deputy Sullivan quietly.

"It's hard to say. Might have been an animal. A deer or something."

The whole group was now in a state bordering on sheer panic. I could see that their feelings were real. This was not just some kind of act being staged for my benefit. I'm no hero, but I did not share their fear. Mrs. Mallette's bleeding ear was a sign of concussion, meaning the air pressure had changed suddenly. Connie had apparently had an hallucinatory or psychic glimpse of those frightening eyes. The metallic clang could not have come from inside the building or I would have heard it, too. It may have been associated with the sudden change in air pressure. I scanned the black skies. There was not a star, not a light visible.

We all filed back to our cars and returned to the McDaniels' home. Mary Mallette's ear stopped bleeding. Keith drove a still-shaking Connie Carpenter home. And, being an all-time idiot, I returned to the TNT area for another look. It was well past midnight as I drove aimlessly up and down the dirt roads among the igloos. Mothman did not pop out of the bushes to cry "Boo!," but I did have one curious experience. As I passed a certain point on one of the isolated roads I was suddenly engulfed in fear. I stepped on the gas and after I went a few yards my fear vanished as quickly as it came. I continued to drive, eventually returning again to the same spot. And again a wave of unspeakable fear swept over me. I drove quickly away from the place and then stopped, puzzled. Why would this one stretch of road produce this hair-raising effect? I turned around and slowly headed back, trying to note trees, fenceposts, and other landmarks in the dark. Once again, when I reached that particular point the hair tingled on the back of my neck and I became genuinely afraid. When I emerged from the other side of this invisible zone I stopped and got out of my car. The air was perfectly still. There wasn't any audible sound . . . not even a bird call. I was reminded of the hour of quiet that settles inexplicably over the jungle in early morning when suddenly, usually around 2 A.M., all of the animals, birds, even the insects, become totally silent for about two hours. If you're not used to the jungle and its ways, this sudden silence can wake you from a deep sleep.

I walked back to the "zone of fear" slowly, alert for any rustle of bushes, measuring my own breathing and emotions. I was perfectly calm until I took one step too many and was back in the zone. I almost panicked and ran, but I forced myself to look around and proceed slowly. By now I had figured out that I was probably walking through a beam of ultrasonic waves and really had nothing to be afraid of. After I had gone about fifteen feet I stepped outside the zone and everything was normal again. Now I had to walk through that damned spot again to get back to my car! It was too dark, almost pitch-black, and I was too unfamiliar with the TNT area at the time to attempt to go around the zone. Although I knew it was harmless, I dreaded reentering it. I actually considered remaining there, only yards from my car, until daybreak. But I finally steeled myself and walked once more through that invisible stream, scared out of my wits in transit yet privately pleased with my discovery.

In daylight I returned to the same spot. The zone of fear was gone. I searched for power transmission lines, telephone microwave towers, and anything that might have radiated energy through the area. There was nothing. Nor did a daytime exploration of the power plant reveal anything Connie might have mistaken for red eyes.

Mrs. Mallette's bleeding ear and my discovery of the ultrasonic zone of fear convinced me that UFO-type phenomena were present in the TNT area even though the police and press had not received any reports. I asked Mrs. Hyre and the McDaniels to be alert for any rumors of sightings. Within days I tracked down dozens of UFO witnesses throughout the Ohio valley. At 2 A.M. on the morning I was first prowling the TNT area, a young man living further up the Ohio River got up to go to the bathroom and saw a brilliantly illuminated object floating in the air just above the water. It was circular in shape and appeared to have windows in it covered over with curtains like crumpled aluminum foil. Two hours later, Mr. and Mrs. Charles Hern of Cheshire, Ohio, saw something very similar. Their home was directly opposite the TNT area on the Ohio side of the river. Mr. Hern was walking his dog when he noticed a red light on the opposite riverbank. At first he thought it might be a trapper in a boat checking his muskrat traps. Then he realized it was on the bank, not on the water, and in the glare of the light he could see figures moving about. He called his wife outside and they both watched for several minutes trying to figure out what it was. The figures seemed to be very small in stature.

Dazzled and disbelieving, the Herns woke up their neighbors, Mr. and Mrs. Walter Taylor, who joined them. Red and orange lights flashed on and off, and one light seemed to be directed toward the water most of the time. Finally the lights went out and a bright greenish light came on. Then the object rose straight up into the air and disappeared into the sky.

"I've lived on this riverbank since I was twelve years old," Mr. Hern told Mary Hyre and myself, "and I know every boat light, but this was definitely something I've never seen before."

"It's a funny thing," Mrs. Hern added. "We were so stunned we didn't even talk about it afterwards. We just sat silently at the kitchen table. We even forgot to say our 'thank yous' that morning."

As soon as Mrs. Hyre began publishing UFO reports in the *Messenger* dozens of other people came forward with their own stories. She was able to print only a small percentage of all the reports she received.

IV.

Dr. Morgan, the Parkersburg psychiatrist, was watching a football game on television in his home in a suburb of the city that December when he was overcome by a strange sensation. A voice began to speak to him, announcing that it came from a spaceship somewhere overhead. He was becoming a contactee!

(A year later, Woodrow Derenberger was a guest on Long John Nebel's radio talk show in New York and I was one of the panelists. Long John phoned Dr. Morgan on the air and he described his experiences in a beeperphone conversation.)

While Dr. Morgan was tuning in to that phantom reality of the superspectrum, Woody was entertaining more interesting visitors at Mineral Wells. A man identifying himself as Captain Bruce Parsons of the NASA security police at Cocoa Beach, Florida, called on him and invited him to Cape Kennedy, home of our space program. Shortly after Christmas, Woody, his wife, and children flew to Cape Kennedy to spend a week with Captain Parsons. By day they toured the great rocket-launching installation. But each evening Woody was taken to a room somewhere on the Cape where he was questioned for hours, covering every detail of his visits with Indrid Cold. One of his questioners was a man identified as the head of NASA and called simply "Charlie."*

According to Woody, at the end of the week his interrogators showed him a star map and pointed to a speck on it telling him, "That's where they're from." They said they had interviewed several other contactees, all with stories similar to his own. When he asked why they didn't release their UFO information to the public, they allegedly replied that it would only cause panic. Women would commit suicide, throw babies out the window, and this kind of panic could sweep the world, they said.

Derenberger brought home a flock of souvenirs as proof of his trip: photographs and even a scrap of the material used in our astronauts' spacesuits. This, Woody says, is the same kind of reflective material worn by Indrid Cold under his coat on that rainy November evening.

*The head of NASA at that time was Dr. Thomas O. Paine.

8:
Procession
of the Damned

I.

While Mothman and Indrid Cold attracted all the publicity and turned everyone's eyes to the deep skies of night, the strange ones began to arrive in West Virginia. They trooped down from the hills, along the muddy back roads, up from the winding "hollers," like an army of leprechauns seeking impoverished shoemakers. It was open season on the human race and so the ancient procession of the damned marched once more. A doctor and his wife driving along a country road in a snowstorm saw a huge, caped figure of a man struggling through the snow, so they stopped to give him a ride. He vanished. There was nothing but whirling snow-flakes and night where he had stood.

Black limousines halted in front of hill homes and deeply tanned "census takers" inquired about the number of children living with the families. Always the children. In several instances, the occupants of the big black cars merely asked for a glass of water. The old fairy trick, taken up from the Middle Ages and dusted off. A blond woman in her thirties, well-groomed, with a soft southern accent, visited people in Ohio and West Virginia whom I had interviewed. She introduced herself as "John Keel's secretary," thus winning instant admission. The clipboard she carried held a complicated form filled with personal questions about the witnesses' health, income, the type of cars they owned, their general family background, and some fairly sophisticated questions about their UFO sightings. Not the type of questions a run-of-the-mill UFO buff would ask.

I have no secretary. I didn't learn about this woman until months later when one of my friends in Ohio wrote to me and happened to mention, "As I told your secretary when she was here . . ." Then I checked and found out she had visited many people, most of whom I had never mentioned in print. How had she located them?

There were other weird types on the loose. In early December one of them tried to waylay Mrs. Marcella Bennett, one of the ladies who had had the frightening meeting with Mothman in the TNT area on November 16. She and her small daughter, Teena, were driving along a deserted back road outside of Point Pleasant when she became aware of a red Ford Galaxy following her. It was driven by a large man, a stranger, she said, who appeared to be wearing a very bushy fright wig. She slowed down, expecting the vehicle would pass. Instead, it tried to force her off the road. She accelerated and the other car raced around her, shot down the road, and disappeared around a bend. When she circled the bend she was alarmed to find that the Ford was now parked crossways on the narrow dirt road, blocking it. Badly frightened, she warned her daughter to hold on and jammed the gas pedal to the floor. The other driver, seeing that she didn't mean to stop, pulled over hastily and let her pass. She had never seen the man before. And she never saw him again. Molestations of this sort were rare, virtually nonexistent, in Point Pleasant before Mothman arrived.

Mrs. Mary Hyre entertained the first of her long string of peculiar visitors early in January 1967. She was working late in her office opposite the county courthouse when her door opened and a very small man entered. He was about four feet six inches tall, she told me in a phone call soon afterward. Although it was about 20°F. outside, he was wearing nothing but a short-sleeved blue shirt and blue trousers of thin-looking material. His eyes were dark and deepset, and were covered with thick-lensed glasses. He was wearing odd shoes with very thick soles which probably added an inch or two to his height.

Speaking in a low, halting voice, he asked her for directions to Welch, West Virginia, a town in the southeastern tip of the state. She thought at first that he had some kind of speech impediment. His black hair was long and cut squarely "like a bowl haircut" and his eyes remained fixed on her in an unflinching, hypnotic way.

"He kept getting closer and closer," she reported. "His funny eyes staring at me almost hypnotically."

He told her a long-winded, disjointed story about his truck breaking down in Detroit, Michigan. He had hitchhiked all the way from Detroit. As he talked, he inched closer and closer to her, and she became frightened, thinking she had some kind of a nut on her hands. She pulled back from her desk and ran into the back room where her newspaper's circulation manager was working on a telephone campaign. He joined her and they spoke together to the little man.

"He seemed to know more about West Virginia than we did," she declared later.

At one point the telephone rang, and while she was speaking on it the little man picked up a ball-point pen from her desk and examined it with amazement, "as if he had never seen a pen before."

"You can have that if you want it," she offered. He responded with a loud, peculiar laugh, a kind of cackle. Then he ran out into the night and disappeared around a corner.

The next day Mrs. Hyre checked with the sheriff's office to find out if there was any mentally deficient person on the loose. The answer was negative.

II.

On the afternoon of January 9, 1967, Edward Christiansen and his family returned to their new home in Wildwood, New Jersey, after a trip to Florida. They had just moved into the new house, some distance from the place where they had lived at the time of their November UFO sighting. Neither their address nor phone number was listed in the then-current phone book. They entered their house by the back door. The front door was still heavily bolted and locked, the way they had left it when they had gone to Florida.

At 5:30 P.M. there was a knock on the front door. Mrs. Arline Christiansen was in the kitchen preparing dinner.

"Check and see who that is," she told her seventeen-year-old daughter, Connie. "If it's a salesman, don't answer."

Connie took a peek and reported back, "It's the strangest looking man I've ever seen."

Mrs. Christiansen went to the door, unbolted and unlatched it. It was growing dark and was bitter cold outside. There was no car in view and this seemed peculiar because the Christiansen home was removed from other houses in a rather isolated spot. A tall man stood on the doorstep.

"Does Edward Christiansen live here?" he asked. Arline admitted he did. "I'm from the *Missing Heirs Bureau*," the man continued. "Mr. Christiansen may have inherited a great deal of money. May I come in?"

It was an approach that was hard to resist. She stepped back and invited him in, calling out to her husband.

Edward Christiansen is six feet two inches tall and heavy-set. The stranger towered over him and must have been at least six feet six inches tall. He was also enormously broad and might have weighed at least three hundred pounds. He wore a fur Russian-style hat with a black visor on it and a very long black coat that seemed to be made of thin material . . . too thin for the cold weather.

"This will only take forty minutes," he said as he removed his hat and revealed an unusual head, large and round while his face seemed angular, pointed. He had black hair which was closely cropped to his head, as if his head had been shaved and the hair was just growing in again. There was a perfectly round spot on the back of his head as if that area had recently been shaved. His nose and mouth seemed relatively normal, but his eyes were large, protruding, like "thyroid eyes," and set wide apart. One eye appeared to have a cast, like a glass eye, and did not move in unison with its companion.

Edward Christiansen told him at the outset that a mistake had been made, that he could not believe that anyone had left him any money. The man assured him that he might, indeed, be the Edward Christiansen he was seeking and, in order to verify it, he would like to ask some questions. He removed his coat. There was a badge on his shirt pocket which he quickly covered with his hand and removed, placing it in his coat pocket.

"It looked like a gold or brass badge," Connie told me later. "But it wasn't an ordinary police badge or anything like that. We just got a glimpse of it . . . but it seemed to have a big *K* on it with a small *x* alongside and there were some letters or numbers around the edge. It was obvious he didn't want us to see it."

He was not wearing a suit jacket. Underneath his thin outer coat he was wearing a short-sleeved shirt made of a Dacron-like material. His trousers were of a dark material, gray or black, and were a little too short. When he sat down they rode high up his calves. He wore dark socks and dark shoes with unusually thick rubber soles.

Arline and Connie were most fascinated by a strange feature on his leg. When he sat down they could see a long thick green wire attached to the inside of his leg. It came up out of his socks and disappeared under his trousers. At one point it seemed to be indented into his leg and was covered by a large brown spot. Connie seemed to have studied him the most carefully and gave the best description.

In many ways, this odd man shared the characteristics of Mary Hyre's tiny visitor of only a few days earlier. Mrs. Hyre said the little man had unusually pale skin, almost a sickly white. The Christiansens said their visitor had an unnatural pallor. They assumed he was sick. His speech was also strange, with a high "tinny" voice that seemed especially peculiar coming from such a large man. He spoke in a dull, emotionless monotone in clipped words and phrases, "like a computer." Connie said that he sounded as if he were reciting everything from memory. Mrs. Hyre told me her tiny visitor had spoken in a hard-to-understand singsong manner, "like a recording." Both men wore unusually thick rubber-soled shoes. Both were ill-dressed for the weather, and both had eccentric haircuts. Small points, perhaps, but significant in these cases.

After the man had introduced himself (none of the family could remember his name; they all said it was something common like Brown or Smith, but they did remember that he said his friends called him "Tiny"), the family dog, Gigi, snarled and barked at him. He spoke to the dog and calmed it.

When Tiny had seated himself, Mrs. Christiansen told him they were about to eat and asked him if he wanted to join them. He replied that he was on a diet but that he would like a glass of water in about ten minutes. He seemed to wheeze, they all noted, like a man with asthma, and he appeared to have difficulty breathing.

Tiny produced a small notebook and a pen and assured the family that this was not any kind of confidence game. He was looking for an Edward Christiansen who was due to inherit a large sum of money and he would need information about Ed's past history to determine if he was the man. He then proceeded to ask a long series of questions. Did Ed have any scars or birthmarks? Ed said he had a scar on his back from an operation and an appendix scar. Tiny asked for every detail—the length, width, and exact position of those scars. He also asked for a complete list of all the schools Ed had attended, and the number and type of auto vehicles the family owned. At one point he asked the couple if they would be willing to fly to any place in the United States to collect the inheritance, explaining they would have to be present when the will was read. Ed and Arline agreed they could make themselves available for such a trip.

According to Connie, Tiny's face gradually grew redder and redder as he talked and after a few minutes he turned to her and asked: "May I have that glass of water now?" She fetched the water for him and he took out a large yellow capsule which he gulped down. He returned to normal after taking it.

Tiny mentioned three specific names and asked Ed if he recognized any of them. He did not and later he was able to remember only one of them—Roy Stevens. Connie said she thought another of the names was Taylor, but she wasn't sure. At this time Ed did not know about Gwendoline Martino's "Gwen Stevens" wrong numbers in December, nor had Gwen heard about Tiny and the three names until I interviewed the family in late February 1967.

We had started out by discussing their UFO sighting in November, then I began to ask my routine far-out questions. When I asked them if they had received any unusual visitors after their sighting, they looked at each other with the shock of recognition. I separated them and interviewed each member of the family individually. All of their statements coincided exactly. Since five witnesses were involved, Mr. and Mrs. Christiansen and their three children, all of above-average intelligence and very observant, I regarded this as an outstanding MIB-type [Men in Black] report. I did not publish it until two years later, withholding the details to preclude possible hoaxes.

Tiny concluded his interview less than an hour after he arrived. It was probably precisely forty minutes, just as he promised. He donned his hat and coat and told Ed he would be notified by mail within ten days.

Arline was in the kitchen when he left and she decided she was going to watch him and see where he went. She stepped out the kitchen door and stood in the dark watching the big man as he walked toward the road. "His shoes squished loudly as he walked," she noted. When he reached the road, he made a gesture with his hand and a black 1963 Cadillac drove through the trees and pulled up. It was driving in the pitch-dark with its headlights out so she couldn't see the driver. Tiny climbed into the car and it drove away, its headlights still out.

The next morning Ed was alone in the house when the phone rang. A female voice explained she was calling about the missing heir interview. "We've located the Edward Christiansen we were looking for in California," she explained. Ed said he had felt sure he wasn't the right one, thanked her, and hung up. When he told his family about the call, they all dismissed the incident from their minds until my interview with them.

The wire running up the leg is one feature I have been unable to fit into my research in other MIB cases. It has never been repeated. Was Tiny wearing electric socks? Or was he a wired android operated by remote control?

As for his badge, I suspect that the *K* was really the Greek letter *sigma* [Σ], which has turned up repeatedly in other

UFO cases, and is often used by scientists to express the strange or unknown.

III.

Two days after Tiny, the pop-eyed missing-heirs investigator, invaded Cape May, Mothman, the pop-eyed pterodactyl, visited Tiny's restaurant in Point Pleasant. At 5 P.M. on January 11, 1967, Mrs. Mabel McDaniel was walking near the drive-in restaurant when she saw an object soaring down Route 62.

"I thought it was an airplane, then I realized it was flying much too low," she said. She had been living with Mothman witnesses for two months but never expected to see the critter herself. Nor did she want to. Knowing that she was psychologically prepared to, maybe, even hallucinate a sighting, I interviewed her very carefully afterward. Her story held up. This was a real sighting.

She froze in her tracks, scarcely believing her eyes.

"I thought I could see two legs . . . like men's legs . . . hanging down from it. It circled low over Tiny's and then flew off." She could not see any head or neck, the wings were motionless, and it was completely silent. In a way, it sounded almost like a hang-glider. But hang-gliding was almost a completely unknown sport in 1967.* Mrs. McDaniel was nervous and excited afterward but suffered no ill effects.

---

*Hang-gliders are lightweight frames covered with nylon. They look something like kites and the rider hangs underneath on bars and straps. They are launched from steep hills or cliffs. Route 62 runs along the edge of the Ohio River and the terrain is very flat.

IV.

Gwendoline Martino and her daughter returned from Europe in January and visited the Christiansens a few days after Tiny rode off in his darkened Cadillac. At 3 A.M. on January 13, 1967, Gwen and Connie, who were sharing a room, were awakened by a loud sound seeming to come from directly overhead. The sounds were distant at first, like someone hammering on metal with a rubber mallet or, possibly, walking over a metal surface. The noises grew steadily louder until they were deafening. "The whole house seemed to shake," Gwen said. When she started to get up to investigate, the sounds stopped instantly. As soon as she was back in bed, they began again. The two women debated whether they should wake up Ed Christiansen, a heavy sleeper. Gwen started to get out of bed again, and again the noises stopped. Finally they faded away.

Two evenings later Mr. and Mrs. Christiansen returned home to find their children in a very disraught state. They had heard the strange hammering sound again, followed by heavy footsteps crunching through the thick snow outside the house. Connie's nineteen-year-old boyfriend was present and he had looked out a window in time to see a tall figure hurrying away from the house. It was wearing a long white cape and when it reached a five-foot-high fence it leaped effortlessly over it and disappeared on the other side.

The next morning Ed Christiansen examined the area for footprints. He found a set of large human tracks deeply imbedded in the snow, leading to the fence and continuing on the other side. These footprints went on to another building some distance away and stopped abruptly at the wall of the structure. There were no other footprints around the building, an old abandoned shed, and the witnesses were puzzled as to where the person could have gone. Like our hairy monsters, little green Martians, and Mothman, the caped intruder had vanished into nothingness.

V.

Enter Tad Jones, a rarity among UFO witnesses because of his very common name. A gentle, handsome man in his thirties, Mr. Jones was a deeply religious person who did not smoke or drink. In 1967, he lived in Dunbar, a suburb of Charleston, West Virginia, and managed an appliance store at a place called Cross Lanes. Urbane, intelligent, and articulate, he was one of the most impressive UFO witnesses I have met in my travels.

At 9:05 A.M. on the morning of January 19, 1967, Tad was driving to his store along the newly completed multi-lane highway, Route 64, about ten miles outside of Charleston. A large object was blocking the road ahead of him and he first assumed it was a vehicle being used by a construction gang still working on the highway. But as he drew closer he saw that it was hovering in the air, about four feet off the ground.

"It was a large metal sphere," he said. "Since it was broad daylight I got a very good look at it. It was about twenty feet in diameter and was the color of dull aluminum."

He slowed his car and studied the thing for about two minutes.

"There were four legs attached to it," he continued, "with casterlike wheels on the bottom of each one. And there was a small window about nine inches in diameter on the side facing me. But I couldn't see anything inside the sphere. On the underside there was something like a propeller. It was idling when I first drove up, then it started spinning faster and the whole object began to rise upward. It disappeared into the sky and I drove on to my store."

Shaken and puzzled by his sighting, he decided to call the police and report it. His story quickly found its way into the local papers.

The next morning a crude note was slipped under his door in Dunbar. Written on ordinary notebook paper in block letters, it stated: "We know what you have seen and we know that you have talked. You'd better keep your mouth shut." He decided it had to be the work of some local prankster.

In nearby St. Albans, Mr. Ralph Jarrett, a chemical engineer and the local UFO authority, was shaving that morning when his telephone rang. He put down his razor and went into the bedroom to pick up the extension.

"I heard a very clear 'beep-beep' sound," Jarrett said. "The beeping continued for about two, maybe three minutes. Then the phone went dead and the dial tone came on. I've heard all sorts of code transmissions on shortwave, but nothing quite like that."

He went downstairs to breakfast, opened his copy of *The Charleston Gazette*, and read about Tad Jones's sighting . . . the first he had heard of it. Jarrett, an agressive, loquacious middle-aged man, was a highly qualified investigator. He later contacted Jones and conducted a thorough study of the case. He discovered the object had been hovering *directly above* a major gas line which passed under the road. (There have been other sightings of UFOs directly over buried gas lines.)

A few days later, another note was slipped under the door of Jones's home in Dunbar. This one was written on a piece of cardboard which had been burned around the edges. It repeated the earlier threat, adding, ". . . there want [sic] be another warning."

I arrived on the scene several weeks later and during my questioning he remembered another incident which seemed unimportant to him at the time. About a week after his sighting, he was driving along the same highway at the same time in the morning when he came upon a man standing by the road in approximately the same spot where the sphere had hovered. Thinking the man was hitchhiking and was stranded in this isolated stretch of road, Jones slowed his truck and called out to him, "Want a lift?" The man did not reply but merely waved him on. The next morning this same man was in the same place but this time Tad did not slow down.

"He was very tanned," Jones recalled, "or his face was very flushed. He looked normal and was wearing a blue coat and a blue cap with a visor . . . something like a uniform, I guess. I noticed he was holding a box in his hand. Some kind of instrument. It had a large dial on it, like a clock, and a wire ran from it to his other hand."

Later we checked the local gas companies to find out if they had had a man "walking the line" in that area. The answer was negative. I also asked about instruments such as Tad had described. No such instruments were in use.

When Mrs. Hyre and I visited the spot on Route 64 we found a series of very strange footprints in the mud beside the road. One group of footprints were identical to those I had found behind the power plant in the TNT area the previous December. They looked like huge dog tracks and were so deep the animal who made them must have weighed two hundred pounds or more. I couldn't relate them to Mothman, and there were a lot of dogs in the area, so I didn't think much about them at the time. Tad made plaster casts of these new prints, however, and none of the local wildlife authorities could identify them. They were *not* dog tracks. Zoologist Ivan Sanderson later rejected the "big dog" explanation, also, and told me similar tracks frequently turned up in places where paranormal events had occurred. And, in fact, I have since come across them myself in several separate spots around the country.

Aside from the dog tracks, we found a single footprint of what appeared to be a large, naked human foot. This was planted in the center of a muddy section with no other footprints of any kind around it. But a short distance away I came across some old friends . . . a type of footprint that has appeared at many UFO sites around the country. They look like the prints made by ripple-soled shoes but their spacing is always peculiar. They don't start anywhere and they don't lead anywhere. Ripple soles had been in fashion in the early 1960s and then had faded out. I once owned a pair myself. But these phantom prints had a ridge around the edges. Years later, when the first men walked on the moon, I realized the photos of the prints left by their moon-walking shoes were identical to the footprints I had seen over and over again in my travels. Obviously, the Martians and Venusians buy their equipment from the same companies that supply our space program.

VI.

Connie Carpenter's sighting of Mothman in November 1966 triggered off a long series of weird situations. She heard loud beeping sounds outside her bedroom window on several occasions. Then, in February 1967, someone tried to abduct her.

Early that month she and Keith Gordon were married and they moved across the river to a house in Middleport, Ohio. They did not have a phone and their new address was known only to their families and close friends. Middleport is a town of about three thousand people. Connie was still attending school. An excessively slender girl, she would never win a Raquel Welch lookalike contest.

At 8:15 A.M. on February 22, 1967, she started out for school. Keith was already at work. As she began walking down the quiet, tree-lined street a large black car pulled up alongside. Since all young people are automobile conscious, she said she could positively identify it as a 1949 Buick. The driver opened his door and called to her, asking for directions, so she walked over to his car. He was a clean-cut young man of about twenty-five, she said later, and was wearing a colorful mod shirt, no jacket, despite the cold weather. His thick black hair was neatly combed and he appeared to be very suntanned. He spoke with no noticeable accent. The car, though nearly twenty years old, was so well kept it looked like new. Even the interior had a look of newness about it.

When she reached the vehicle, the young man suddenly lunged, grabbed her arm, and ordered her to get in with him. After a brief struggle she managed to break away. She ran back to her house and locked herself in, completely terrified. She cowered in the house until her husband came home from work. And she decided to stay home the next day, too. At 3 P.M. she heard someone on the porch and there was a loud knock on the door. She waited awhile then cautiously went to the door. There was no one on the porch and no car in sight, but a note had been slipped under the door. It was written in pencil in block letters on a piece of ordinary notebook paper.

"Be careful girl," it read, "I can get you yet."

That night Connie and Keith went to the local police. The note was turned over to officer Raymond Manly. In March 1967, I visited the police station, hoping to recover the note so I could compare the handwriting with other notes I had collected. Manly had lost it somewhere along the way. When I asked to see their file on the case they produced a printed form containing Connie's name and address and one scribbled line, "Dark Buick, young man." The police chief assured me that no such car existed in Middleport and that it was obviously a case of some maniac trying to abduct a young girl. Officer Manly told me he was keeping the house under constant surveillance. I had to break the news that the Gordons had moved back to the West Virginia side of the river shortly after the incident. Despite my sheaf of credentials and press cards, both men were overly suspicious of me and asked me repeatedly if I really wasn't "from the government." This fear of government agents was already universal in 1967, long before the general breakdown of faith in the government of the 1970s.

The UFO enthusiasts had done their job well. Their twenty-year campaign against the air force had really shut the government off from many UFO reports.

In the mid-1950s I had experienced a variation of this paranoia while traveling through the Orient. The CIA had already earned an odious reputation abroad, its butter-fingered agents often operating as wandering journalists, particularly in the Himalayas where they were trying to foment revolutionary activity against the Chinese who were then settling down in Tibet. More than once I was openly accused of being a secret American *agent provocateur*. Officials would "lose" my passport for days at a time while they checked me out forward and backward. In Baghdad, and again in Singapore, I was actually grilled by the authorities who were apparently convinced I was after state secrets or was planning to overthrow the government. Since I knew very little about the CIA in those days I was perplexed by all this attention.

Eventually I learned that the CIA had a habit of enlisting very young people between the ages of seventeen and twenty-five, frequently involving them in bizarre scenarios. Considerable evidence exists indicating that Lee Harvey Oswald was a CIA pawn early on.

Today the CIA has an annual budget in excess of $11 billion, and it doesn't have to account to the president or Congress. A large part of this budget is probably wasted on bureaucratic nonsense, and another large part is spent on what can only be termed malicious mischief. Technically, the CIA has no legal authority or responsibilities within the continental United States, but if you open a phone book for any moderate-sized U.S. city you will find a local CIA office listed. They also maintain thousands of "fronts," offices disguised as legitimate businesses, throughout the country.

During the recent Watergate debacle investigating reporters documented the fact that some of the participants were not only long-time CIA agents, but also that these same men had been involved in the abortive Bay of Pigs invasion of Cuba in 1961, and some had been present in Dealey Plaza in Dallas on the day President Kennedy was assassinated. It is noteworthy that reporters, editors, and citizens engaged in the investigation of President Kennedy's death suffered harassment and telephone problems identical to those experienced by UFO researchers. Some of these tactics will be examined in detail further on.

However, I can not accuse the CIA as being the source of the weird incidents outlined here. Rather, *the phenomenon is imitative.* This paranormal mimicry is difficult for many to understand but I come across constant examples. Early in January 1973, for instance, a reliable witness in Ohio observed an unusual-looking helicopter which she was able to describe in detail. When she sketched it for a local UFO enthusiast he was flabbergasted. He was an aeronautical engineer specializing in helicopters and he knew the thing she drew was a new secret helicopter *that was still on the drawing board!*

Even closer to home, a few days after Tad Jones's sighting on Route 64, *True* magazine hit the stands with an article of mine about flying saucers. It was illustrated with drawings of all kinds of odd-shaped objects, many of them the pure products of the artist's imagination. It included an exact replica of Jones's sphere, complete with wheeled legs and propeller. An object exactly like this had never been described in the UFO literature before . . . or since. The artist had produced his layout many weeks before. Somehow the phenomenon had mischievously duplicated the artist's conception for Jones's benefit.

9:

"Wake Up
Down There!"

I.

A young couple, very much in love, sprawled together in the back seat of an old jalopy on a deserted dirt road in the isolated back hills east of Ravenswood, West Virginia. It was a starlit, moonless night in the spring of 1967, just warm enough so the pair were able to strip to the buff comfortably. Things were rather pleasant on that squeaky back seat until about 10:30 P.M. when a blinding bluish light poured in through the windows of the parked car.

"At first, I thought it was the police," the young man told me later. "Then we both felt a funny tingling sensation that scared us half out of our wits. I jumped up and stared into the light. It wasn't a flashlight or spotlight. It was more like a big ball of bluish fire hovering a couple of feet off the ground directly alongside the car. There was a funny sound, too, like a low hum."

His girlfriend screamed, he reported, and the light seemed to back away slightly while the humming increased in volume.

"The next thing we knew," the young man continued, "it was gone. Just like that. We jumped into our clothes and got the hell out of there. Another funny thing, when we got into town it was after 12:30. We couldn't figure it out. It seemed like we only looked at that light for a couple of seconds. But somehow it must have taken two hours."

Their first inclination was to run to the police but they decided against it, since they weren't supposed to be on that road doing what they were doing in the first place. ("Her old man would've killed me!") They drove around for several minutes until their hysteria subsided and then he dropped her off at her home.

The next morning both the boy and the girl woke up to find themselves heavily "sunburned" from head to foot. The boy's eyes were almost swollen shut for two weeks afterward. It was not an easy matter for them to explain how they managed to get a total, and quite painful, sunburn at night in the early spring.

Shortly afterward he heard that I was in the area and sought me out to tell me the story. His skin was still reddish and his eyes were still bothering him when I met him.

The actinic ray burns were proof of his story. And I knew that UFOs often zero in on lovers in parked cars. Many—most—of the monster episodes in my files took place in remote lovers' lanes. Young love has to run enough hazards without the fear of a hairy weirdo hammering on the windshield.

What concerned me was the two-hour time lapse or spell of lacunal amnesia which apparently took place. What could have happened to the pair during that forgotten period?

The phenomenon has an almost pornographic preoccupation with our mating practices. One of its most celebrated games is the manipulation of romantic relationships. Early investigators of the fairy episodes, such as novelist Sir Walter Scott, noted that fairies seemed to delight in bringing people together and fostering love, or, conversely, indulging in conspiracies to force lovers apart. The Bell witch of Tennessee is supposed to have manipulated the love life of a Bell daughter, almost tragically. Brad Steiger, one of America's best-known investigators of the paranormal, has been involved in several poltergeist cases in which the mischievous poltergeists tried to wreck romances and marriages.[1] Nothing can quite affect a new groom's virility like being physically hurled from his wedding bed by an unseen force and pelted with flying ashtrays thrown by invisible hands. Unbelievable though it may seem, such things do happen.

Flying saucer contactees often have their marriages disrupted, even destroyed, after they begin their liaisons with the space people. And there are many cases in which flying saucer enthusiasts have been brought together—literally hurled together—through their mutual interest.

Could it be that some people are programed to love by this mysterious force?

II.

A public relations officer for the United Nations, Donald Estrella, accompanied me on one of my trips to West Virginia in 1967. In those days the UN was keenly interested in the UFO enigma. Mr. U Thant, then secretary general of the organization, held private meetings with author John Fuller and Dr. J. Allen Hynek, two leading UFO authorities. The late Drew Pearson created a sensation when he revealed that Mr. Thant regarded flying saucers as second in importance after the war in Vietnam. (Thant later denied the Pearson story.)

When Don Estrella saw all the bizarre things I was investigating, things which—to his surprise—seemed to have

[1] Brad Steiger, *Haunted Lovers* (New York: Dell, 1971).

little relevance to wonderful spaceships from another planet, he told me about three unrelated events that had happened to him over a span of several years.

"Seven or eight years ago," he said, "I was taking a vacation trip with four friends through the New England states. We were riding in a high-powered car along a deserted country road somewhere in New Hampshire, I believe. We were going quite fast when suddenly we hit something. This was in broad daylight and it was as if we suddenly crashed into an invisible brick wall. The whole front of the car was smashed in. Luckily, none of us were hurt but we were a bit stunned. We got out and looked around. There was absolutely nothing on the road. We never could figure out what had happened."

Experience had taught me that paranormal events are often interlaced with puzzling yet seemingly normal things like strange phone calls. Had he ever received any odd calls?

"There was one thing," he said slowly. "About five years ago I took a train out to see a friend of mine on Long Island and when I got there he accused me of playing a hoax on him. He said he'd received a phone call about half an hour before I arrived. A voice that sounded very distant had said, 'Hello, Don.' My friend told him that I hadn't arrived yet. The voice then began to recite a series of numbers meaninglessly. My friend thought it was some kind of gag and hung up."

Finally I asked him if he had ever had any really odd encounters with peculiar strangers. He looked at me bewildered and astonished.

"There's one that's always bothered me. It happened around the time of that phone call thing. One night when I was walking home to my apartment I became aware of a man following me. When I looked at him, he stopped and grinned at me . . . but there was an air of evil about him. I can't pinpoint it exactly."

"Was he possibly some kind of sex deviate?" I suggested.

"No . . . I don't think so. He was short and slight, and wore a black coat and black trousers. His face was dark and foreign-looking. I don't know why, but that evil grin is burned into my memory."

Don said he hurried into his apartment and never saw the man again. A mere chance encounter on a busy New York street. Perhaps.

The foolishly grinning man is a staple item in psychic lore. Black-suited with a dark complexion and craggy foreign face, he has been described to me in many places by many people.

As for strange phone calls, I have investigated so many that I am now practically a telephone engineer. They are hard to nail down because there are so many cranks, hoaxers, and "phone phreaks" out there today. But the calls that interest me most fall into patterns that exclude natural explanations.

At 8 A.M. on March 24, 1961, two women in Prospect, Oregon, a town of about three hundred people, were talking together on the phone when suddenly a strange man's voice broke into the line and snapped, "Wake up down there!" One of the ladies regarded this as an affront and she proceeded to express a very strong opinion. The voice started to rattle on in a rapid-fire language that sounded like Spanish but the line seemed to be dead. The two women could not hear each other. After the man suddenly stopped, the line became live again.

The next day, at the same hour, the women were on the phone again, and again the strange voice interrupted with, "Wake up down there!"

This time the women listened quietly as the voice said something in the foreign language, and then it recited the numbers forty and twenty-five over and over. No one in Prospect spoke Spanish. There was no accounting for the incident.

Voices counting off meaningless numbers also cut in on TV reception in UFO flap areas. Usually people who experience this sort of thing dismiss it as police calls or the work of some Ham radio operator. They don't realize that TV sound is broadcast on FM channels reserved for that purpose and there is little chance that a shortwave or CB (Citizen's Band) transmission could interfere.

But the phenomenon is not always restricted to electrical apparatus. After I published a couple of pieces about it I received dozens of letters from people throughout the country recounting their own experiences. To my surprise, most of these people had heard the voices late at night, usually waking them up with a sharp command. For example, a man in the Southwest claimed he had been jarred awake on several different nights by the sound of a deep male voice ordering, "Wake up, number 491!" A woman in Ohio heard the voice while driving, "873. . . . You are 873." And another woman in Kansas wrote, "Please tell me who these people are that keep reading numbers to me. They sound as if they are standing right next to me but there is no one there."

Do we all have a number tatooed in our brains? Hardly. There are three billion people so some of them should be numbered 2,834,689,357. But all of the numbers that have come to my attention contain only two or three digits.

Another version of this phenomenon are the Morse code-like beeps that blast out of car radios, telephones, and TV sets when UFOs are active. On January 31, 1968, a woman in California called me long distance to tell me of a string of unusual events around her home. Her phone was "going crazy," the house lights were flashing on and off periodically and the electricians couldn't find the source of the problem, and other weird things were happening. As she talked I recognized certain patterns which suggested that a repeatable experiment might be possible. So I gave her some advice which would have sounded insane to anyone overhearing the conversation. I instructed her to go outside at exactly 9 P.M.

that night with a flashlight and if she saw anything in the sky to signal to it.

The next day she called me back excitedly. Her husband, who had been skeptical of the whole UFO business, had been converted, she announced with delight. She had followed my instructions and, sure enough, at 9 P.M. that night a large orange sphere appeared directly over her home. She flashed the light three times but there was no response from the object. After a few moments it scurried off. She and her husband reentered the house where the television was on. As soon as they entered the living room three loud, very loud beeps shot out of the TV set. Her husband was completely flabbergasted.

I have given the same crazy advice to other UFO sighters, always with similar results. Sometimes after watching an object their telephones will suddenly ring . . . and there will be no one on the line. Or their doorbells will ring by themselves.

Obviously these things are manifestations within the electro-magnetic (EM) spectrum. The voices, however, seem to come from a more mysterious superspectrum.

In hypnosis there is a simple technique called posthypnotic suggestion. The hypnotist can tell his subject that fifteen minutes after he comes out of his trance he will suddenly feel an impulse to climb up on a chair and crow like a rooster. When the subject is brought out of his trance he behaves normally for fifteen minutes, then he suddenly climbs onto a chair and crows. He can't explain why he did it. It seemed like a rational action at the moment.

There is a kind of posthypnotic suggestion involved in many UFO and psychic incidents. The witness is driving along a road late at night. He hears a beeping sound and lapses into a trance . . . as if he had been preconditioned to lose consciousness at the sound of the beep. Later, he awakes to the sound of another series of beeps. Now he finds he is some distance from his original point and he's baffled about what happened in the intervening minutes—or hours—for he can't remember a thing.

Several variations of this hypnosis-inducing tactic occur. Some witnesses see an approaching aerial object with numbers clearly marked on it. As they study the numbers they lapse into a trance. In some cases, ancient lettering like Greek or Chinese appear on the object. The effect is the same. Months, even years, later the same percipient may again see the same numbers or letters on an object, or even on a set of license plates or a sign, and again falls into a deep trance.

III.

The U.S. Air Force and the CIA were blamed for the many weird telephone problems that plagued the tiny bands of UFO investigators around the country in the 1960s. They were convinced that the government was out to get them. But these things have been happening from the earliest days of the modern UFO age when, in June 1947, before the air force or the CIA were even committed to UFO investigation, pilot Kenneth Arnold was checking into the Maury Island sightings in Tacoma. He and a fellow pilot ran their investigation from a hotel and some unidentified person repeatedly called the local newspapers and told reporters everything that was transpiring in that hotel room. Arnold tore the place apart looking for hidden microphones, but there didn't seem to be any.

The official air force report on the sighting of a Florida scoutmaster, Sonny Desvergers, in 1952 states: "Captain Corney [an air force intelligence officer] was asked about the facts of supposedly anonymous threatening telephone calls that Mr. Desvergers had received. He stated that Desvergers had called him approximately two weeks ago and stated that he had been receiving anonymous threatening telephone calls while at work in the establishment in which he is employed. The gist of the calls were threats telling Desvergers to lay off of his story and that if he didn't he would be sorry and several other things."

Witnesses to landings and low-level overflights are often singled out for harassment, even when they don't report their sightings. Publicized contactees like Woodrow Derenberger receive the full treatment.

Like many sincere contactees, Woody decided to write a book about his experiences and, like most contactees, ended up paying for the cost of printing himself. Contactee books, and there are hundreds of them, have a very limited fringe market of only two or three thousand people, so Madison Avenue publishers understandably give them short shrift. In Woody's little effort he stated:[2]

> As I write this book, I keep getting phone calls warning me to stop. They have even called my wife at her place of employment, telling her to stop me or they will. These people have also called my friends making the same threat.
>
> I have no way of knowing who these people are, yet they are calling too often to be crank calls. Several times I have written material that has disappeared from my home. When I leave home for any reason, I always lock all doors and windows, yet several times when we returned home, we found our home had been ransacked, drawers pulled out, papers strewn all over the floor, and valuable tapes missing, and my tape recorder broken. . . . I have mailed letters, dropped personally by me in the Post Office letter box, that have failed to reach their destination.

[2] Woodrow W. Derenberger, with Harold W. Hubbard, *Visitors from Lanulos* (New York: Vantage Press, 1971).

After Woody's contact became widely known, two gentlemen dropped into the appliance store where he worked and walked directly up to him.

"We think you know who we are, Mr. Derenberger," they said flatly. "We'd advise you to forget all about what you've seen."

They left as abruptly as they'd arrived. Woody described them as being short, stocky, dressed in black suits, and having olive complexions. For some reason he concluded the Men in Black were really from the Mafia.

No matter where he moved—and he moved several times in 1967—the phone pranksters and black Cadillacs managed to find him, he claims.

Meanwhile, his pretty young wife and their two children also met Indrid Cold and his colleagues from the planet Lanulos. Mrs. Derenberger was frightened of them and felt they were engaged in something evil. They were just like us, she told me, traveled about in ordinary automobiles, and were probably infiltrating the human race in large numbers.

Woodrow Derenberger's story troubled me from the outset, and for many reasons. It did not fit the mold of the usual UFO contact tale. While the telepathy element was common enough, the total physicality of his experiences seemed *too real.* They defied easy classification and would not fit into any of the pigeonholes I had constructed. Either he was the world's most convincing liar, and had somehow trained his wife, children, and friends to back up his lies, or he had had a very special set of experiences beyond the limits of ufology.

By March 1967 the crowds had given up in discouragement and Mr. Cold was able to safely land his spaceship on Woody's farm. Woody went aboard, according to his story, and took a flight all the way to Brazil and back. The interior of the spaceship was disappointingly normal, with bunks and equipment of obvious terrestrial manufacture. Later that year, Derenberger would be flown to Lanulos . . . a pleasant little planet where the people ran around nearly nude. Most contactees who claim to have visited other planets, and there are many, usually described a futuristic world. There was something mundane about Woody's descriptions of that nudist colony in outer space. Too mundane.

In his later adventures, Woody usually met the spaceships in some isolated spot, often near a highway under construction—a seemingly trivial detail yet one that is most significant. Cold or one of his partners would pick Woody up in a Volkswagen and drive him to the rendezvous point.

His world was now thickly populated with space people named Kemi, Clinnel, Demo, Ardo, Kletaw, etc. They assumed real personalities and were very real to him. But I knew that in most UFO contacts the entities use names adopted from ancient Greek and from mythology, so I was puzzled by these "fairy" names. However, many of Woody's experiences had definite fairy tale overtones. And two of this friends had a classic fairy experience. A young man named Jim Hacket, and his cousin Darla Sartor, were out skywatching at a place called Bogle Ridge one night when they saw a group of red, green, and white lights descend from the sky and drop into a gully close to their position. A moment later there was a bright flash and Jim felt his face tingling, like a mild electric shock. Then he heard voices outside the car . . . voices which Darla could not hear. Suddenly there was a sharp rap on the window, causing the pair to jump with alarm. A man holding some kind of red light stood outside the car and Hacket received a mental message to get out of the car.

"Is she your wife?" the man asked.

"No, she's my cousin."

The man told him to tell Darla to stay in the car. Then he led young Hacket off into the darkness. When he returned, his shoes, socks, and watch were missing. He said the man had taken them. It had been raining and the ground was muddy so his shoes had been coated with mud and water.

Jim and Darla visited Woody the next day and the contactee accompanied them to the same spot on Bogle Ridge that night. Indrid Cold, Karl Ardo, and Demo Hassan were waiting for them. Woody explained what happened and the spacemen said Hacket had encountered "humanoids" who were no-good thieves. He was lucky he had lost only his shoes, socks, and watch. But they would run the culprits down and recover the items, they promised.

The next morning when Jim stepped out his door to pick up his morning paper he was surprised to find his shoes, now neatly shined, sitting on the step with the laundered socks and the watch inside.

The contactee lore is filled with silly episodes like this. The entities serve as good guys and bad guys alternately. Phantom muggers can materialize out of the darkness and attack the contactee with baseball bats, only to be thwarted by the sudden arrival of the good guys who beat them up and cart off their carcasses—and the baseball bats and any other evidence. Many of our black-suited "Silencers" are engaged in similar games.

IV.

Jim Hacket was lucky. He only lost his shoes. Elsewhere throughout the Ohio River valley, dogs, cows, and horses were dying suddenly and mysteriously, usually from surgical-like incisions in their throats. Animal disappearances and deaths go hand in hand with the UFO phenomenon. The most puzzling aspect of these deaths is the absence of blood. Often the carcasses seem drained of all blood. The wounds don't bleed. No blood is in evidence in the grass or dirt where the victims lay.

Among my grimmer memories of 1966–67 are those times when I knelt in farm fields to examine dead animals, particularly dogs, who had suffered amazingly clean and expert cuts. These deaths were not localized, but came in nationwide waves simultaneously with UFO waves. This pattern has been repeated since. Prior to the October 1973 flying saucer flap there was an epidemic of animal deaths throughout the Midwest from Minnesota to Mississippi, causing quite a stir in the local press.

"Two points confounding investigators have been the absence of blood and footprints," the *Kansas City Times* reported, December 22, 1973. "Even on warm days, with the carcass freshly killed, there has been no bleeding on or around the animal. Some believe the cattle were drained of blood. No human tracks have been detected near each mutilation, even in fresh snow."

In December 1973 and January 1974 there were wholesale disappearances of pet dogs from Connecticut to California. Small towns like Voluntown, Connecticut, lost a large part of their dog population in a few days. Fifteen dogs vanished from Woodstock, New York, in the Catskill Mountains during the same period. As in previous waves of animal mutilations and disappearances, authorities tried to blame witchcraft cults, cattle rustlers, and dognapers, who sell the poor animals to hospitals for experimental purposes. But the total absence of evidence of any kind seems to rule out these conventional explanations.

Europe has been plagued with phantom animal killers for generations. Sweden had a plague of this sort of thing in 1972. The extensive vampire legends of Middle Europe were undoubtedly based on such incidents. Vampires were cloaked beings, often accompanied by strange aerial lights, who could paralyze humans and animals in their tracks. As recently as twenty years ago there were a series of "vampire" killings in Yugoslavia. Four bloodless human bodies were found with slashed throats in a field near Klek Mountain, according to one report.

As I have noted, UFOs, hairy monsters, and Mothmen all appear to have the ability to ferret out human females during their menstrual period. I began to seriously wonder if blood and flesh were not vital ingredients in the mysterious transmogrification process. Did energies from the superspectrum need earthly biological materials to construct temporary entities? It does seem as if many UFO and monster sightings are staged as distractions, luring crowds of people to places like the TNT area while animal mutilations and disappearances are taking place almost unnoticed only a few miles away.

Soon after the Mothman's first appearance in November 1966, police found the body of a dog in the TNT area. It was completely charred, yet the surrounding area was unburned. I wondered if it might not have been sacrificed in some secret magical ritual by some unknown local warlock: a ritual that brought Mothman into being?

The UFO waves of the 1960s were accompanied by the occult explosion—the rapid spread of witchcraft and magical practices. An interesting side effect of the flying saucer phenomenon is that many of the people attracted to the subject, people with very materialistic and pseudo-scientific outlooks, gradually drift into the study of psychic phenomena, abandoning the extraterrestrial theory along the way. In retrospect, flying saucers were partly responsible for the occult explosion.

The most confusing feature of the phenomenon is its use of allegorical situations and complicated diversions meant to cover up some more covert activity. Hairy monsters are seen carrying dead dogs, so people assume other missing dogs provided dinner for the smelly apparition. Actually the dogs may have served some other purpose altogether . . . a purpose that might turn our hair gray instantly if we knew the full details.

In messages passed along to Italian contactee Eugenio Siragusa, the mischievous entities have tried to explain their "volumetric logic" in cosmic double-talk. Dr. Jacques Vallee has called it "metalogic," suggesting that the entities have a logic system quite different from ours and when they try to translate things on our level their statements come out absurd. He does not consider their *need for deceit* which is based upon their urge to manipulate us through beliefs and what the British call "acceptances." Once Woodrow Derenberger accepted Indrid Cold's existence, and the existence of Lanulos, his view of reality could be manipulated to include those beings and places.

In March 1967, a truly astonishing UFO "attack" took place in West Virginia, apparently supporting the vampiric theories I was entertaining at the time. While other UFO investigators had been collecting endless descriptions of things seen in the sky, I was out examining dead animals in remote fields, pondering the real meaning behind the bloodless carcasses.

On the night of March 5, a Red Cross Bloodmobile was traveling along Route 2, which runs parallel to the Ohio River. Beau Shertzer, twenty-one, and a young nurse had been out all day collecting human blood and now they were heading back to Huntington, West Virginia, with a van filled with fresh blood. The road was dark and cold and there was very little traffic. As they moved along a particularly deserted stretch, there was a flash in the woods on a nearby hill and a large white glow appeared. It rose slowly into the air and flew straight for their vehicle.

"My God! What is it?" the nurse cried.

"I'm not going to stick around to find out," Shertzer answered, pushing his foot down on the gas.

The object effortlessly swooped over the van and stayed with it. Shertzer rolled down his window and looked up. He was horrified to see some kind of arm or extension being lowered from the luminous thing cruising only a few feet above the Bloodmobile.

"It's trying to get us!" The nurse yelled, watching another arm reach down on her side. It looked as if the flying object was trying to wrap a pincerslike device around the vehicle. Shertzer poured on the horses but the object kept pace with them easily. Apparently they were saved by the sudden appearance of headlights from approaching traffic. As the other cars neared, the object retracted the arms and hastily flew off.

Both young people rushed to the police in a state of hysteria. The incident was mentioned briefly on a radio newscast that night but was not picked up by the newspapers.

In cases like this we have to ask: Did the UFO really intend to carry off the Bloodmobile? Or was it all a sham to "prove" the UFOs interest in blood. Later I tried to check to find out if any Bloodmobiles had actually vanished anywhere. The Red Cross thought I was a bit nuts.

But I often found myself seriously wondering if we only hear about the people who get away!

V.

A few nights after the remarkable Bloodmobile incident, Point Pleasant police officer Harold Harmon was making a routine patrol through the dismal, unlit TNT area when a dark object hovering a few feet above a small pond caught his eye.

"It was definitely a solid machine of some kind," he told me later. "I could even see what appeared to be windows in it. It rocked unevenly like a boat hitting waves, and then it floated silently away over the trees."

Another nationwide UFO wave was underway that March, but the now-jaded national news media ignored it.

Scientists from the newly commissioned Colorado University UFO project trotted around the country trying to investigate new reports while the projects's head, Dr. Edward U. Condon, complained that it was like a fire department that answered only false alarms. That spring some of the scientists spent weeks in the Harrisburg, Pennsylvania, area observing the "meandering nocturnal lights" that busied themselves there nightly. Their learned conclusion was that the Pennsylvanian skies were "most remarkable."

Ships in the Atlantic were reporting huge luminous "cigars" discharging small globes of light which sailed toward New York and Long Island. And on Long Island and neighboring Connecticut, those globes were cutting nightly capers. During my frequent treks out to Long Island, I saw several of the objects myself and I collected some eyewitness testimony that boggled my already much-boggled mind. One family of seven people swore they had seen a circular object land near a wooded area on Long Island. They stopped their car to watch and were astonished when they saw two figures, normal-human-sized beings, exit through a door in the object as a large black car crossed the field and stopped nearby. The two beings got into the car and it drove off. The object took off quickly and disappeared into the night sky. Similar incidents had been reported in South America, France, and England, but this was the first time I had come across one in the United States. The family was terrified. They knew they should report it to someone but they kept silent until they heard me on a radio program a few days later.

Meanwhile, the Ohio valley was lit up by these things nightly, from Cairo, Illinois, in the south, where the Ohio River linked with the Mississippi, to the northernmost tip of the river in Pennsylvania.

On March 12, 1967, a woman in Letart Falls, Ohio, was driving home from church at 11:30 P.M., accompanied by her twenty-year-old daughter, when, as they rounded a cor-

ner in a wooded area, a huge white thing appeared directly
in front of their car. They said it had curved wings about ten
feet wide. There was a head on the creature and it appeared
to have very long hair. It was in view of their headlights for
several seconds before it flew upward and vanished from
sight. The witnesses were very religious and assumed they
had seen an angel, or even Jesus Christ himself. After their
sighting their telephone went haywire and their television
was suddenly subjected to heavy interference. I found a
number of UFOs had been seen in the Letart Falls area,
with concentrations around a large gravel pit there.

Sightings in the Northeast were keeping me busy at that
time. But I talked with Mary Hyre frequently. She was
receiving more UFO reports than she could print and some
other strange things were happening in Point Pleasant.
Three very tall, dark-complexioned (not Negroid) men were
causing the local police some consternation. These men
knocked on doors late at night, purportedly selling magazines though we couldn't find anyone who had ordered
subscriptions from them. They spoke fluent, unaccented
English and were described as "good-looking" with heavily
tanned skin. Their height and broadness impressed the witnesses the most. Although these men continued to appear
throughout the region for a month, Mrs. Hyre and the
police could not find out where they were staying. They
were always on foot. Apparently they did not have a car.

Mrs. Mabel McDaniel worked in the local unemploy-
ment office on Main Street in Point Pleasant and during the
second week in March a strange man blundered into the
office. He wore a black coat and black cap and behaved in
a most peculiar manner.

"He didn't look like a colored person, but still was very
dark," Mrs. McDaniel said, "and his English was so poor I
never did really figure out what he wanted. His eyes were
funny-looking, kind of starey and glassy. From what I could

get from him, he was looking for an insurance company, only he kept saying he wanted 'trip insurance.' "

He told her he had also visited the office of the *Messenger* (he did not, according to Mary). He spoke in the garbled, singsong manner of so many of our weirdo visitors and moved in an unsteady, almost drunken way.

It seemed to me that something phenomenal was building up in the Point Pleasant area. I decided to shelve my other projects and return to the Ohio valley. This time I was accompanied by Daniel Drasin, a young movie producer who was planning to do a UFO special for the Public Broadcasting Laboratories (PBL) of the educational television network. Don Estrella also asked to go along. Both men knew very little about the UFO situation at that time, and in keeping with my habit I told them nothing. I wanted them to see for themselves the incredible scope and complexity of the thing.

So late that March our little entourage hopped into rented cars and took off on an eight-hundred-mile journey into the twilight zone.

10:

Purple Lights
and April Foolishness

I.

"My phones have gone crazy," Mary Hyre noted, "even my unlisted numbers. Strangers call me at all hours of the day and night. Sometimes I get funny beeping sounds. Did you ever hear about anything like that?"

I had to admit I had. However, it had become my policy to say very little about these matters to anyone, even close friends. After Mary and I had concluded our interview with Charles Hern and his wife in Ohio, Mr. Hern had escorted us to the door and remarked, "You know, we've told you about everything we've seen . . . and you haven't told us a damned thing!"

I was so taciturn that the UFO buffs had surrounded me with an aura of mystery (they tend to surround *everything* with mystery). James Moseley, editor of *Saucer News* (now defunct), once told Gray Barker, "He gives you the impression of not only knowing as much as we about flying saucers —but actually knowing a lot more—a lot that he is not telling."

The truth was more mundane than mysterious. I was keeping many of my findings a secret to prevent pranksters from setting up hoaxes (many of those findings are being revealed here for the first time). I maintained a "low profile" to curb rumors and prevent possible panic in the areas I was visiting. I avoided personal publicity, unlike most of the other self-styled UFO investigators who spent most of their time staging press conferences and building up scrapbooks. Finally, some of the things I was studying seemed so absurd on the surface—especially to the hardcore believers in extra-terrestrial visitants—that revealing them would only produce more gossip, controversy, and nonsense.

Dan Drasin and Don Estrella expressed growing amazement—and some fear—as they traveled with me up and down the valley, listening to my strange questions and the even stranger answers we were getting from witnesses. A young woman in Point Pleasant was having telephone problems. Every night when she returned home from work at 5 o'clock her phone would ring and a man's voice would speak to her in a rapid-fire language she could not understand. "It sounds something like Spanish . . . yet I don't think it is Spanish," she complained. She protested to the phone company, but they insisted they could find nothing wrong with her line.

We visited her home and I examined her phone in a manner that had become routine for me. I took it apart. Drasin and Estrella watched me silently with a "he's really gone bananas" expression. What did telephones have to do with flying saucers?

When you unscrew modern telephone earpieces you will often find a small piece of cotton which serves as a cushion for the magnet and diaphragm. You shouldn't find anything else. But when I opened this woman's handset I was startled to find a tiny sliver of wood. She said no one, not even the repairmen, had ever opened up her phone before. The wooden object looked like a piece of a matchstick, sharpened at one end and lightly coated with a substance that looked like graphite. Later I showed it to telephone engineers and they said they'd never seen anything like it before. I put it in a plastic box and stored it away. Years later while visiting a magic store in New York (sleight of hand is one of my hobbies), I glanced at a display of practical jokes and discovered a cellophane package filled with similar sticks. Cigarette loads! Somehow an explosive cigarette load had gotten into that Point Pleasant telephone! Who put it there, when, how, and why must remain mysteries.

Soon after my investigation, the woman's phone calls ceased. Maybe I exorcised the phone by removing the stick.

Another family was having telephone problems, and many other troubles besides, on the Camp Conley Road on the southern edge of the TNT area. The woman in Point Pleasant who suffered the calls from a bizarre metallic voice speaking in an incomprehensible language was their daughter-in-law.

"It didn't take us long to learn that when our TV started acting up it was a sure sign that one of those lights was passing over," James Lilly, a no-nonsense riverboat captain, told us. "I didn't think much of all the flying saucer talk until I started seeing them myself. You've got to believe your own eyes."

At first the Lillys kept their sightings to themselves. But gradually rumors began to circulate and carloads of people gathered on Camp Conley Road every night to watch the space people fly by.

"We've seen all kinds of things," Mrs. Lilly said. "Blue lights, green ones, red ones, things that change color. Some of them have been so low that we thought we could see diamond-shaped windows in them. And none of them make any noise at all."

Automobiles near the Lilly home began to stall inexplicably. And the Lillys' little ranch house became haunted soon after the lights started their nightly fly-overs. Kitchen cabinet doors slammed in the middle of the night. Once their living room door, which they locked with both a chain and snaplock at night, was standing ajar when they got up in the morning. They heard loud metallic sounds, "like a pan falling," and Mrs. Lilly heard "a baby crying." "It sounded so plain," she said, "that I looked around the house even though I knew there was no baby here. It seemed to come from the living room . . . only a few feet away from me."

One of my sillier-sounding questions is: "Did you ever dream there was a stranger in the house in the middle of the night?" When I directed this question at the Lillys, Jackie Lilly urged her quiet sixteen-year-old daughter, Linda, to tell about the "nightmare" she had had that March. She was reluctant to discuss it, but with a little coaching from the sidelines she explained how she woke up one night and saw a large figure towering over her bed.

"It was a man," she said. "A big man. Very broad. I couldn't see his face very well but I could see that he was grinning at me."

"Jim was working on the river that night," Mrs. Lilly added. "And Linda woke me up with a terrible scream. She cried out there was a man in her room. I told her she was dreaming. But she screamed again."

"He walked around the bed and stood right over me," Linda declared. "I screamed again and hid under the covers. When I looked up again, he was gone."

"She came running into my room," Mrs. Lilly said. "She cried, 'There is a man in my room! There *is!*' She's refused to sleep alone ever since."

When I asked for a description of the stranger, Linda said she thought he had been wearing a "checkered shirt."

Bedroom phantoms in checkered shirts are old hat to investigators of psychic phenomena. I have come upon this again and again. So often that I have written long articles about it. In some cases these ghosts-in-plaid are accompanied by the odor of hydrogen sulfide and sudden chills or sudden blasts of heat, while other episodes are probably purely hypnopompic. That is, they are the residue of dreams which overlap briefly into the waking state . . . a phenomenon well-known in psychiatry and parapsychology.

I once enjoyed a hypnopompic experience myself. In the winter of 1960–61 I contracted walking pneumonia . . . and I walked with it until I dropped. Early one morning while I was still quite sick and my system was laden with antibiotics and drugs I woke up and saw a large black form hovering at the foot of my bed. It wasn't a man in a checkered shirt but was roughly the shape of a Cocoa Cola bottle.

"What do you know? I'm having an hallucination," I told myself as I lifted my head and studied the apparition. The blob slowly receded, growing smaller and smaller until it disappeared. The experience was never repeated.

II.

Drasin and Estrella returned to New York City in late March while I decided to remain on in Point Pleasant. Dan was convinced that something exceptional was happening in the Ohio valley and he planned to collect a camera crew and return. We had seen a number of odd aerial lights but the oddest of all was so bewildering I didn't even bother to take notes.

We were standing on a hilltop outside of Point Pleasant one night when Mrs. Hyre called our attention to a bright red light slowly moving toward us. It had the shimmering, prismatic appearance of the classic UFO light and Dan, who was a student pilot, agreed it wasn't a plane. No normal wing lights or taillights were visible. The sky was crystal-clear and there was only one small cloud overhead. The light moved very slowly and appeared to be at a low altitude. There was no sound whatsoever.

We watched as the light slowly approached the little

cloud and disappeared into it, or over it. Then we waited for it to reappear. Seconds ticked into minutes. The light did not come out from behind the cloud. "Maybe it went straight up," Mary suggested.

Suddenly there was the distinctive drone of an airplane engine and the obvious silhouette of a small plane emerged from the cloud, wing and taillights flashing. It buzzed off at an altitude of three or four thousand feet. And we laughed at ourselves, momentarily convinced that our UFO had just been an airplane.

However, the more I thought about the incident the more incredible it seemed. We should have been able to see the plane's silhouette clearly before it entered the cloud, and it should not have taken so long to pass through such a small cloud. Something was definitely out of kilter.

Later, I began to study the mystery airplanes and phantom helicopters that have appeared all over the world, and several reports of UFOs that seemingly turned into conventional airplane configurations surfaced. One of the most recent comes from Canada where a group of outdoorsmen on the Cowichan River in British Columbia watched a low-flying object in October 1973.[1]

"It didn't make a sound and it was something we had never seen before," one of the witnesses reported. "There were three red lights rotating around the top part and there were blinking red lights going in the opposite direction around the middle part. There was another light at the very top—a red flashing one.

"Then, from the bottom, a white light shone out like a spotlight. It moved its beam up the river as if it was looking for something. By this time we were all pretty scared. We thought sure the others at the camp must have seen it, too, but afterward they said they hadn't seen a thing. There was a bend in the river between us so I couldn't say for sure whether they did or not."

The witnesses claimed they got a good look at the thing, that it was circular, about eighty feet in diameter, hovering about two hundred feet in the air, and had been in view for a full fifteen minutes.

How did it depart?

"Well, if we told people about this, they'd think we were crazy," the witness said. "But all of a sudden it looked as if it had turned into an airplane. It made a noise like a plane and it looked like a plane, only all the lights went out except for a little red one. It went right past us and disappeared over the trees."

Throughout West Virginia I had heard stories of large, gray, unmarked airplanes hedgehopping the treacherous hills. I knew the air national guard kept some cargo planes at the Charleston airport and that some training flights involved hedgehopping to keep below radar beams. But none of the flights reported to me proved to be the work of the national guard.

Drasin and Estrella had hardly started out for New York when all hell began to break loose. Late on the afternoon of March 31, a workman in the Point Pleasant lumber yard saw a glowing object hovering over the home of Mrs. Doris Deweese. Shortly afterward, Mrs. Deweese watched a luminous object zip across the sky and crash into a small shack on a neighboring hillside. The shack housed the transmitter for Sheriff Johnson's police radio. It started to burn.

What followed was straight out of the Keystone Kops. The police and fire department rushed to the snow-covered hill and bogged down on the mushy dirt road. There was much frantic scurrying and cursing as the men battled the blaze. Part of the hillside was badly scorched. The transmitter inside the shack was not affected by the fire but it was burned out, as if it had been struck by lightning. So in the critical days that followed, the sheriff's department was without its main transmitter.

I was disenchanted with the TNT area because of the crowds that were now streaming back there nightly to watch for the newest sensation—flying saucers. I started searching for a private place where I could carry out my observations quietly. Don, Dan, Mary, and myself had interviewed a number of people in the little community of Gallipolis Ferry, a couple of miles south of Point Pleasant on Route 2, and I had been impressed by their testimony. House lights frequently dimmed there and television sets often acted up late at night. Great blobs of light had been seen on top of the wooded hills in the sparsely settled animal preserve called the Chief Cornstalk Hunting Grounds just south of the village. One resident was having trouble with poltergeist phenomenon . . . lights moving through his house, rappings on the doors and windows, the sounds of babies crying and "women screaming," telephones malfunctioning—the works. Rolfe Lee, a farmer with a big spread in the area, confessed that he had seen so many UFOs over his land that he didn't pay attention to them anymore.

Officer Harold Harmon and I slipped away to Gallipolis Ferry on the night of March 31 while nearly everyone else headed for the TNT area. We soon saw a number of bright starlike objects which flitted about the sky with rapid zigzag movements. Two local teen-agers were sitting on a nearby hilltop next to a roaring bonfire, hoping to lure the UFOs down. I called up to them and asked them to put the fire out, knowing that bright lights tended to repel rather than attract the objects.

Harmon fiddled vainly with his police radio. He could get nothing but static. Later I learned that all the police forces for miles in both directions had constant trouble with their radios that week. Heavy magnetic interference totally disrupted communications among law authorities while the

UFOs carried out their mysterious missions. The destruction of Sheriff Johnson's transmitter was just one small part of the scenario. Telephones, too, went bonkers that week. It seemed as if half the phones in the valley were either out of order altogether, or were clogged with crazy beeps and buzzes.

Accompanied by the two teen-agers, I left Harmon and hiked into the nearby hills in the total blackness. As my eyes became acclimated to the night I began to distinguish a number of vague purple shapes hovering over a woods on Rolfe Lee's property. At first I thought they might be stars low in the sky, gleaming through the natural haze. But when I flashed my six-celled light at one of these purple blobs it suddenly and jerkily moved to one side, as if it were jumping out of my light beam. Fascinated, I repeated the experiment several times. Then I tried flashing the light at obvious stars to see if this wasn't just some trick of my eyesight. The stars didn't move, naturally.

We sat on the hilltop studying the purple blobs for several minutes when suddenly the whole forest in the valley below lit up and glowed with a bright, eerie purple light. There were no houses or roads down there. It would have been a long hike in the dark and the boys were reluctant to join me, so we just sat and stared at the glowing forest until the light faded.

III.

The next night, Saturday, April 1, Mary Hyre and I drove up Five Mile Creek Road below Gallipolis Ferry until we reached a hilltop which commanded a view of the hills and valleys I had visited the night before. There was a single farmhouse on the hill and the people who lived there went to bed at 9:30 each night, being early risers. So the whole area was silent, deserted, and without lights throughout the night.

A few minutes after we arrived, Mary pointed out a small reddish light low on a steep wooded hill south of our position. It appeared to be blinking on and off, and bobbing up and down in a manner quite different from any of the stars on the horizon. While we watched breathlessly, barely speaking, it slowly circled the distant fields and woods and crossed in front of us, edging closer and closer. The farmhouse was about seventy-five feet in front of us. The object now appeared to be square or rectangular. It could not be mistaken for a star. It vanished momentarily behind some trees north of the farmhouse and when it reappeared it was much closer. Now we could make out a dark form. The red glow seemed to be a window. It hovered about fifty feet off the ground. I thought I could see a shadowy human figure in the "window" but Mary thought it was some kind of partition. This was the only point on which we disagreed.

We sat transfixed for several minutes, fully expecting the object to land directly in front of us and ask to be taken to our leader. I finally got out of the car and flashed my powerful beam directly at the object. It responded instantly, quickly shooting straight up into the sky, the red light going out completely.

"I guess I blew it," I groaned. But there would be other nights and more funny lights.

The following night we returned to the same hilltop. The brilliant night sky was filled with stars . . . and things not on my star map. We could easily recognize the UFOs because they were brighter and more brilliantly colored than normal stars. Some were red flashers, some were cold purple blobs, and some were multi-colored. Mrs. Hyre confirmed that they jumped out of the way of my flashlight. I picked out an especially large object and flashed: -../././.../-.-.././/-./-.. ("descend"). Mary gasped as it began to lose altitude.

"It looks like it's going down a flight of stairs," she noted. We were watching the famous "falling leaf" motion which has been described by many UFO witnesses.

About 12:30 A.M. Mrs. Hyre decided to call it a night. She drove off leaving me alone in my car sitting, like an idiot, waiting for something to happen. And it did. One hour later, at 1:35 A.M. on April 3, 1967, I had my best sighting. A clearly defined circular object suddenly zipped down from the sky and passed parallel to my car. It was so colorful that it is burned into my memory. The greenish upper surface was topped by a bright red light. There were reddish "portholes" or circular lights around the rim. The colors were so brilliant they were almost unearthly. It disappeared behind some trees to my left. I felt it was very close . . . perhaps only a few hundred feet from my car. Although it had been in full view for several seconds I never even thought of picking up the movie camera on the seat beside me.

I had three interesting physical reactions to this sighting. First of all, although I am used to prowling graveyards and TNT areas alone late at night, I was scared to death. My first thought was to start the car and get the hell out of there. But I managed to brace myself. I did lock the car doors. Second, while I was watching the object I thought I heard a sizzling or hissing sound. Later I realized I couldn't be sure if the sound had been real. Third, the next morning my eyes were sore and reddened. They felt like they were full of sand. I had a mild case of conjunctivitis and it persisted for several days.

In my notebook I scribbled, "2 A.M., drove to turnaround point [a driveway by a barn down the road], turned and returned to original parking position . . . unable to see anything in ravine . . . no lights or signs of acitivity . . . still scared . . . not anxious to get out of car . . . "

Another note reads, "No sign of moon which was supposed to rise at 1:59 A.M." This referred to something that had happened the night before. After the object with the reddish "window" had disappeared, Mary and I sat in the darkness for a long time when suddenly a great glowing object appeared behind some trees on a distant hill. It was red and large and we both thought we could see a human figure moving about on the hill. We really thought something had landed there. After a few minutes the object slowly rose upward and to our mutual embarrassment we saw that it was the moon. I had never seen a moonrise exactly like that one so I decided to deliberately watch the moon the following evening. I checked the papers for the time the moon was supposed to come up. But it never did.

That night, as I said, was cloudless and star-filled but the moon *never* appeared. I stayed in the area until 3:30 A.M. and the moon was still conspicuously absent when I left.

The night after that the moon appeared right on schedule.

Sheriff Johnson, Deputy Halstead, Mary Hyre, and I went back to Five Mile Creek Road the next afternoon to look for my saucer. Deputy Halstead carried a Geiger counter. As Johnson followed my car up the hill he was startled when his car radio suddenly sprang to life, emitting police calls from the adjoining county. The amazing thing was that *his radio was turned off at the time!* It had to be turned on with a key and the key was not even in the lock!

We searched for scorched marks, broken tree limbs, radioactivity, anything that could have provided evidence of my sighting. But as Halstead and I clambered around the ravine I was chagrined to find that my estimates must have been way off. The object must have been further away from me than I thought, and therefore it had to be bigger than I thought (I estimated it was only fifteen or twenty feet in diameter).

In my favor was the fact that there were widespread UFO sightings on the nights of April 2–3. South of Charleston,

West Virginia, a large group of people, including several state police officers, watched a formation of fifteen lights maneuver over a forest and descend.

Every night I went to the hill at Five Mile Creek Road, sometimes alone, sometimes accompanied by a few others. And every night I saw a variety of strange aerial objects. Only two airplanes passed over on a regular schedule, one at 11 P.M. and another at 2 A.M. Each night from three to eight unidentified "stars" appeared. They were always in the same position at the beginning of each evening and a casual observer would automatically conclude they were really just stars. However, on overcast nights these unidentifieds would be the only "stars" in the sky, meaning they were below the clouds. While the rest of the night sky slowly rotated, these phony stars would remain in their fixed positions, sometimes for hours, before they would begin to move. Then they would travel in any direction, up, down, clockwise, etc.

They had a number of curious traits. When a plane would fly over they would suddenly dim or go out altogether. As soon as the plane was gone they would flare up again.

It was always impossible to judge their size, altitude, or distance. Sometimes I thought they were relatively close only to find they were actually miles away, traversing the river. Boatmen on the river were obviously watching them also. Occasionally a searchlight from a riverboat would suddenly shoot into the sky, aimed straight at an object I was watching, and the object would skitter out of the way.

I doubted that these funny lights were spaceships from Andromeda and I made a strenuous effort to find rational explanations. Dr. Donald Menzel, a Harvard astronomer, advocates an air inversion theory, contending that these lights are ordinary lights reflecting off layers of warm or cold air and producing a mirage effect. This theory wasn't workable on Five Mile Creek Road simply because there weren't enough light sources. A large radio antenna some miles down the river did produce some interesting effects. When there was a haze the flashing red lights on the antenna were an eerie sight from my hill and never failed to excite first-time visitors to my lookout post.

Three or four days after my monumental UFO sighting I was sitting in Mary's office when she became very thoughtful.

"You know, there's something I've been meaning to tell you," she began hesitantly. "I don't know why, but it always seems to slip my mind. That night that I left you early . . . the night you saw that colored disc . . . when I got to Route 2 and started for Point Pleasant I saw a big globe of light right on the river. I couldn't figure out what it was . . . but I didn't stop. The funny thing is, I forgot it completely. I didn't remember it until a day or so afterward. Then I forgot it again. I can't understand it. I've always had a very good memory."

Lacunal amnesia, loss of the memory of specific incidents or moments in time, is a common part of the phenomenon. In December 1967 Faye Carpenter, Connie's mother, had a more baffling attack of amnesia. The night that "Jack Brown" visited Connie (Chapter Two), Mrs. Carpenter had opened the door for him. He was in his shirt sleeves, no jacket or coat although it was extremely cold. She was not going to let him in . . . but she did. And she had absolutely no memory of his visit afterward even though she had been present when he talked with Connie, Keith, and Larry.

In the days following Mr. Brown's visit, a poltergeist settled in the Carpenter household. Securely fastened pictures fell off the walls. Small objects disappeared from shelves and reappeared in unlikely places. The manifestations lasted about two weeks.

IV.

During her news-gathering rounds, Mary Hyre was approached by a professional woman in Gallipolis, Ohio, the
town directly across the river from Gallipolis Ferry, West
Virginia. She said she heard I was in the area and she wanted
to talk to me. My motel, the Blue Fountain, was on the
outskirts of Gallipolis so I arranged a meeting with the lady.
She held a very responsible job and insisted on anonymity,
as so many witnesses do, so I will call her Mrs. Bryant.

We met in a private office in a major company in Gallipolis. Mrs. Bryant was a reserved, well-spoken middle-aged
woman who looked slightly fatigued from overwork. She was
very secretive and suspicious at first, but after I showed her
my parcel of credentials she relaxed somewhat. It was obvious she had been through a great deal and she was concerned I would not believe her. She had gone to the local
authorities, she said, and they had laughed at her. I assured
her that I wouldn't laugh, that I was accustomed to hearing
incredible stories from credible people.

"Last November . . . I think it was the second or third,"
she began, "I was out behind this building, getting ready to
go home. It was seven or eight o'clock. Suddenly there was
a little flash, like a camera flash gun going off, directly above
me . . . and then I saw a thing . . . some kind of flying
machine. I couldn't move. I guess I was frozen with fright.
This thing landed right there in the parking lot not twenty
feet away from me. It was like a big cylinder. Anyway, it
didn't make the slightest bit of noise. It just drifted down
and stopped. Like I say, I couldn't move. I guess I started
praying. Then two men came out of it and they walked over
to me."

She studied me anxiously as if expecting me to laugh.

"What did they look like?" I asked.

"They were just normal-sized, normal-looking men, but
their skins were a funny color . . . dark, like maybe they were

heavily tanned. The light was pretty bad there so I couldn't see them all that well."

"Were they Negroes?"

"No. No, they didn't have Negroid features. Their faces seemed kind of pointed. You know, pointed noses, pointed chins, high cheekbones. There was a kind of evil look about them. I was afraid I was going to get robbed or attacked."

"How were they dressed?" I leaned back and lit my pipe.

"As near as I could tell, they were wearing some kind of coveralls, something like a uniform. Then they started talking to me."

She kept watching me, reluctant to continue.

"What did they have to say?" I prompted, trying to avoid leading questions.

"Well, it was all pretty silly. They just wanted to know my name, where I was from, what I did for a living, things like that. Sometimes it was hard to understand them. Their voices were sort of singsongy and high-pitched. It was like listening to a phonograph record played at the wrong speed. And they kept asking me for the time. They asked 'What is your time?' two or three times. Finally they just walked back to the thing and it took off. Then I could move again. I was scared out of my wits but I decided not to tell anyone. Then a couple of days later I heard about a man up near Parkersburg who had the same thing happen to him."

"His name is Woodrow Derenberger," I volunteered. "Have you met him?"

"No. I just heard something about him on the radio." She paused and moistened her thin lips. "I wonder . . . did he ever see those men again?"

"He says he did."

She looked relieved.

"Well, I saw them again. I saw them in broad daylight. Walking right down the main street in Gallipolis. This time they were dressed in normal clothes. They looked like anybody. They sort of nodded to me when they passed me. I got scared all over again. Real scared. That's when I went to the police and told them what I saw. They laughed at me and said I was probably just imagining things." She paused again and shook her head sadly. "You see, I've been to the police before . . . about my cattle rustlers. I guess they think I'm some kind of a nut. I went to the FBI, too. They came out to my place but said they couldn't find anything. After that somebody tapped my telephone. Maybe it was the FBI."

I was scribbling in my pocket notebook. A year or two earlier I would have classified Mrs. Bryant as a paranoid-schizophrenic. But she didn't seem like a common run-of-the-mill nut.

She and her two teen-aged children lived on a farm outside of Gallipolis. She kept cows there and beginning in 1963–64 she started to have trouble with cattle rustlers who butchered the animals in the field.

"Whoever they were," she observed, "they didn't seem to want the choice cuts. They just took the brains, eyeballs, udders, and organs that—you know—we'd normally throw away."

Had she ever caught the culprits in the act?

"Several times," she said. "I'd see them out in the field and go after them with a shotgun. But they always got away. They're tall men and they wear white coveralls . . . which is kind of stupid because they really stand out in the dark. And they can certainly run and jump. I've seen them leap over high fences from a standing start."

Her home burned to the ground during that period and she built a new one-story ranch house on the same site. One night when she was alone in the new house, she said, she woke up and found herself unable to move. She felt a wave of almost overpowering heat as she heard the kitchen door open. She had double-locked it before going to bed. While she lay there helplessly, she said she saw a tall figure walk through the kitchen and apparently go out another locked door on the other side. After it left, she was able to move.

Other strange sounds pervaded the house, she claimed. She and her children often heard heavy footsteps on the roof and loud metallic clangs.

After interviewing her, I drove out alone to her house to talk to her children. The Bryant farm was quite isolated on a hilly back road. The house stood on a knoll overlooking the surrounding fields. Her teen-aged son was a down-to-earth boy, used to the responsibilities of being the man in the family. He confirmed his mother's stories about the rustlers and added some interesting details. He pointed out some nearby trees. One night, he said, as he and his mother were walking up the road they saw a large glowing object hovering directly above the trees. "She was scared real bad," he noted. Their telephone often went dead for no reason. Other times they got calls that just consisted of strange beeping sounds and "electronic music." He also mentioned the big gray "flying boxcars" that often flew over the area at treetop level. "It's a wonder they don't crash," he said. "If they flew any lower they'd have to put their wheels down."

When I examined the kitchen of the little house I found that the locked door through which the nocturnal phantom had supposedly exited led to nowhere. There were no steps outside, just a very steep drop of about ten feet to the ground.

Later I checked with the local police about rumors of disappearing dogs and cattle in the area, and I brought up Mrs. Bryant's name. "That poor woman," I was told. "She's always seeing things. Just a couple of months back she came in here with some story about spacemen walking around Gallipolis. Before that it was cattle rustlers."

So Mrs. Bryant still sits on her farm, watching the strange lights in her fields, and when her phone rings she waits a long time before she picks it up.

11:

If This Is Wednesday, It Must Be a Venusian

I.

James Lilly stood on his lawn surrounded by reporters from Charleston and Huntington newspapers, Sheriff George Johnson and his wife, and a host of others. Hundreds of automobiles lined the Camp Conley Road, dark and silent except for the glows of cigarettes. Other cars cruised in slow streams along the rutted roads of the TNT area to the north.

"It's just about that time," Jim Lilly announced, glancing at his watch. It was exactly 8:30 P.M. "They come over every night right about now."

Horns suddenly began to bleat and excited shouts echoed through the trees.

"Right on time," Lilly chuckled. "You can set your watch by 'em."

"My God! What is it?" A reporter and novice UFO-watcher cried out as a brilliant white light slowly glided into view. It arched gracefully overhead about one hundred feet above the trees. Car doors slammed up and down the road as families scrambled out of their vehicles to watch. Newsmen floundered with their expensive cameras.

"What in hell is the matter with this? The shutter didn't trip!"

The light passed slowly toward Point Pleasant, the ground below lighting up in its glow as it passed.

"Where's that guy Keel?" someone asked.

"He's probably up there riding in that damned thing," someone else answered.

A light plane suddenly circled over the TNT area, all its lights ablaze.

"Here comes Doc Shaw again," Jim Lilly laughed. "Who does he think he's fooling."

But voices were crying out in the dark, "There goes another one!"

The plane cut its engine for a moment and glided.

George Johnson turned to his wife. "Well, you wanted to see a UFO."

"It was like seeing a ghost," she shuddered.

The air was filled with the sounds of auto engines grinding away impotently and drivers snarling and cursing because their cars wouldn't start.

The light traveled on to the ravine that passed behind North Park Road, then it dipped down and moved low along the bottom of the ravine. Betty Kelly, thirteen, looked out the kitchen window of the Kelly house and screamed.

"Ma . . . it's back!"

The glowing thing was appearing nightly behind the Kelly home. It seemed to settle in their backyard at times and the glow faded slightly so they could see a definite object. They even thought they saw a triangular doorway in it and what appeared to be frosted glass windows. Their neighbors had all been watching, too, but had wisely avoided publicity. They didn't want their street to become another Camp Conley Road or TNT area.

When Betty cried out, Bill Kelly, her father, grumbled in the living room. He was an electronics engineer and he had just taken the back off the family's brand-new color TV set. The set had blown out the night before when the object had paid a visit. "Somebody should do something about these things," he complained.

The object began to glow more intensely and then it vanished.

"Where did it go?" Mrs. Kelly asked her daughter.

"I don't know—it—it just went." She started to cry. She would be so nervous and upset that she wouldn't go to school the next day.

The phone rang. Bill Kelly looked at it as if it were a snake. He picked it up slowly, listened and scowled, then replaced the receiver. His wife glanced at him expectantly.

"Another one of those calls . . . beeep, beep, beep," he nodded.

On top of a hill east of Point Pleasant Mary Hyre and I stood by our cars looking down at the village.

"Where did it go, John?"

I was straining my eyesight through a cheap telescope.

"I think it went down that ravine by North Park. But I can't see it now."

"At least it was right on schedule."

Flickering red and green lights suddenly appeared.

"A plane," I noted.

"Probably Doctor Shaw. He told me he's been spooking the people at the TNT area."

"It's hard to mistake an airplane for one of those UFO lights."

"Look!" she called out sharply. "Something is following that plane."

A few hundred feet behind the plane I could see a large black object, almost as big as the plane itself but completely without lights.

"Mothman! Is it Mothman?"

I fumbled with my telescope. It's very difficult to zero in on an object in the night sky with a handheld telescope. I couldn't even locate the plane.

The plane crossed the river and headed for the Gallipolis airport. The thing following him was quickly lost in the black sky.

We returned to Mary's office and found all the phones ringing. People were seeing flying objects all up and down the valley. Some had probably just seen the good doctor's nocturnal sortie, but others described what sounded like genuine UFOs.

That was April 5, 1967, a Wednesday. I had collected and analyzed some seven hundred UFO reports from 1966 and discovered that the greatest number of sightings, 20 percent, took place on Wednesdays. I called this "the Wednesday phenomenon." The events of 1967 conformed to this curious pattern, as have the sightings of later flaps. The major events of October 1973 were concentrated around Wednesdays, particularly Wednesday, October 17.

So here was another curious contradiction. The entities professed to be ignorant of our time frame; yet the objects managed to fly to a rigid schedule that could be measured by our clocks and calendars.

When I interviewed attorney Robert Wright in Sistersville, West Virginia, he told me the things have turned up every Wednesday throughout the summer of 1966, "like clockwork."

No one except the U.S. Air Force had attempted even a superficial statistical analysis of UFO sightings before, so my findings were greeted with howls of derision by the scientists who posed as experts on the phenomenon. Then Dr. David Saunders of Colorado University fed several thousand sightings into a computer and found the Wednesday phenomenon remained stable. That day produced the largest number of sightings, well beyond the laws of chance and averages.

In March 1967, Ralph Jarrett talked me into violating my

"low-profile" policy and I appeared with him on the Jackie Oberlinger show on WCHS-TV in Charleston. In the course of our discussion I mentioned that the best time to see a UFO was 10 P.M. on a Wednesday. Mrs. Oberlinger, a vivacious blond lady and very much a local celebrity, took me at my word. On Wednesday, March 29, she and a group of her friends gathered in her backyard in Charleston and, sure enough, at exactly 10 P.M. three globes of brilliant white light passed directly overhead in a V-formation.

The Wednesday phenomenon works. I've been studying it for years and I still can't say *why* it works. Researchers in other parts of the world have now followed my example and found similar time patterns in the sightings in their own countries. The table below is a breakdown of sightings recorded in 1950, as analyzed by Saunders, United States; Ballester-Orlando, Spain; Bonabot, Belgium.

DISTRIBUTION OF UFO REPORTS—1950

DAY	United States	Spain	Belgium	TOTAL	Percent-Age
Sunday	40	6	23	69	9.8
Monday	53	8	42	103	14.7
Tuesday	44	15	43	102	14.6
WEDNESDAY	57	19	56	132	18.8
Thursday	51	10	55	116	16.5
Friday	40	12	38	90	12.8
Saturday	32	13	44	89	12.7
Totals:	317	83	301	701	99.9

(Originally published in *Bulletin du Gesag*, Belgium, June 1972.)

II.

Soon after arriving in Point Pleasant and getting a handle on the scope of the situation, I phoned the Lockburn Air

Force Base in Ohio and outlined what was happening to a Lieutenant Hoffman, the base UFO officer. He was very polite, but he was also disinterested and it was clear the air force was not going to launch any kind of investigation.

Perhaps an investigation was already underway. As I wandered around Main Street in early April I noticed a surprising number of strangers who just didn't seem to fit in. They had the indelible look of federal officers . . . conservative ties, square clothes, recent haircuts. There must have been fifteen or twenty of them. I saw them in the local restaurants and drugstores, everywhere.

"Is there a convention in town?" I asked Mary Hyre.

"So you noticed them, too?" She smiled. "Everybody's been asking me about them. But so far I haven't found out a thing."

I decided to trap one of them into a conversation, but they all vanished before I could do so.

One night Roger Scarberry, Steve Mallette, and myself were driving around the TNT area when we came upon a large black Cadillac parked in the shadows. I slammed on the brakes, got out of our car, and walked over to the other vehicle. A well-dressed, distinguished-looking man was sitting behind the wheel holding a microphone in his hand. I tried to engage him in a conversation but he would only grunt. Obviously he wanted to be left alone. I never saw him again.

My days were spent tracking down witnesses and in early evening I would cruise through the TNT area before going to Five Mile Creek Road for skywatches that usually lasted until 3 or 4 A.M. Then I would drive back to Point Pleasant, cross the rickety old Silver Bridge into Ohio, and grab a few hours sleep at the Blue Fountain.

Three or four miles south of my secret hilltop there was a heavily forested ridge. The object with the reddish "window" which Mary and I had seen on our first night seemed to have come from there. Each night at exactly 10 P.M. a bright red glow would appear on that ridge, as if someone had just turned on a powerful light. Thinking there might be a house there, or a road (and we were watching auto taillights), I returned in daylight but found it would have been a very long hike to reach it. No buildings were visible there. I drove through the roads in the Chief Cornstalk Hunting Grounds, hoping to find a road up that particular ridge but apparently it was inaccessible.

On Thursday, April 6, Mrs. Hyre accompanied me to Five Mile Creek Road and we watched as the light came on, right on schedule. Suddenly we saw an identical-type light behind the trees north of our position in the very spot where I had seen the glowing disc descend. I knew there were no houses or roads in that direction. We divided our attention between the two lights. Both seemed to be moving through the trees very slowly. I got out of the car with my flashlight and flashed it three times in the direction of the southern ridge. An instant later there were three extremely bright flashes. Mary nearly jumped out of her skin.

"They answered you!" she declared.

The red light rose upward until it was a hundred feet or so above the trees. Then it went out, as if someone had turned off a switch. The light in the north dipped down behind the trees and disappeared.

AFFIDAVIT

To whom it may concern:

I, Mrs. Mary Hyre of 219-Sixth Street, Point Pleasant, W. Va., a reporter for the Athens (Ohio) *Messenger*, hereby swear that I was present at the following event and personally witnessed it as described.

On the evening of April 6, 1967, I accompanied Mr. John A. Keel of New York City to an isolated hilltop on Five Mile Creek Road south of Gallipolis Ferry, W. Va. Shortly after 11 p.m. I observed a pale red object of undetermined size moving in a controlled manner slightly above tree-top level over a hill about 500 yards south of our position. There are no houses or roads on that hill. The object appeared to move cautiously and slowly through the sky to the far end of the sloping field, the light flickering on and off in an irregular pattern.

As the object drew closer, Mr. Keel got out of the car and flashed a powerful flashlight directly at it three times. The object immediately returned the signal by flashing a brilliant white light three times. Then it rose upwards and the pale red light went completely out.

State of West Virginia)
) To-wit: Signed:
County of Mason   )   *Mary Hyre*
                                   Mary Hyre

This day personally appeared before me in my office, county and state, Mary Hyre, known to me personally, and acknowledged the above statement to be true and that she personally signed her signature in my presence.

Given under my hand this _21_ day of _June_ 1967.

My commission expires _June 12 1977_

                               Howard Schultz Notary Public

Mrs. Mabel McDaniel and two other women went to the hill with me the following night. About 10:15 the usual reddish glow appeared on the southern hill. Then a second one popped up a short distance from the first. I flashed my light at them but nothing happened. So I climbed a fence and walked into a field to try to get a closer look. The two objects slowly came together. As I crossed the field I suddenly noticed something new . . . a pale bluish ball of light hovering high in the trees of an orchard behind the nearby farmhouse. The light moved about from tree to tree as though it were following my movements. I flashed my light at it and it flared with dazzling brilliance, dimmed, and vanished. Simultaneously, the lights on the southern ridge grew brighter for a moment and then also went out. I slowly made my way back across the field in the dark, climbed the fence, and returned to Mrs. McDaniel's car. I was surprised to find all three women in a very frightened state.

"I think we'd better leave," Mrs. McDaniel said nervously. They drove off quickly.

Five minutes later, as I sat alone in my car, the reddish glow flared up again on the ridge. For the first time, it changed color from red to a glaring white and rose slowly upward, bobbing like a Yo-Yo toward the river in the west. Apparently some boatmen on the river saw the object also, for a bright searchlight suddenly shot up from behind the hills, aimed directly at the luminous thing. When the searchlight appeared, the object halted in mid-flight, dropped downward, and went out. The searchlight continued to scan the sky.

The next day I talked with Mrs. McDaniel and told her what I had seen.

"Too bad you didn't stick around," I remarked.

"We were pretty scared," she began. "We . . . oh, you'll probably think we were being silly."

"Did that blue light frighten you?"

"It wasn't the light," she said hesitantly. "We saw that. And then we saw a tall man in the field. We all saw him climb over the fence and cross behind our car. We thought it was you coming back. Then your flashlight went on way out in the field and we knew it wasn't you. We ran the windows up and locked the doors and waited for you to come back."

I had certainly not seen anyone else in that field. Had their eyes been playing tricks? Or were there phantoms on that hilltop?

That weekend I drove into Ohio to check out some of the many weird events happening there. One of my all-time favorites happened in the little village of Duncan Falls. Here is the verbatim entry from my journal:

Sometime in late October 1966 (witness does not remember exact date) Mr. Leonard "Shy" Elmore, 72, of Duncan Falls, Ohio, was taking a stroll around 4 A.M. when he encountered a strange "building" which frightened him badly. Like many elderly people, Mr. Elmore does not sleep well and often takes long walks late at night. On this particular morning, he was walking along a road two blocks from his home when he saw a strange "L-shaped building that looked like a galvanized iron shed" sitting in the middle of a large field. Since he had never noticed this "shed" before he walked closer to take a better look. Something about it frightened him . . . later he could not explain why it had scared him . . . and he turned and started to hurry away. Although it was dark and he could see no windows or doors in the "shed," he claims that he distinctly heard a normal male voice come from it. "Don't run . . . don't run," the voice called. "I didn't 'sactly run," Mr. Elmore told me, "but I walked pretty fast."

He hurried home and got his rifle and returned to the site. To his astonishment, the "shed" was gone. This incident upset him very much and, according to his wife, he was a nervous wreck for several days afterwards. He decided to call the sheriff and report what he'd seen. The sheriff promised to come out and take a look . . . but never did. Mr. Elmore told me his story in a direct manner without embellishments or wandering speculations.

No Men in Black came around to bother Mr. Elmore. I was the first reporter to talk to him. When he showed me the field I was perturbed to find that it was right next to the Duncan Falls Elementary School. An unusual number of sightings and Fortean* events seem to be concentrated around schools and the largest percentage of witnesses consists of children between the ages of seven and eighteen. Another statistical oddity is that the majority of the adults

* A Fortean event is any event which does not have a rational scientific explanation. The word was coined after Charles Fort. There is even an International Fortean Organization (INFO); Box 367; Arlington, Virginia.

who claim their autos were pursued by UFOs or monsters are schoolteachers, especially teachers specializing in abnormal children—the very bright or the mentally deficient. This is why I was so interested in the West Virginia "census takers" who were mainly concerned with the numbers and ages of the children living in the Ohio valley.

12:

Games Nonpeople Play

I.

"Woodrow Derenberger is pregnant!"

The word flashed up and down the Ohio valley, and many people took the absurd rumor seriously. The space people had selected Woody for a unique experiment, so the story went, and he had gone into hiding to nurture his rapidly swelling stomach. He would soon be giving birth to a very special baby; part earthling, part extraterrestrial. The child was slated to grow into a great leader.

The events of 1966–67 had fractured everyone's sense of credulity. Almost anything now seemed possible. A pregnant man was no more absurd than the winged behemoth, or the gigantic illuminated forms that cruised up and down the Ohio nightly. A fantastic new world was taking shape, populated by spacemen who drove Cadillacs and Volkswagens, psychiatrists who heard bodiless voices in the night, and things that ate dogs and cattle while everyone was looking in the wrong direction.

Like everyone else, I was caught up in the games, mystery

piling upon mystery. Someone somewhere obviously knew every move I was making, or so it seemed. I became very secretive, not even telling my closest friends where I was going or where I had been. Nevertheless, something seemed to be following me. I would drop in unannounced on a remote farm and soon after I settled down to chat with the residents their phone would ring and there would be no one on the line, or a series of loud beeps would ring out. The farmer would act astonished.

"We've *never* had a call like that before!"

The phone would ring repeatedly until I left.

This happened several different times in several different places.

I used a system of "spot checks," visiting homes in flap areas and talking with people who had never reported anything. Mrs. Hyre accompanied me on a number of these spot checks and was amazed at how much had been going on. Her name and face were familiar to everyone in the area and her reputation as a fair, objective reporter was impeccable. People automatically loosened up when they saw her and talked freely. In the hills surrounding Point Pleasant we heard many stories about footsteps on the roof, strange metallic clangings (the most common being the sound of a car door slamming outside the house when there were no cars in sight). One family showed us how the flap covering the entrance to their attic had been mysteriously moved. It was a hole in the ceiling of a bedroom and could only be reached with a high ladder. Others complained of "Gypsies" marching across their property late at night; men in bright reflective clothing and women in ankle-length dresses, all with long hair and dark Oriental faces. (This was well before the hippie explosion of the late 1960s.)

North of Gallipolis, Ohio, I impulsively stopped at an isolated farmhouse one afternoon and when I knocked at the door a grim-faced man answered with a shotgun in his hands. I started to show my credentials and explain who I was but he cut me short.

"I know who you are," he growled. "We don't want anything to do with you. Get out of here."

Puzzled, I reported back to Mary and suggested that she visit the farm to see if she could find out the reason for the man's strange behavior.

The next day we went back. I remained in the car while she talked with him for several minutes. Finally they both came out to the car laughing.

"You're not going to believe this," the farmer began apologetically, "but ten minutes before you arrived here yesterday I got a phone call. It sounded like a neighbor of mine and he said he was calling to warn me about a crazy man . . . a real dangerous type . . . with a beard . . . that had just been to see him. Said I shouldn't have anything to do with him. Ten minutes later you showed up. After you left, I called him back. He was out in the fields. Had been all day. His wife had to go get him. He said he hadn't made that call."

I looked sternly at Mary.

"Is this some kind of a put-on?"

"Absolutely not," she answered, turning to the farmer. "Tell him the rest of it."

"Well, about a week ago something scared my cows real bad," he continued. "You know, we ain't told anyone about this, Mrs. Hyre. You aren't going to put it in the paper, are you?"

"Not if you don't want us to."

"Come on. Let me show you something."

He led us into the field behind his barn. There was a thirty-foot circle of scorched earth on the hillside. I had seen several of these "fairy circles" before.

"That night our cows really acted up," he went on. "They stampeded. They were so scared they went right through the fence over there." He pointed toward a stretch of wire fence that had obviously just been repaired. "It's an electric fence. Now you know that it takes a lot to make cows charge through an electric fence. Anyway, when I heard the ruckus I ran outside and I saw my cows scattering down the road. And there was a big red and white glowing thing sitting right in the field. I've got to say that it scared me half to death. I ran back in my house to get my gun. Didn't take me more than a minute. But when I got outside again the thing was gone. This circle was all that was left. It took the rest of the night to round up my cows."

"Were any of them lost or missing?" I asked.

"No." He paused. "But Herk—that's Hercules—my big old collie dog ran off that night and we ain't seen him since."

Mary had been with me when I had checked into other missing dog incidents. She gave me a meaningful glance and he caught it.

"Say, you don't think that thing took old Herk, do you?"

"No. It was probably just some kind of electrical phenomenon," I answered gently. "Herk will probably come back."

"I hope so. We sure loved that dog." He looked thoughtful. "Electrical, huh. Let me show you something else."

He led us into his barn and showed us a brand-new circuit box.

"I had to have this put in the next day so I could run my milker. The old box was completely burned out. In fact, it was melted . . . like somebody had put a welding torch to it."

"See, it must have been some kind of electrical thing," I said lamely. I knew Ivan Sanderson had investigated an almost identical incident in New Jersey only weeks before. But in that case the cows had been in their stalls in the barn and were found dead.

"Has anyone else been around to talk to you about this?"

"No . . . I haven't told anyone. Just some fellows from the

electric company who turned up the next day. They fussed around with the transformer on the pole by the road. I tried to talk with them but they didn't have much to say."

"Did you know them?"

"Never saw them before. Come to think of it, they didn't have a regular electric truck. Just a panel truck."

"Would you recognize them if you saw them again?"

"Sure would. They was foreigners. You know, Japs or something. Like I said, they weren't very friendly."

"How were they dressed?"

"Oh, you know . . . ordinary coveralls. I did notice their shoes, though. They had on funny shoes with very thick rubber soles. Guess when you work around electricity you need insulation."

Mary shuddered perceptibly.

"Say, do you know these fellows?" he asked.

"Well, I saw a man with thick-soled shoes like that once," Mary began. I cut in sharply, thanking the man, promising to keep him out of the papers, and reminding Mary that we had an appointment elsewhere.

Back in the car, Mary could no longer curb her natural curiosity.

"What do you make of all this, John?"

"The more I find out, the more confusing it becomes."

"That's the way I feel. That phone call . . . sounds like someone didn't want you to talk to him."

"It could work the other way, too," I suggested. "Maybe this whole thing was set up so I *would* talk to him. I just picked his farm out at random. If he had just turned me away with a smile I would never have bothered him again. But when he came to the door with a gun . . ."

"But how did they know you were going to stop there? How could anyone have possibly known?"

"That's the real question. How could anyone have known?"

II.

A few days before leaving New York I called Gray Barker in Clarksburg and he agreed to meet me the following Tuesday in Point Pleasant. As soon as he hung up, I dialed Woodrow Derenberger's unlisted number and spoke to his wife.

"When are you coming to see us again?" she asked.

"I expect to be in West Virginia next week," I replied.

"I know. I hear you're having a secret meeting with Gray Barker on Tuesday."

I was stunned.

"I'm meeting with Gray," I admitted, "but it's not very secret. I didn't know about it myself until a couple of minutes ago, so how on earth did you know?"

There was a pause.

"Charlie Cutler over in Ohio told us about it a couple of days ago," she finally said.

"And how did he know about it?"

"I—I don't know. I suppose he heard it somewhere."

When you enter the unreal world of the contactees, predictions, prophecies, and a mysterious invasion of your privacy become commonplace. Contactees seem to develop heightened perceptions, ESP, and precognition. The changes occur almost overnight. In their meetings with the entities they are served up platters of propaganda along with rumors and nonsense which they accept and repeat as fact. Many of the choicest tidbits in UFO lore were not actual events but were put into circulation by contactees who placed their complete trust in their contacters. The entities spun wild tales about crashed saucers being confiscated by the U.S. Air Force, farmers shooting and wounding spacemen, and so forth. Contactees repeated the stories to wild-eyed UFO enthusiasts and so they spread in ever-widening circles until they appeared in articles and books.

Derenberger never claimed psychic powers. He said he

received telepathic messages from Indrid Cold giving him specific information. Others such as Ted Owens and Uri Geller have also claimed that their psychic abilities came from space intelligencies. Mr. Owens has racked up an impressive record predicting the outcomes of football games. Mr. Geller, an Israeli psychic, became world famous after his alleged contact with a flying saucer on a desert in the Middle East. Both men have been examined and tested by armies of scientists and parapsychologists.

I have probably examined and befriended more UFO contactees than anyone else. Usually their experiences follow certain patterns which they are not even aware of at the time. A long series of seemingly unrelated events occur prior to the first overt contact. These events can begin in childhood and span many years. Then, too, most contactees have active or latent psychic abilities before contact. People who see ghosts or religious apparitions have the same patterns as the UFO contactees. And, in fact, the apparitions described in religious "miracles" usually share the same physical characteristics as our UFO entities; that is, long fingers, dusky complexions, pointed features.

The flying saucer lore of the past twenty-seven years has been built on three main components: (1) the sighting reports, usually poorly investigated by amateurs and believers, or based entirely on fragmented and often inaccurate newspaper stories; (2) the testimony of the contactees; (3) messages received through spirit mediums and ESP. In recent years a new element has been added by the few scientists pulled into the controversy. This is the tiresome use of probabilities to explain that there must be zillions of other planets and therefore there must be uncounted numbers of inhabited places in the universe. In the early 1960s exobiology became the new scientific rip-off. Various foundations and NASA poured millions of dollars into the study of extraterrestrial life. Since there were no samples available for study, and since there is not the slightest bit of evidence that even a single planet exists in any other star system, exobiology was not an easy field. Scientists had to justify their enormous expenditures with reams of speculative papers: We do not even have enough facts, after fifteen years of study, to form a real basis for the coveted probabilities. If Nick the Greek were asked to make book on the existence of extraterrestrial life, he would find the scientific arguments so tenuous that the odds would have to be somewhere around a trillion to one. Of the nine planets in our own solar system, only three—Mercury, Earth, and Mars—are solid, and only one of these three is infested with life. The appearance of life requires a long list of environmental and chemical conditions. For all these conditions to exist simultaneously on a single planet also requires a whole series of improbable coincidences.

Men have always gazed at the night sky and dreamed of other worlds. Four thousand years ago, Enoch became the first space traveler, visiting seven worlds or planets after being roused from his sleep by angelic spacemen. Swedenborg, the great Swedish mathematician, went wandering through the cosmos in the 1700s, and a proper Bostonian named William Denton was given a guided tour of Venus in the 1860s. George Adamski, Howard Menger, and several others visited the moon in the 1950s, preceding Neil Armstrong by more than a decade. Menger, a New Jersey sign painter, brought back some "moon potatoes" that looked like rocks . . . and they didn't cost the taxpayers a cent. Adamski, a California eccentric, found the backside of the moon rich in vegetation and water. Others observed cunningly concealed underground cities there.

Still others have traveled to scores of unknown planets in distant galaxies. Planets with exotic-sounding names adopted from ancient Greek, just as most of the entities who stop lone drivers on isolated back yards claim names from mythology.

For example, on Wednesday, July 26, 1967, Mrs. Maris

De Long and Michael Kisner were driving in a park near California's Big Tujunga Canyon when they heard a bodiless voice which instructed them to watch for something unusual. There was a flash of light in the sky and a glowing disc twenty feet in diameter appeared. Soon they were chatting with "Kronin," master of the Kronian race. He was very tall and both boneless and eyeless, and said he was "a space robot encased in a time capsule."

As soon as Mrs. De Long reached her home after the visit her phone rang. It was Kronin. She later recorded several conversations with him in which he explained the problems of the universe. She had never heard of Cronus, the Roman god of time.

Another entity popular in occult circles for centuries is Ashtoreth, the Phoenician goddess of love. A character called Ashtar has been communicating with UFO fans for years, coming through worldwide at séances, on Ouija boards, and through mental telepathy. Ashtar is a big cheese in the Intergalactic Federation. Contactees have churned out dozens of books filled with his messages.

A woman on Long Island had an encounter with an olive-skinned gentleman in a greenish suit in May 1967 and his name caused me some problems. He called himself Aphloes. I finally figured out that it was from *aphlogistic*, a word derived from Greek meaning "a lamp giving light without flame."

Woodrow Derenberger's Mr. Cold did not fit this pattern. In fact, the name made me suspicious of Woody's story and if I had not talked with others who had shared similar experiences on the same night, I might have rejected Derenberger outright because of it.

In earlier times, fairies, demons, and even human witches practicing their Black Sabbath rites, chose gravel pits, garbage dumps, cemeteries *and crossroads* for their appearances. Modern hairy monsters and UFOs select the same sites, and quite a few UFO contacts have occurred near crossroads or on highways still under construction *at points where old highways once intersected.* Derenberger's first contact with Cold was on a newly completed highway yards from an old intersection.

Across the river, the vast "Indian" mounds of Ohio stand as mute testimony of some earlier culture almost identical to the culture which constructed the great mounds of Great Britain. The latter were joined by straight tracks or "leys" which formed a complicated grid system. I wondered if a similar ley grid may not have once existed in West Virginia and I studied aerial photos and old maps looking for such a system. There are tiny traces here and there, but modern farmers and builders have destroyed most of the old artifacts, just as they had destroyed a great many of the mounds, stone towers, etc., that stood on this continent when the first Europeans arrived.

Had Woody been stopped on a cross-point of some old ley network? The only clue lies in Mr. Cold's uncharacteristic selection for a name. In his study of the British leys, *The View Over Atlantis,* John Michell stated:

> A peculiar feature of the old alignments is that certain names appear with remarkable frequency along their routes. Names with Red, White and Black are common; so are *Cold* or Cole, Dod, Merry and Ley.

It would be in keeping with the twisted logic of the entities to call attention to a West Virginia ley system by staging their landings at specific points along the grid and adopting names like Cold. Apparently this is exactly what they did in 1966–67.

So far as I know, Cold and his mischievous companions never presented themselves to other contactees . . . or they changed their names to suit each occasion. This, too, is a break with tradition. Ashtar, Orthon, and several others with names that sound like synthetic fabrics have contacted thousands of people all over the world in the past twenty years.

In September 1973, just before the great October UFO wave, posters sprang up all over Atlanta, Georgia, proclaiming the eminent arrival of the space people. A Georgia psychic was in mental communication with Zandark, who identified himself as "a member of the United Cosmic Council; a Commander in Chief in Charge of Directing Technical Transmissions Via Mental Telepathy or the Combination of Mediumistic Telepathy Under the Direction of the Confederation of Cosmic Space Beings." Zandark delivered the usual "We come to bring peace" message, claimed credit for building the Sphinx, the Pyramids, "and other structural phenomenas," and complained that contactees were not being taken seriously enough, but were being "branded fools, fanatics, and personal publicity seekers." We were advised to shape up.

Each of Zandark's communications began with the salutation, "Adonai Vassu." When the sitters at the Atlanta séances asked for a translation they were told it meant, "Peace be with you, and love forever."

Unknown to the Georgia group, a contactee in Italy, Eugenio Siragusa, has been in touch with the space people for years and his contacter always signs off with, "May the light of the universal peace be with you . . . [signed] Adoniesis."

Adoniesis is a manufactured word, a sort of Romanization of *Adonai*, an ancient Hebrew word for God; *Vassu* stems from the Latin *vassus*, meaning servant. So *Adonai Vassu* really means "servant of God." Old Zandark is just another angel in disguise! Adoniesis and Adonai are not so far removed from each other. It is interesting that the same terms would turn up at séances an ocean apart.

Even more interesting is the fact that the messages received by psychics everywhere bear remarkable similarities in content, even in phrasing. I have researched obscure contactee-type books written two and three hundred years ago and have found the same identical messages and phraseology were prevalent then. Since much of this literature is very obscure and hard to find, and since many of our psychics and contactees are poorly read, it is doubtful if this is a question of fakers repeating the earlier material. Rather, it seems as if there is a phonograph in the sky endlessly repeating the same material generation after generation as if there were a crack in the record.

Author Brad Steiger interviewed scores of psychics, prophets, and contactees for his study of this phenomenon, *Revelation: The Divine Fire.* He found that people claiming to be in communication with God, angels, spirits of the dead, and spacemen from other planets were all receiving essentially the same information. All spoke of an impending disaster, just as Zandark warned, "The time for your planet is crucial." But the prophets and seers of the last century were getting the same spiel.

William Miller (1782–1849) founded the Seventh-Day Adventists in the belief that the world was coming to an end in 1843. Interestingly, prophets all over the world and tribes of Hopi and Navaho Indians in the Southwest picked that same year. Clearly, they were all tuned in to the same "static." Jehovah's Witnesses were founded in 1872 on a similar premise.

The messages delivered to the children in Fátima, Portugal, in 1917, also discussed the coming disaster, but phrased in obscure theological terms.

Again and again, psychics and contactees have gathered their family and friends together to sit on a hilltop and wait for the predicted end of the world. This charade has been repeated many times in the past twenty-five years with UFO contactees preparing for the wonderful space people to descend in their flying saucers and evacuate a chosen few from our doomed planet.

The world was supposed to end on December 24, 1967. Occult and UFO groups around the world got the message in every language. A Danish cult actually built a lead-lined bomb shelter and spent the holidays cringing in it, waiting for the big blast.

In 1973, a UFO contactee in Wisconsin soberly announced that the comet Kahotek was going to wreck the earth that Christmas. He was recruiting people to be evacuated by his space friends.

Zandark, Orthon, Ashtar, Xeno, Cold, and all their cronies have been leading many of us around by the noses for centuries. First they convince us of their honesty, reliability, the accuracy of their predictions, and their well-meant intentions. Then they leave us sitting on a hilltop waiting for the world to blow up.

When the world was sparsely populated and the signals from the superspectrum were not smothered in so much static from the lower spectrum, men learned to place great faith in these entities and their prophecies. Priests, scholars, and magicians achieved a marvelous understanding of the cosmos and the cosmic forces through astrology, alchemy, and the magical manipulation of matter. But as man followed the angelic dictate, "Multiply and replenish the earth," our planet began to suffer from psychic pollution. The record on that great phonograph in the sky cracked and stuck in a single groove . . . single groove . . . single groove . . . single . . . .

III.

The contactee syndrome is a fundamental reprograming process. No matter what frame of reference is being used, the experience usually begins with either the sudden flash of light or a sound—a humming, buzzing, or beeping. The subject's attention is riveted to a pulsing, flickering light of dazzling intensity. He finds he is unable to move a muscle and is rooted to the spot.

Next the flickering light goes through a series of color changes and a seemingly physical object begins to take form. The light diminishes revealing a boat (if the event occurs on a lake or river), a flying machine of unusual configuration, or an entity of some sort.

What's really happening?

The percipient is first entranced by the flickering light. From the moment he feels paralyzed he loses touch with reality and begins to hallucinate. The light remains a light, but his or her mind constructs something else. This can be compared with normal hypnosis. (I have been an amateur hypnotist for many years.) A hypnotized subject very often thinks he is fully conscious, that the hypnosis isn't working and he is just going along with the hypnotist, but when he tries to move or disobey a command he is surprised to find he can't. The paralysis reported in so many UFO cases is really a form of hypnosis.

In the 1940s medical science discovered the flicker phenomenon; that some human brains are extremely responsive to a flickering light; that such a light can produce an epileptic-type trance accompanied by elaborate hallucinations. In *Battle for the Mind*, William Sargant pointed out:

> It should be more widely known that electrical recordings of the human brain show that it is particularly sensitive to rhythmic stimulation by percussion and bright light among other things and certain rates of rhythm can build up recordable abnormalities of brain function and explosive states of tension sufficient even to produce convulsive fits in predisposed subjects. Some people can be persuaded to dance in time with such rhythms until they collapse in exhaustion. Furthermore, it is easier to disorganize the normal function

of the brain by attacking it simultaneously with several strong rhythms played in different tempos. This leads to protective inhibition, either rapidly in the weak inhibitory temperament or after a prolonged period of excitement in the strong excitatory one.

When the flicker—or pulsing sound—happens to be synchronized with the alpha rhythm of a particular brain, the brain is short-circuited. There are cases in which some people were triggered by the flickering of a motion-picture image and overcome by an urge to strangle the persons sitting next to them. Dr. Grey Walter of the Burden Neurological Institute at Bristol, England, had a patient who passed out while riding a bicycle along an avenue of trees. The trees produced the flicker phenomenon as he sped past them.

"A few subjects yielded epileptic patterns," Dr. Walter noted in his book *The Living Brain.* "Auditory experiences were rare; but there may be organized hallucinations, that is, complete scenes, as in dreams, involving more than one sense. All sorts of emotion are experienced; fatigue, confusion, fear, disgust, anger, pleasure. Sometimes the sense of time is lost or disturbed. One subject said that he had been 'pushed sideways in time'—yesterday was at one side, instead of behind, and tomorrow was off the port bow."

In short, a light flickering at exactly the right frequency can place the witness in a hypnoticlike trance. He views this as paralysis since he loses control of his limbs for the duration of the trance even though a part of his mind remains conscious. He views the hallucinations of the trance as a continuation of the reality he was experiencing a moment before. Like a normal subject of hypnosis, he loses his sense of time. Time can be compressed or expanded, as in a dream. Events which seem to span several hours are actually hallucinated in seconds or minutes, or the reverse can occur.

When he comes out of his trance and looks at his watch he finds that hours have passed even though he thought he only watched the light for a few seconds.

In a religious miracle such as that at Garabandal, Spain, in the 1960s, crowds surrounded the small children as they entered trances and conversed with entities only they could see. The children sometimes remained motionless for hours, but when they came out of their trances they thought only minutes had passed.

The psychedelic lights and flickering strobes so popular with the youth culture in the 1960s actually served to induce trances and produce quasi-religious experiences, particularly when coupled with the mind-numbing beat of hard rock music and hallucinogenic drugs. The euphoria of the big rock festivals was a direct product of this phenomenon. Young people voluntarily, and enthusiastically, submitted themselves to a brainwashing process . . . reprograming themselves, or being reprogramed by an outside force which, as the violence and social upsets of the period demonstrate, was not always benevolent.

When a contactee comes out of his trance he often finds himself suffering from severe headaches and muscular aches and pains for days afterward. Great lethargy is another common symptom, with the percipient indulging in excessive sleep, exhausted. These symptoms are comparable to those of epileptics who have suffered muscular spasms. Excessive thirst, another symptom, is probably caused by something else . . . dehydration from exposure to intense low frequency (VLF) electromagnetic radiation. Such radiation penetrates and dries every tissue.

The mechanism—the light flashes—can be subjective, seen only by the percipient, or objective, seen by others and even photographable. The subjective flashes must be caused by radiation which by-passes the eyes and optical nerves and is received directly by the brain. Objective flashes are masses of energy moving through the visible spectrum. Witnesses whose minds are not tuned to the specific frequency of the flickering of the object are not affected, except by the actinic rays that may be emitted.

When investigating multiple UFO sightings I am not concerned with the chance witnesses of an objective light. Rather I try to seek out those persons who were directly affected by the light. They rarely report their sighting, either because the accompanying hallucination was so bizarre or so terrifying, or because they simply had no memory of the entire event; they suffered lacunal amnesia. When I succeed in finding such people I obtain their entire life history and keep in touch with them for a long period after my interview to observe any changes in personality or outlook that may occur. In some cases, rapid deterioration takes place. The percipient has innumerable secondary hallucinations, just as a person who has taken LSD can go on another "trip" unexpectedly weeks later. He can become mentally unbalanced, abandon his family and his work, develop into a fanatic, and, in several unfortunate cases, end up with a nervous breakdown or commit suicide.

On the other side of the coin, some percipients experience a profound expansion of consciousness, a greatly increased IQ, and a complete change of life-style . . . for the better.

Since this is a historic process, and a continuing one, it is probable that most great leaders had a contact experience at some point in their early life. Canadian psychiatrist Dr. Richard Bucke conducted the first study of this phenomenon in his book *Cosmic Consciousness* published in the year 1900. In religious circles the phenomenon is called "illumination."

In its purest form, illumination is *not* a religious experience. For a few brief moments the percipient understands, truly understands, the workings of the entire universe. He perceives all of history, past, present, and future, totally. He feels he is a part of the superspectrum and is one with the cosmos. Unfortunately, when the brief experience is over he cannot remember most of it because it has been added to his subconscious, and he cannot articulate those parts he can remember. But he has been reprogramed, even prepared for a new role in life. To some the experience is "the call" that propels them into the clergy.

There seems to be a rule that each cosmic force has its imitators. Victims of UFO contact are often suffering from false illumination. Either their minds have misinterpreted the experience, or a lower force has reprogramed them using the same mechanism. In a sense, they have become "possessed." They suffer from hallucinosis—repeated hallucinations. Their lives are manipulated disastrously. Once a person has undergone false illumination he becomes vulnerable to repetitions, just as once a person has been hypnotized he can be easily hypnotized again.

The phenomenon is dependent on belief, and as more and more people believe in flying saucers from other planets, the lower force can manipulate more people through false illumination. I have been watching, with great consternation, the worldwide spread of the UFO belief and its accompanying disease. If it continues unchecked we may face a time when universal acceptance of the fictitious space people will lead us to a modern faith in extraterrestrials that will enable them to interfere overtly in our affairs, just as the ancient gods dwelling on mountaintops directly ruled large segments of the population in the Orient, Greece, Rome, Africa, and South America.

However they arrived at their 1953 decision, the CIA/air force plan to debunk, downgrade, and ridicule flying saucers was, in retrospect, the most responsible course the government could take. But they underestimated the scope of the phenomenon and its ability to manipulate humans and generate propaganda.

IV.

On May 20, 1967, Steve Michalak was out prospecting near Falcon Lake, Manitoba, Canada, when he saw a large circular object land. It seemed to be made of glittering metal "like stainless steel." He approached it and thought he could hear voices mumbling inside. He called out but received no answer. Instead, the object spewed out some kind of gas or flame which caught him full in the chest and sent him reeling backward as it took off. Both his shirt and the skin underneath were burned with an odd checkerboard pattern.

Mr. Michalak became extremely ill, suffering a week of blackouts, nausea, headaches, and a weight loss of twenty-two pounds. It took him many weeks to return to normal. Then, on September 21, 1967, 124 days after the initial incident, the burns on his chest returned and his body began to swell. He was hospitalized and again returned to normal. But the malady returned every 109 to 124 days. In August 1968, after a year of recurring illnesses, he visited the Mayo Clinic in Minnesota at his own expense. Doctors there told him they had treated another UFO victim from California who suffered from the same thing. His problems stemmed from "a foreign substance" in his blood, he was told.

When scientists from the air force-financed UFO study conducted by Colorado University visited Michalak, they asked to see the place where the saucer had landed. He admitted that he had been searching for the spot himself, without success. He was puzzled by his inability to locate it. Despite his inexplicable injury, the scientists viewed this inability as proof that his story was a hoax. In their final report they implied he was not telling the truth.

Actually there are a great many cases in which the witnesses found they could not relocate the site of their experience. Buildings and landmarks clearly seen at the time seem to vanish. Roads and highways disappear. This bewildering phenomenon is well-known in psychic lore also, probably because many psychic experiences are hallucinatory, too. There are innumerable stories about restaurants that seemed to dissolve after the witnesses stopped there. Tales of disappearing houses are common. A weary traveler stops at an old abandoned house for the night, just like in the movies, and later learns the house he stayed in does not exist . . . or had burned down years ago.

True to the reflective factor, as I was writing this I received a letter from F. W. Holiday, the British investigator, in which he tells the following:

> A family in the south of England still spend their weekends driving around woods looking for a mysterious lake they encountered some fifteen years ago. Out in the middle they saw a huge rock with a sword driven into it. Later they went back to do some research but there was no trace of such a lake. No one had heard of it and it isn't on the maps.

One could fill a book with such incidents, and, indeed, some authors have. Long ago I classified such episodes as distortions of reality. Throughout history people have been straying through Alice's looking glass, seeing things that don't exist, visiting places that spill off the maps into some hallucinatory other dimension. Fifteen years ago there was a lake in England with a sword jutting out of a stone, waiting for some king to come along and pull it out, shouting, "Excalibur!" This is no more ridiculous than stumbling upon a secret flying saucer base nestled in the hills of New England and bustling with activity. Contactees have claimed such things.

An engineer named Rex Ball swears he came upon a mysterious underground installation in Georgia in 1940, manned by small Oriental-looking men in coveralls and a few American military officers. When he was caught in the tunnels, one of the officers issued the curt command, "Make him look like a nut!" He woke up in a field, uncertain whether his experience had been real or a dream.

That seems to be the battle cry of the phenomenon. "Make him look like a nut!"

13:

Phantom Photographers

I.

"How much did Keel pay you to say these things?" a middle-aged man with a cultured voice demanded over and over again as he systematically called several of the witnesses named in my syndicated newspaper columns. All those long-distance phone calls must have cost him a lot of money and all he succeeded in doing was raising the ire of people who had already been plagued by an endless stream of unwelcome visitors, crank phone calls, and crazy letters. Some of them forwarded their mail to me, not knowing if they should answer, or how.

Our UFO enthusiasts are compulsive letter writers. A major portion of the mail received by witnesses are letters scribbled on sheets of cheap ruled paper in pencil demanding, "Send me everything you know." Others are neatly typed and cover forty or fifty pages. Threatening letters are not uncommon, some are laborious paste-ups using words clipped from magazines and newspapers . . . "Do not talk about flying saucers." Others are painfully written in block letters in red ink. Almost unreadable mimeographed forms are sent out by many of the teen-aged UFO investigators who spring up after each flap, asking such vital scientific questions as: "Which planet did they come from?"

Unfortunately, no qualifications are necessary to join the various nationwide UFO correspondence clubs. Anyone who could scrape up the five or ten dollars could receive an impressive-looking membership card which gave them carte blanche to harass local police and witnesses. Members of the "little old ladies in tennis shoes" brigade found instant identity in joining such clubs. Then they trooped about their state, lecturing on the coming of the Brothers, appearing on local radio and television as the local "experts," and, more often than not, bringing more ridicule to an already ridiculous situation.

Although they are largely a harmless, humorless lot, a few of the ego-tripping characters in ufology are not above creating a few hoaxes of their own, placing prank calls, and, of course, circulating the idiotic rumors. Ivan Sanderson referred to them as "neurots," short for neurotics. Dr. Edward Condon of Colorado University labeled them "obstructionist." On several occasions I did find that some of these card-carrying ufologists had warned witnesses to report only to them. Members of competing correspondence clubs often engaged in open battles, trying to reach witnesses first and accusing each other of all kinds of misdeeds. Donald E. Keyhoe, head of the Washington-based NICAP, had spent years building and publicizing his case against the air force. The only tangible result of his campaign was the quality of the people attracted to ufology, and to his ideas. Paranoid-schizophrenics and obsessive-compulsive personalities dominated the field.

Many of these groups collapsed inwardly in a short time because of the conflicting egos and the excessive paranoia (members often regarded their fellow members as "agents of the air force"). Even NICAP, which had been founded in 1956 by a physicist who was hot on the trail of the secret of flying saucer propulsion systems, came apart at the seams in the late 1960s. The few qualified members of its headquarters staff departed in an atmosphere of rancor, taking choice files and mailing lists with them, and Stuart Nixon, the office boy during the Keyhoe regime, became director of the organization.

The air force and CIA did not have to try to disrupt the ufological movement. It is by its very nature a self-disrupting network of disoriented people.

In the spring of 1967, following the publicity that attended Mothman and the UFOs, mobs of strangers descended on Point Pleasant. Cars filled with students from neighboring colleges would arrive unannounced at the homes of witnesses named in newspaper accounts, often late at night, and expect to be welcomed. Mary Hyre and all the others were subjected to silly interviews by people who obviously didn't have any notion of how to go about investigating anything. Some of these investigators were tactless and impolite, as only teen-agers can be, to the point of being offensive. One by one the witnesses fell silent, refusing to talk to any more strangers, so newcomers saw a new mystery —someone had obviously ordered everyone in the Ohio valley to shut up.

While reporters from all the neighboring cities were flocking to Point Pleasant and writing extensively about the UFO and monster sightings, the little local daily, the *Point Pleasant Register*, ignored the whole situation. When a girl on the *Register* staff was pursued by a UFO one night that spring, Mary Hyre printed the story in the *Messenger*. The young editor of the *Register* remained steadfastly anti-UFO throughout the fracas.

It was then my policy to publish only reports in which the witnesses allowed their names to be used. I avoided "blind" items. But as time went on and I saw what was happening to some of these people, I realized they had to be protected, not from Men in Black or sinister government agencies but from the UFO believers themselves. This unfortunate problem persists, and this is why I have used blind items here, or, in some cases, altered the names of the witnesses or their location. This is a common policy in medical books and scientific literature, but it is sad that it becomes necessary in studies of this kind.

II.

One Sunday afternoon in the spring of 1967, I was walking along Forty-second Street and Third Avenue with a lady friend. There were very few people on the streets at the time. Suddenly a tall, thin man came around a corner. His face was gaunt and pointed, and he was carrying a camera. He raised the camera and deliberately took our picture, then he turned and *ran* up the street. My friend knew nothing about Men in Black, and it is not unusual to see tourists snapping pictures in New York City. I deliberately refrained from making any comment.

"That was strange," she remarked. "And he was such an evil-looking man. Why did he take our picture?"

I could only shrug. The man, incidently, was not dressed in black. He was wearing a sports jacket and slacks but his clothes seemed to hang very poorly on his thin frame.

A few days later, Dan Drasin phoned me. He was preparing to go back to West Virginia with a camera crew.

"You know, this probably doesn't mean anything," he said slowly, "but the other day I was walking through midtown Manhattan and an Indian took my picture. He was even wearing a black suit."

Dan knew of my concern with the MIB, but he was not well-known to the UFO enthusiasts (I had tried to tell myself that the photographer on Third Avenue was a ufo-nut of some kind).

"Probably just a tourist," I offered.

"Probably."

In West Virginia, Mrs. Hyre was continuing to have problems. A luminous object appeared over her house and projected a powerful beam of light into her backyard. She was not home at the time but her husband and several neighbors saw it. Then one evening her confused "little man" reappeared on the streets of Point Pleasant. She was certain it was the same man who had visited her office in January. This time he was wearing a khaki-colored uniform but had on the same thick-soled shoes. When he saw Mary approaching him he looked alarmed, took off on a dead run, and leaped into a black car driven by a very large man.

"By the time I got out in the line of traffic," Mary said, "he was gone across the bridge into Ohio. I didn't get the license number but the color looked orange."

Three days later, on May 8, Mrs. Hyre arrived home from a civic meeting around 11:30 P.M. Just as she was opening her front door a large black car squealed to a stop directly outside her house. She stood on her porch and watched as a man got out of the vehicle, raised a camera to his face, and snapped her picture.

"His flash gun was very bright," she reported. "It blinded me momentarily. While I was standing there rubbing my eyes he got back into his car and it drove off. I couldn't see if there was anyone else in the car." She paused. "Now why do you suppose anyone would want to take my picture like that?"

Why indeed. Our Men in Black were now engaged in a new game. Or perhaps the game had been going for years but no one had ever noticed it before. As if I didn't have enough trouble already, now I was chasing phantom photographers all over the landscape.

On a rainy night in April a man from Ohio had been driving along Route 2 near the Chief Cornstalk Hunting Grounds when a large black form rose from the woods and flew over his car. "It was at least ten feet wide," he claimed. "I stepped on the gas and it kept right up with me. We were doing over seventy. It scared the hell out of me. Then I saw it move ahead of me and turn toward the river."

Months later, late in October, he returned home from work and found a prowler in his apartment.

"When I opened the door I saw this man standing in my living room," he reported. "I think he dressed all in black. I couldn't see his face, but he was about five feet nine. I started to fumble for the light switch when he took my picture. There was a big flash of light, so bright I couldn't see a thing. While I was rubbing my eyes the burglar darted past me and went out the open door. I guess I arrived just in time because nothing was missing."

Burglars with flash guns!

Sixty miles north of Point Pleasant, a young family in Belpre, Ohio, was having the full range of UFO-associated problems. The man in the family, I'll call him Ben, had seen a UFO hovering near a chemical plant on the river. He'd heard you could signal to the objects so he flashed his car's spotlight at it. The spotlight went out instantly and later he found that all the electrical systems in his car had burned out.

His sighting marked the beginning of all kinds of weird happenings. First, his telephone went crazy. Like so many others, he had not reported his sighting to anyone yet he began to receive the beeping calls, and calls from "metallic voices," urging him to attend undefined meetings (he never went). A poltergeist moved into Ben's house. Drawers opened by themselves. Objects disappeared. A heavy cabinet pushed against a window was moved by some force. (Later I tried to move this cabinet by myself and found it was too heavy.) Ben's wife began to notice unusual people in the neighborhood. Ben received a mild scare that August as he was walking down the Main Street in Parkersburg and saw two black-garbed Oriental-looking men who grinned at him broadly as if they knew him. They appeared to be confused or drunken, he noted, and seemed to have difficulty walking. Ben knew nothing of the MIB lore, but the men so alarmed him that he crossed to the other side of the street.

He had more UFO sightings. And more freak phone calls. Finally he mentioned his troubles to Parke McDaniel . . . they worked together . . . and Mrs. Hyre and I drove to Belpre. Two weeks before our visit, according to Ben's wife, a black car had stopped in front of their house and a man in a black suit had apparently taken photos with a large camera. Two of their neighbors had also witnessed this and corroborated their story. The photographer did not pay any attention to any of the other houses on the street.

On Long Island, less than thirty miles from New York City, UFOs, Men in Black, and phantom photographers were all very busy that summer. Eventually I gathered reports of the photographers from as far away as Seattle. An aerospace engineer in the Northwest reported: "For some three days photographs were taken of our house. We thought they might be realtors or someone doing a film on the area. Then began the telephone interference, mail stoppage and misdirection, etc."

The engineer, a well-educated man with a responsible position in a major aircraft company, involved himself in UFO research as a hobby. At first he assumed the photographers, telephone harassers, and all were agents of the government. Then something uncanny attacked his new home.

"Twice a very powerful specterlike influence visited the house which projected FEAR of an incredible nature," he wrote. "I am certain that anyone who did not understand these things would have been driven in very short order to the state mental hospital. Another attack was interference with the time constance of a heart beat. I would be awakened with a pulse of over two hundred! However, I always awakened because I sleep with plastic ear stoppers and in each of about thirty to thirty-five instances the noise awakened me."

I had heard of this heart-beat phenomenon in Massachussetts and several other places, and put it down as more psychological than physiological. When Mary Hyre complained of hearing a loud, pulsing heart-beat sound late at night I knew she had suffered one severe heart attack and worried that she was really hearing her own heart beat. Then Linda Scarberry and the McDaniels complained of hearing the same sound.

Roger Scarberry was haunted by something else . . . by dreams of a great eye floating in the sky over Mary's house. Point Pleasant was filled with omens and portents. A man and a woman carrying a camera visited Steve and Mary Mallette, wanting to take pictures of them. Mrs. Mallette took down the license number on their Volkswagen and when Mary had the police check it out it proved to be nonexistent. This business with license numbers was repeated over and over, and in many places. Witnesses would carefully note the plates on the black Cadillacs and mysterious panel trucks, but when the police ran a routine check the computers came up with a blank.

When you consider the many millions of licenses issued in the United States, the odds against your being able to manufacture an unlisted number are astronomical. Yet our MIB always manage to come up with unused numbers. (There were more incidents of this type during the October 1973 wave.)

Phantom photographer reports have been rare in England, but in 1973 two leading British ufologists, Brinsley Le Poer Trench and J. B. Delair, came across an incident involving the Bogart family who live in a forest near Maresfield, Sussex. The Bogarts' isolated cottage has been plagued with apparitions, strange sounds, and poltergeist activity. And a large number of low-flying luminous objects have been seen repeatedly in the vicinity.

"On more than one occasion Mrs. Bogart alleges that she has been perturbed to find a yellow Volkswagen car (having smoked-glass windows) following her discreetly at a distance," Delair reports.* "Once this involved the vehicle slowly following her down a woodland cart-track leading to Piltdown Lake, of it then stopping some distance from her, of two medium-sized individuals emerging and hurriedly taking photographs of her, and of the individuals quickly reentering the car and driving off in the opposite direction. On another occasion, in Maresfield, the same vehicle (or one exactly similar) seemed to be 'kerb-crawling' several yards behind her. Mrs. Bogart has no idea to whom the Volkswagen belongs, or why it should apparently follow her about in such furtive fashion, nor why she should be so mysteriously photographed."

III.

If you review the thousands of UFO contact reports you will find that many of them begin with the appearance of an entity holding some kind of "flashlight" which is shone directly at the witness. In cases in which the percipient was taken aboard a saucer, a light flashes and he is told his picture has just been taken. In other instances, some of which have already been described, the entity approaches the witness and suddenly flashes a light at him which causes paralysis.

Woodrow Derenberger was among the very few contact claimants who did not describe such flashes.

In trying to nail down the exact chronological order of events in the contactee experience, I found that the witnesses observed the flash *first* and then they saw the entity

* *Awareness*, Autumn 1973 (J. B. Delair, ed. 19 Cumnor Road, Wootton, Boar's Hill, Oxford, Berkshire; England).

approaching with some kind of flashlight. A second flash paralyzed them or rendered them unconscious.

The phenomenon takes yet another form. The witness is stepping out his door, or getting out of his automobile, when there is a sudden burst of light "like a flash gun going off." No photographer or camera is visible. There is no sudden paralysis or ill effects. The witness just scratches his head in bewilderment and goes about his business. However, those who see these flashes have usually had psychic experiences previously. They have seen a UFO, a monster, or a ghost, or they are gifted with ESP or precognition.

In 1967, I was living in one of those glass buildings in Manhattan, part of a huge apartment complex. I was on a high floor facing an identical building across a small park, but I also had a splendid view of lower Manhattan. In the evenings while hammering away at my typewriter in front of a wall-to-wall window, I began seeing sudden flashes of blue light in the space between the two buildings. At first I assumed there was a photographer in the other building. Then I saw the same kind of flashes high in the air, further down the avenue. I watched them night after night. When friends were in my apartment the flashes seemed to stop. I thought of them as "psychic flashes" because very often my phone would ring immediately after I saw one.

Later I moved to another apartment on the other side of town, with no real view of the sky, although my study faced a small courtyard favored by fighting cats and a few scrawny trees hopelessly battling for survival. There were no more psychic flashes until the summer of 1971 . . . just prior to a major change in my life. Suddenly there were brilliant flashes outside my window, although there were no photographers, or people of any kind, in the courtyard or across the way. A couple of times I went down into the courtyard to see if I could find out what was causing the flashes but there was no possible explanation. A month later I was called to

Washington, D.C., to serve as a consultant to the Department of Health, Education, and Welfare. I worked in the Capital for a year, heading a special project under Elliot Richardson, then-secretary of HEW.

I haven't seen any of those flashes since.

Were they a part of some subtle programing process? My life has gone through many abrupt changes, and each major change has been preceded by some form of inexplicable phenomena. In observing other witnesses, this also seems to be true in their lives. Are these things clues to a psychic force which controls us all?

14:
Sideways in Time

I.

You are driving along a deserted highway late at night when suddenly you see a flash of light in the sky ahead. The light draws nearer and a peculiar feeling overtakes you: a kind of tingling sensation. Your car radio, which is turned off, begins to emit a loud beeping like Morse code. Your headlights dim and then your engine sputters and stalls. You coast to the side of the road, overcome by a great wave of sheer terror.

Suddenly it is morning. You wake up in your own bed with absolutely no memory of having driven home, undressing, and retiring. When you try to recall the night before, it all seems hazy and unreal. Maybe it was all a dream, you tell yourself. But you feel exhausted, as if you had been on a drunken binge and your eyes are very sore. Within a few days you have forgotten the whole incident, if it was a real incident, but occasionally you wake up at night sweating profusely from a recurrent nightmare. You dream that you are in some kind of hospital operating room with strange figures gathered around your outstretched body.

Thousands of people have shared this kind of experience in recent years. It may have happened to your next-door neighbor even though he or she has never mentioned it to you . . . or to anyone else. Such people are "silent contactees." Others traveling that same highway may have seen that same light and even reported it to the local police or newspapers. But the silent contactee remains uncertain of the reality of it all and keeps quiet.

For every publicly known contactee like Woodrow Derenberger there are thousands of silent ones. Some later manage to recall fragments of what happened and then their mind plays tricks and colors what they can remember with false details . . . confabulations. The terror they felt becomes linked with awesome monsters and apparitions. The operating room becomes a chamber on a spacecraft.

Like all the other things discussed here, this is not a new phenomenon. Black magicians, witch doctors, and shamans of other ages evolved explanations as fanciful as those of modern UFO buffs. They thought spirits kidnapped humans and somehow dismantled their bodies and reconstructed them, or even created an exact duplicate in some fashion. The changeling concept in religious and occult lore is a variation of this. Small children are supposedly whisked away and substituted with bodies that look just like them but are really programed in an entirely different way.

A person who consorted with the devil supposedly had a mark somewhere on his flesh as a souvenir of the experience. A modern UFO contactee develops these "devil's marks," sometimes in the form of a wart or boil, sometimes a rash or blotch that looks like a birthmark. In occult lore, pains in the stomach or solar plexus occur during the experience, just as UFO contactee Mrs. Barney Hill thought the spacemen were probing her stomach with a long needle. Blood is drawn from the chin, neck, or the tips of the fingers and the affected areas remain sore for several days afterward. A number of contactees have had a reddish mark on the side of their neck, just below the ear, and recalled that an entity had touched them there causing them to pass out. A few contactees have claimed that the entities simply scraped their arms with some kind of instrument and apparently removed a few cells "for study." Actually each cell of your body contains the elaborate memory system called the genetic code. If someone wanted to construct a duplicate of you, and had the necessary technology, they would need only a cell or two from your body. Or a sample of your blood might do it.

It is, of course, really impossible to tell what is actually going on from these meager clues. The memory of the contactees is unreliable; the phenomenon deliberately sets up false trails and creates manifestations designed to support the beliefs of false frames of reference. By drawing blood conspicuously from a few people who let their stories be known, they establish an explanation for the thousands of dead animals who have their blood drained during flap periods. We blame the devil, vampires, or space people.

Nothing in the paranormal world is as it seems.

Let us examine three different cases of UFO contact, each belonging to a different category, but all probably caused by the same cosmic mechanism.

The first is the story of Eugenio Siragusa, the Italian contactee who is the center of a growing cult.[1] I have chosen him rather whimsically because we share the same birth date. He was born on March 25, 1919. I was born on March 25, 1930. Here's a summary of his story in his own words.

> I was 33 years old . . . and for the requirements of my job, I was up very early that morning. Having arrived at the "Martyrs Square," I was waiting for the bus as usual when suddenly, I spotted in the sky, a kind of luminous object of

[1] C.E.F.C.; 12, rue des Bossons; 1213 ONEX; Geneva, Switzerland.

a white mercurial color, which zigzagged very rapidly. This luminosity continued to intensify; it approached and I saw an object similar to a spinning top which stopped above me. I admit that I was petrified. What could this object be? A wave of thoughts flowed into my mind when suddenly, a brilliant ray left the object and struck me, it pierced me completely, while an indescribable serenity flowed into me. Upon that all my fear left me and a moment later, the brilliant ray became thinner and disappeared, as if absorbed by the machine, just like the spot on a television set when it is turned off. As the ray disappeared, this object, which I later understood to be one of these "flying saucers," began to move and left an arc in the sky before disappearing.

When I pulled myself together, I rapidly discovered more and more that something extraordinary had happened to me: a sort of redimension of my personality, my voice even changed to a gentle tone.

Ever since then an inner voice has begun to instruct me on geology and cosmology; it opened my mind to the mysteries of Creation and of my former lives. This redimension of my existence was possible thanks to continued ESP contacts which were established between certain Extraterrestrians and myself. This extra sensory perception was continually developing within me; it lasted 11 long years before I could actually, physically meet my extraterrestrial instructors. One day, at last I had my first meeting with them. Here is briefly how these events unfolded:

One night, in 1962, I suddenly felt the need to go on the Etna (Sicilian volcano which overlooks Catania). I got into my car and drove off. On my way I had the distinct sensation that instead of it being me, it was the car which was guided by a superior force. As I was winding up the mountain, I approached Mount Manfre at an altitude of 1370 meters. After having stopped my car on the side of the road, I continued by foot along a path which led up to an extinct crater. I had gone up half way on this steep path when I suddenly saw on top of the hill, in the darkness, two silhouettes standing out in the moonlight with shining silver space suits. They were tall, well built, with blond hair which fell over their shoulders. They wore brilliant armlets around their wrists and ankles which had the color of gold; they also wore a luminous belt around their waist, and a strange metallic plate on their chests. When I saw them, my blood froze and I felt a cold sweat flow out of me. I had hoped for this moment for eleven years, but as the spot was isolated, the nocturnal obscurity and sudden meeting were not situations which would give me courage. One of the Extraterrestrians then directed a green light towards me, which was projected by an object he had in his hand. Instantly a strange sensation calmed me and gave me an indescribable serenity; my heart which in the beginning seemed to exploded in my chest, set itself to throb regularly. Looking at their two faces enlightened by the moon, I could admire their soft features and their austere and serene look. Suddenly, one of them spoke to me in Italian: "We have been waiting for you," he told me. "Record in your memory what we are going to tell you"; they gave me a message to send to the governors and the responsible of the earth. In this message there was the "reprimanding" warning to all those responsible, to stop the atomic explosions as well as to grant humanity the well-being of true progress, but with Justice, Freedom, Love and Fraternity. Following this meeting, we had several conversations during other meetings; I was told that they are part of an Inter-Galactic Confederation, to which adhere the inhabitants of many planets. They are the tutors of human kind, including our planet. We should consider them as thus like big brothers who are concerned about the bad turning we have taken, making us risk to bring the use of the atomic bomb. They come all this way to us to warn us in time of the danger we are heading into, because the Cosmic Counsel condemns the people of Earth for their inhuman behavior: the people to which the truth is hidden, are governed by lies; shameful crimes are considered acts of heroism; violence becomes a necessity; racial hatred appears as a normal thing to our civilization; religion has been deformed and brought to fanaticism. . . .

Then one day, on a stern tone and with deep sadness in their voices, they told me: "A highly evolved humanity sends to you astronauts and missionaries from a distance of several light years to enlighten you on the nature of your existence, but instead of being thankful for their efforts, you ignore them and mock all the teachings they bring to you; know that an evolution which has failed is a planetarian catastrophe, and this will be the inevitable consequences of your acts." They then added: "In a past life, everyone of you has worked towards the establishment of the civilization which exists today; you have all collaborated in participating in the development of humanity. Understand that you are preparing yourselves today! As tutors of your kind, we can do nothing else but condemn your acts; know this: you are rigorously supervised by a superior race who will never permit you to come to the disaster of a 'nuclear war.' "

Mr. Siragusa was reprogramed in the classic manner of all fanatics, and he has been used to disseminate propaganda couched in terms understandable and acceptable to us. The messages include references to reincarnation, politics, and religion, but not within the loftier intellectual framework of some alien "superior culture." Instead of telling us things we do not know, they tell us the things we want to hear and believe. Our own fear of nuclear annihilation was epidemic in the 1950s and early 1960s. So many of the UFO messages of that period were stern warnings about our misuse of atomic energy. As our own paranoia subsided, so did these threats from outer space.

II.

The most widely publicized UFO contact of October 1973 was also the least important. Two fishermen in Pascagoula, Mississippi, suffered a rather routine hallucination which hurled them onto national television and attracted the attention of UFO-philes, crackpots, and astronomers. The case has been so widely discussed that I will just summarize it very briefly here.

"It is my opinion that he told the truth when he stated that he believes he saw a spaceship, that he was taken into the spaceship, and that he saw three creatures," Scott Glasgow, a New Orleans polygraph (lie detector) specialist declared after examining Charles Hickson in October 1973. Dr. J. Allen Hynek, an astronomer, also interviewed Hickson and his friend Calvin Parker.

"There is no question in my mind that these men have had a terrifying experience," Hynek stated. "Under no circumstances should they be ridiculed. Let's protect these men."

Hickson, forty-two, and Parker, eighteen, would need all the protection they could get.

The two men had been fishing from a pier on the Pascagoula River when at 8 P.M. on October 11, 1973, they heard a loud pulsing, humming sound. Then they saw a brilliant flickering blue light moving over the water toward them.

Both men became paralyzed. "I felt immobilized," Hickson said later. "I couldn't move. But I know I was scared to death."

As the light drew closer it took on an egg-shaped appearance. Young Parker lost consciousness, fainting dead away, so the two-witness sighting now became a one-witness event. Hickson said two five-foot-tall beings came out of the object. They were grayish with wrinkled skin, no necks, pointed ears, and crablike claws. They picked up the two men ("It was like just floating in the air") and carried them into the object where "a big eye," somewhere between the size of a large softball and a basketball, moved over their bodies, apparently studying them. Then they were deposited back on the river pier to the exact spot where they had been picked up.

When the light withdrew, the two men came to their senses and ran in terror to the local sheriff's office. Following their experience, Hickson and Parker suffered blinding headaches. "At first, those dreams I had was awful," Charlie Hickson told NBC News reporter Ralph Blum, "and the headaches was so bad—like a pressure on my skull."

The day after the incident a small wound opened up on Hickson's arm and bled profusely for a few hours. Then it closed just as mysteriously as it had come.

The pier from which the men were fishing was under constant surveillance by a TV system at a naval installation across the river. The men monitoring the system saw nothing unusual that night. They were also in full view of a nearby drawbridge, and the tollbooths for a neighboring highway. The men manning those positions did not see anything unusual on the river. They saw no lights; additional proof that the episode was hallucinatory.

Ralph Blum learned another interesting fact when he asked Hickson why he was not carrying a watch. "Never could. People said I had electricity," Hickson explained. "To give you an example, before I went into the service, I tried two or three wrist watches. But they wouldn't keep time on me. They'd either lose time, or gain time. Or they'd just stop. . . . I never did find one that would keep correct time. I even tried Elgins, these railroad pocket watches? And they don't keep correct time. So I don't tote a watch."

Obviously Mr. Hickson's physical makeup includes some unknown but not unheard of force which interferes with watches. He could be surrounded by that special energy field or aura which attracts UFO-type phenomena. Calvin Parker was just unfortunate enough to be present when the phenomenon zeroed in on Hickson. Since the light was not operating on his alpha wave frequency, Parker wasn't entranced . . . he was knocked unconscious. Hickson entered a hypnoticlike trance and hallucinated.

Besides all the press attention, crank phone calls, and

attending nonsense, Calvin Parker suffered a nervous breakdown. Yet, despite the uproar in Pascagoula, the men were
never properly investigated by qualified persons . . . aside
from the air force. A hydraulic engineer from Berkeley
visited them, hypnotized them, and when they began to
relive their terrible fear he cut the session short. Afterward
he soberly informed reporters that he was certain the men
had been examined by "robots from outer space."

The air force investigation was another story. Deputy
Tom Huntley accompanied the two men to the Keesler Air
Force Base. "When we got there it was something amazing," Huntley told Ralph Blum afterward. "We were in an
unmarked car but the guards were expecting us and waved
us through the moment I said who we was. I looked back
through my rear-view mirror, and damn if two cars full of
air police hadn't fallen in behind us. They had more air
police stationed at each crossing all along the road. We
pulled up in this concrete area behind a building. The police
had halted all traffic. Doctors were waiting, and man, *they*
looked like space creatures—all wrapped in white and
masked and gloved. They went over Charlie and Calvin
from head to toe. They ran a radioactive check. They
swabbed between the boys' fingers, along the tops of their
shoes, even under the heels. Then they put each swab into
a little bottle and labeled each bottle."

It was clear the air force doctors knew what they were
doing and had probably done it many times before. After the
examination was completed, Huntley, Hickson, and Parker
were escorted to another building.

"It was something," Huntley said. "Armed air police at
each door and all along the route! Four of 'em in the conference room! And the brass—colonels, majors—the whole
base command must have been there. And a heap of doctors."

The men were closely interrogated for several minutes.
Some of the questions asked were identical to the questions

I ask in my own interviews. Questions about diet (some contactees seem to favor a high starch diet), marks or punctures on their bodies, family history, etc.

The intriguing part of this is the extensive security measures taken. It sounds as if the whole base had been put on alert for the occasion, and the two contactees were so closely guarded during their visit that it seems as if the air force expected them to blow up the base. To me, this Keesler Air Force Base investigation was far more interesting than the UFO contact itself.

Perhaps someone in the air force had read my 1967–68 articles in *Flying Saucer Review* advising investigators to "find out what they had for breakfast."

III.

Woodrow Derenberger regarded the ufonauts as "time travelers." He noted some interesting distortions of time during his jaunts to the far-off galaxy of Ganymede (actually Ganymede is the name of one of Jupiter's moons). When he went off on a trip with Indrid Cold, a trip that seemed to take hours or days, he always found on his return that only a few hours of earth time had passed. He rejected the notion that he may have hallucinated his interstellar voyages, so time-traveling was the only answer acceptable to him.

In many of the cases outlined here I have pointed out the entities' obsession with time. Their behavior as described by various witnesses further suggests their problems in adjusting to our time frame. For example, their rapid-fire unintelligible "language" noted by witnesses all over the world as sounding like "a speeded up phonograph record" could be caused by their failure to adjust to our time cycle when they enter our space-time continuum. They are talking at a faster rate because their time is different from ours. When they manage to adjust, they have to forcibly slow themselves down, articulating their words slowly, in a singsong manner. For high-speed radio transmissions we record signals at a normal speed, then broadcast the tape at very high speed. The receiver records it at the same high speed and then slows the tape down again to play it back. Our entities are like those radio receivers, playing back the message at slow speeds until they hit upon a speed we can interpret.

The entities also foul up in other ways. They arrive in clothes that are out of style, or not yet in style. Their vehicles are out of date. If they use slang, they might come up with archaic terms like "twenty-three Skidoo" or "hubba hubba." The poor bastards not only fail to understand who or what they are, but also where they are or what time period they're in. Some of these mistakes seem intentional and have some allegorical purpose. But others seem to be just . . . mistakes.

This brings us to one of the most puzzling contact stories in my files.

At 1:15 A.M. on the morning of Sunday, December 10, 1967, a young college student from Adelphi, Maryland, was driving home alone outside of Washington, D.C. As he was crossing the then-partially completed cutoff on Interstate 70, leading from Route 40 to Route 29, he saw a large object on the road directly ahead. At first he thought it was a tractor-trailer jackknifed across the road. Then he realized it was a bone-white reflective object shaped like an egg and standing on four legs. As he pulled to a stop a few feet from the object he could make out two figures standing next to the thing. Their appearance terrified him.

One of the men walked to his car with a broad grin on his face. He was about five feet ten, wore light blue coveralls, thick-soled boots or shoes, and he had a ruddy or suntanned complexion with large eyes "like thyroid eyes." The grin remained fixed on his face throughout the episode.

"Do not be afraid of me," he said several times in an audible voice. His name, he said, was Vadig. He spoke with Tom, the witness, for several minutes, asking ordinary questions about where he was from, where he was going, what he did, etc.

Finally he said pointedly, "I'll see you in time," and walked back to the object. A small door opened and a metal ladder folded down. A hand reached out and helped Vadig aboard, then the thing rose silently into the air and disappeared. Tom told his three roommates about the encounter, but they didn't take him seriously so he didn't mention it to anyone else.

Tom was working his way through school by serving as a waiter part-time in a chain of restaurants in the D.C. area. He had not mentioned this to Vadig. But one Sunday night in early February 1968, Vadig entered the restaurant where he was working and sat at one of his tables. Vadig was now wearing a conventional suit with a black outer coat.

"Do you remember me?" Vadig asked.

"I sure do." Tom answered, very surprised. They exchanged a few words and Tom brought him a cup of coffee.

"My presence here would be detrimental to the family trade," Vadig said at one point with a chuckle.

He asked Tom if he would be willing to meet with him the following Sunday. Tom agreed and Vadig left the restaurant.

"I'll see you in time," he promised.

After work the next Sunday, a waitress drove Tom home and dropped him off. As she pulled away, a big black car with its lights out glided from the shadows and halted at the curb. Mr. Vadig called out to Tom. Another man was in the car. Tom later recalled only that he wore a gray coat, had black hair, and never spoke. Tom got into the car.

"It was a very old Buick," he reported. "But it was very well kept. It looked brand-new. It even *smelled* brand-new."

They drove for about thirty minutes to a remote spot on a back road in Maryland. When Tom got out of the car he was astonished to see the egg-shaped object waiting for them. He was put into a circular room containing nothing but a couple of bucket seats and a gray TV screen. Vadig and his companion disappeared into another part of the ship.

After a few minutes the TV screen came alive, the object shuddered, and Tom watched the image of the earth receding to a tiny speck on the screen. Three or four hours passed. He was still dressed in his waiter's uniform and did not have a watch. But it seemed like hours before another planet appeared on the screen, grew larger, and then the craft landed with a thump.

The young waiter found himself in a place not too unlike the earth. He and Vadig got into a wheelless vehicle that traveled along a kind of trough.

"This is Lanulos," Vadig announced with pride in his voice.

He repeated the name several times so it would stick in Tom's memory.

Their vehicle traveled through a large city with low, flat buildings and signs written in some kind of Oriental-looking characters. The people, male and female, were all nude.

"There were some real lookers there, too," Tom commented.

After the tour, they returned to the egg-shaped craft and took off again. Tom sat alone in the same circular room watching the television screen for hours. Finally they arrived back on earth at the same place from which they had left. Tom, Vadig, and the silent man returned to the old Buick and drove for about thirty minutes until they reached his apartment house.

"I'll see you in time," Vadig declared, then the car drove off.

Tom ran into his apartment, determined to wake up his roommates and tell them of his adventure. He found they were sitting up, waiting for him. But what amazed him most was the clock on the wall. The waitress had dropped him off around midnight. Now it was only 1:30 A.M. The whole trip, including the thirty-minute rides to and from the UFO, had taken less than two hours!

His excitement and bewilderment were real and his roommates took him seriously this time.

A month later, Woodrow Derenberger visited Washington and appeared on a number of talk shows. Tom was sleeping when one of his roommates burst into his bedroom exclaiming, "Tom, there's a guy on the radio talking about *Lanulos!*"

All four were flabbergasted to hear Woody describe experiences very similar to Tom's. They called the radio station and spoke to him after the program.

By sheer coincidence, I was in Washington at the time and agreed to go with Woody when he interviewed the young man. But I sternly warned Derenberger and his wife not to ask any leading questions. Naturally, I suspected the whole thing was some kind of put-on. Either Tom and Woody were in cahoots, or Tom, who was a psychology major, was working on a paper about the gullible UFO buffs, I thought.

It quickly became apparent that Tom and his roommates were quite sincere. They were too involved in their studies to read UFO literature and, in any case, some of the details in Tom's story could not be found in any of the superficial UFO lore. I finally had to conclude Tom was on the level. He was not looking for publicity and I decided I would not write up his story.

However, Woody told others about him (I think even Woody was surprised by such direct confirmation of his own experiences) and some Washington UFO enthusiasts convinced Tom he should reveal his adventure to the world. Two years later he lectured before a UFO club and appeared on Long John's radio program in New York. Since he had chosen to come out publicly, I finally devoted a paragraph to him in one of my books. After the book was published, Tom wrote me an angry letter.

Ever since those appearances . . . I have been pestered and plagued by a horde of kooks. They call, write, stop to visit, etc. They drove me crazy. Some of my very close friends began to advise me of the dangers to my reputation that these types of individuals were posing. I decided to tell them all once and for all that I desired no more public contact. . . . Although the experiences I had were completely true, I sometimes wish I had never revealed them to anyone. The only reason I made them known was because I thought I could help to verify and help uncover some of the mystery that shrouds the UFO phenomenon. . . . I should have kept my mouth shut like I had planned to when you first interviewed me.

Tom married a beautiful girl and she didn't learn of his weird meetings with Vadig until months after the ceremony. Like so many others before him, myself included, he learned that the only thing more bizarre than the phenomenon itself is the unruly mob of true believers, cranks, and irresponsible self-styled investigators who pursue the subject; moths attracted to the flame. They tormented Charles Hickson and Calvin Parker in 1973, just as they had arrived by the carload in Point Pleasant in 1967.

15:
Misery
on the Mount

I.

Daniel Drasin was about eighteen when he filmed a riot in New York's Washington Square, titled it *Sunday*, and won a number of motion-picture awards. Now still in his mid-twenties, handsome, quiet-spoken, intelligent, and perceptive, he was well into a promising career in the film industry. The West Virginia UFO documentary was an important break for him and he plunged into the project with a mixture of awe and enthusiasm. As I was on my way to Washington, D. C., from Point Pleasant, he was headed in the other direction with a skeleton crew hoping to get some authentic movies of those funny lights in the sky.

When I reached Washington I parked my car on Connecticut Avenue, one of the main thoroughfares, in broad daylight for a few minutes. Some of my clothes and camera cases were in the back seat so I carefully locked the doors. While I was gone someone smashed in the vent on the side window and robbed my car. They left behind my clothes and some of my cameras. They took my briefcase, tape recorder and all my notebooks, exposed films, taped interviews with witnesses, cheap telescope and other items with little or no value to anyone except me. Strangely, they had removed my irreplaceable address book from one of the cases and left it on the seat. I called the police. When they finally arrived their attitude was not very sympathetic. Anyone who would leave anything plainly visible in a locked car at 2 P.M. on a main street in Washington was plainly a fool, or so they suggested.

My problems were minor compared to Dan's, however. He was seeing plenty of aerial lights but his battery powered cameras malfunctioned when he tried to photograph them. Finally, he thought he had managed to get some footage. Then the precious films were later accidently ruined in a processing lab back in New York. Members of his crew began to have troubles with their telephones, and a female production assistant was awakened one night in her apartment in Brooklyn by a loud beeping noise. She got up, looked out the window, and saw a large luminous sphere hovering directly outside her building.

During his second visit to Point Pleasant Dan uncovered some Mothman witnesses I had missed. And he also came across some more baffling Men-in-Black-type reports. People up in the back hills had been seeing mysterious unmarked panel trucks which sometimes parked for hours in remote spots. There seemed to be several of these trucks in the area and the rumor was that they belonged to the air force. Men in neat coveralls were seen monkeying with telephone and power lines but no one questioned them.

A woman living alone on an isolated island north of Vancouver, British Columbia, Canada, had two curious encounters with the same kind of beings. She had moved into a tiny one-room cabin on Keats Island in October 1967 and was soon seeing UFO lights nightly. On January 29, 1968, following a close sighting of "a long dark body with dim red and yellow lights at both ends," she was surprised by two visitors. Both wore "neat, dark coveralls" and claimed to be employees of the hydroelectric company. They offered to help her put up a stovepipe. The younger of the two climbed on the roof of her cabin while the other handed him the pipes. "I could hear the man on the ground directing him and the one on the roof would answer, 'Yes, Master.'"

After the pipe was installed, the pair joined her for tea. They seemed "a little stiff." When they left she wondered how they had known she was there because "the cabin couldn't be seen from the road [and] the stove was out when they arrived, so there was no smoke from the chimney."

On May 2, she again encountered two men. "One was the 'boss' Hydro man in his neat coveralls," she reported.[1] "The other was a different, younger man of about 19–20. As I entered the path, the boss man indicated with his hand for the young man to get behind him. They got well off the path and waited for me, the young man a little behind his boss. The fellow stared at me as if I was some kind of freak. . . ."

This time she didn't invite them for tea. One odd thing she noticed during both meetings was their slow, careful way of walking. They looked at their feet and stepped very uncertainly.

The next day a jeep came along the road, containing four men inspecting lines . . . "carelessly dressed, workaday men, none in coveralls. The boss wasn't obviously so. They expressed no surprise at seeing me there, no concern or any particular interest. I told them two of their men already had been around the day before, inspecting the lines. They assured me yesterday's men weren't Hydro men, that somebody had been 'pulling my leg.'"

Somebody was also pulling a lot of legs on cosmopolitan Long Island. In West Virginia I had heard some stories about three men who looked "like Indians" and were accom-

[1]Canadian UFO Report, #13,1972–73

panied by a fourth man, more normal-looking and very shabbily dressed in contrast to the other three. So I was nonplused when I heard identical descriptions from people on Long Island.

An elderly woman who lived alone in a house near the summit of Mount Misery, the highest point on Long Island, had received a visit from this quartet in early April 1967, immediately after a severe rainstorm.

"They had high cheekbones and very red faces, like a bad sunburn," she told me. "They were very polite but they said my land belonged to their tribe and they were going to get it back. What frightened me was their feet. They didn't have a car . . . they must have walked up that muddy hill . . . but their shoes were spotlessly clean. There was no trace of mud or water where they walked in my house."

That same week another visitor came to Mount Misery. This was a woman with striking white hair who claimed to represent a local newspaper. She carried a book "like a big ledger" and asked the witness a number of personal questions about her family background. When I later checked with the newspaper I found they employed no one of that description.

The local Mount Misery expert was Miss Jaye P. Paro, a radio personality then with station WBAB in Babylon, New York. Miss Paro is a dark-haired, dark-eyed young lady with a soft, haunting voice. At that time she conducted an interview show, largely devoted to the historical and psychic lore of the region. Soon after she reported some UFO sightings around Mount Misery she began to receive all manner of crank calls, both at the station and on her unlisted home phone. Metallic voices ordered her to meet them on "the Mount" (she didn't go).

Through Miss Paro I met several local UFO witnesses and contactees. Long Island, I discovered, was crawling with contactees of all ages and both sexes. One of these was a lovely young blonde, whom I will call Jane, who lived near

Mount Misery with her family. Jane was not illiterate, but she seldom read anything other than the comic strips and "Dear Abby." She knew nothing about UFOs and cared less. She was a "fallen Catholic," having abandoned religion when she reached adulthood. She was a very sensitive woman, more ethereal than sensual. There was almost something mystical about her appearance and grace.

Mount Misery is a heavily wooded hill with a few narrow dirt roads slicing through it and a number of large mansions set back among the trees. The late Henry Stimson, secretary of war during World War II, maintained a lavish estate on the summit. For decades the Mount was known as a haunted place, the site of a number of mysterious deaths and disappearances. In the spring of 1967, young couples necking on the back roads began to see low-flying UFOs, particularly around a field that was used as a junkyard for old cars. Others claimed to see a giant hairy monster with gleaming red eyes.

After Miss Paro began to broadcast reports of what was happening on Mount Misery, the usual mobs started to cruise the area nightly to the consternation of the scattered and snobbish residents. Jane and her boyfriend Richard joined the stream of cars one night in early May and eventually found themselves alone on a back road near High Hold, the old Stimson place.

Richard, who was driving, suddenly complained of feeling unwell. He stopped the car and a moment later slumped over the wheel unconscious. Jane was terrified. But before she could focus her attention on him, a brilliant beam of light shot out of the woods next to the road "like a floodlight." It dazzled her and she fell back in her seat unable to move.

The next thing they knew, they were driving along Old Country Road at the base of Mount Misery.

"How did we get here?" Richard asked her, baffled. "What happened?"

"Let's go home," Jane choked. They never discussed the incident again until I arrived on the scene.

A few days later, on May 17, Jane answered the phone (she had her own phone in her room) and a strange metallic voice addressed her. "Listen carefully," it said. "I cannot hear you." It instructed her to go to a small public library nearby and look up a certain book on Indian history.

She did as she was instructed. On May 18 she went to the library at 10:30 A.M. The place was deserted except for the librarian, who struck Jane as being unusual. The woman was "dressed in an old-fashioned suit like something out of the 1940s, with a long skirt, broad shoulders, and flat old-looking shoes." (Remember, this was in 1967, long before the 1940s styles became popular again.) She had a dark complexion, with a fine bone structure, and very black eyes and hair. When Jane entered, the woman seemed to be expecting her and produced the book instantly from under her desk.

Jane sat down at a table and began to riffle through the book, pausing on page forty-two. Her caller had told her to read that page.

"You won't believe this," she told me, "but the print became smaller and smaller, then larger and larger. It changed into a message and I can remember every word of it.

" 'Good morning, friend,' it began. 'You have been selected for many reasons. One is that you are advanced in autosuggestion. Through this science we will make contact. I have messages concerning Earth and its people. The time is set. Fear not . . . I am a friend. For reasons best known to ourselves you must make your contacts known to one reliable person. To break this code is to break contact. Proof shall be given. Notes must be kept of the suggestion state. Be in peace. [signed] A Pal.'

"The print became very small again, and then the normal text reappeared."

As soon as Jane left the library she became quite ill and

vomited several times during the next two days. She approached Miss Paro with her story and was advised to get in touch with me. Her experience on the Mount, her phone call, and the remark about "autosuggestion" all stirred my interest. In those days none of the UFO enthusiasts knew anything about these factors and a hoax seemed very unlikely. And, unknown to Miss Paro and Jane, I was in touch with a distant contactee who was communicating with "Apholes." The signature "A Pal" seemed close enough to Apholes to take seriously. I suspected that Jane had been programed for a set of special experiences and I kept in constant touch with her in the months which followed, maintaining an extensive record of her experiences.

In early June, Jane began to see the "librarian" wherever she went. On June 6, while wandering through a local department store, the woman appeared behind a dress rack. She wore the same old-fashioned clothes and tried to speak to Jane in "broken English." There was something wrong about her speech and movements. "It was as if . . . she were dead," Jane said. When asked if she lived around Babylon, the woman laughed in a strange hysterical way, "like an emotionally disturbed person." (This weird laugh has been described by many contactees.)

"Is there any A-U here?" the woman asked. Jane didn't know what she meant. Just that week I had been pondering the significance of gold in UFO and religious lore. Gold is the seventy-ninth element and the chemical symbol for it is AU.

Jane offered to give the woman a lift but she declined and wandered off.

Unable to sleep that night, Jane got up at the crack of dawn the following morning and went for a walk on an impulse. The dark-skinned woman stepped out of an alley and approached her shyly. "Peter is coming," she announced.

This statement shook Jane. She remembered that Catholic lore predicts that the final pope will be named Peter.

"Why are you interested in our Mount?" the woman continued, then repeated, "Peter is coming very soon."

Next a large black Cadillac came down the street and stopped next to them. It was "brand-new, very shiny and polished," Jane recalled. The driver was an olive-skinned man wearing wraparound sunglasses and dressed in a neat gray suit, apparently of the same material as the woman's clothes. The rear door opened and a man climbed out with a big grin on his face. He was about five feet eight inches tall, with dark skin and Oriental eyes. Jane thought he looked like a Hawaiian. He had the air of someone very important and was dressed in a well-cut, expensive-looking suit of the same gray material that was shiny like silk but was not silk.

He solemnly shook hands with the girl, "his hand was as cold as ice," and stared at her steadily with his jet-black eyes, grinning all the while.

"Do you know who I am?" he asked. "I am Apol [pronounced Apple]."

The Cadillac pulled away and drove off, leaving the three of them standing on the street. Apol produced a piece of folded paper and handed it to Jane.

"Wear this always," he told her. "So 'they' will know who you are."

"Who's they?" she asked.

"They are the very good people," he answered.

The paper, a piece of very old parchment, contained a small metal disc about the size of a quarter. As they talked they walked slowly toward the center of town until they stood in front of the post office. Jane impulsively announced she was going to mail the disc to someone. She went into the post office, got an envelope, and sent the disc and parchment to me special delivery. The two strangers smiled broadly at each other.

When she came out of the post office, Apol told her a number of things about her childhood that no one could have known and advised her to avoid iodine. (She had a minor health problem which required her to avoid iodine in her diet.)

The car reappeared and the two people got into it and drove off. "I felt very strange while I was talking to them," she recalled. "I was whoozy . . . like I was in a daze or something."

If it hadn't been for the metal disc I would have classified the entire episode as hallucinatory. The next day I received the special delivery envelope and was very disappointed by the contents. The disc looked like a blank identification tag similar to those that come with flea collars. The parchment seemed to be the remnants of a very old envelope. After examining it, I put the disc back into the paper exactly as I had received it, then placed the whole thing in a small envelope which I sealed with Scotch tape. I put this into a larger manila envelope and mailed it back to Jane special delivery.

She phoned me the next day.

"Why did you bend the disc and tear up the paper?" She demanded.

She had just received the envelope and found that the parchment in the sealed inner envelope had been ripped into three pieces. The metal disc was bent, as if it had been folded double and then unfolded again. It had also turned charcoal black and smelled like "rotten eggs."

The implication was clear. Someone had the ability to intercept the U.S. mails and tamper with things in sealed envelopes!

II.

While Jane was holding clandestine meetings with Mr. Apol and his mysterious lady friend, Jaye P. Paro was being entertained by the redoubtable Princess Moon Owl, a character who would become a legend on Long Island by the end of 1967. At 3:30 P.M. on June 11, 1967, Jaye entered the studios of WBAB and found a very weird woman waiting for her. She was at least six feet tall, was very dark (Negroid), with large, glassy eyes, and wore a costume largely made up of feathers. She was gasping and wheezing, having great difficulty breathing. Jaye thought she was having a heart attack.

"I am Princess Moon Owl," she declared between wheezes. "I am from another planet. I came here by flying saucer."

Jaye slapped a tape on a tape recorder and offered to interview her for the air. The Princess was delighted, pulled herself together, and delivered a hilarious thirty-minute monologue about life on the planet Ceres in the asteroid belt. She seemed to be familiar with all the New York/Long Island UFO buffs and eccentrics, denouncing some as "phonies" and praising others. As the interview progressed, Jaye became increasingly uncomfortable. Cerians had a problem with body odor. "She stank like rotten eggs," Jaye said afterward. The smell was slight at first but gradually became overpowering. The Princess admitted to being "Seven Ooongots" old . . . or about 350 Earth years.

While the interview was in progress, I was sitting in my New York apartment and my telephone was going crazy. It rang several times but there was no one on the other end. (Until this period I had had very few problems with my personal phone.) Later that afternoon I received a call from a middle-aged woman who said she was Princess Moon Owl and that I could reach her through "contactee Paro." The woman's voice did not resemble the voice on Jaye's tape, which I heard later.

The taped Moon Owl sounded like a man faking an Aunt Jemima accent. He was a very bad actor. I accused Jaye of a hoax and advised her not to put the interview on the air. If it was not a hoax, then Moon Owl was the victim of demonic possession (Jaye's description of the Princess's behavior certainly indicated this). Jaye aired the tape anyway and Long Island's lunatic fringe went wild with joy. At last a genuine space person was in their midst.

Once she had established her credentials on WBAB, Moon Owl began to systematically telephone all of Long Island's prominent UFO enthusiasts. They accepted her authenticity without question. What troubled me was the fact that she managed to vector in on a number of unlisted numbers, and she obviously knew a great deal about the local personalities. The most suspicious things of all were her transparent references to a major UFO convention scheduled to be held that June 24 in New York's Hotel Commodore. James Moseley, publisher of *Saucer News*, had rented the hotel's auditorium and practically an entire floor for the event and was staging press conferences and radio and television appearances to promote his investment. Princess Moon Owl seemed to fit too neatly into the publicity campaign.

Meanwhile, Jane's phantom friends were visiting her daily and helpfully giving her surprising information about my own "secret" investigations. My interview with the Christiansens of Cape May, and the details of their pill-popping visitor, Tiny, was then known only to a few trusted people like Ivan Sanderson. But on June 12, Mr. Apol and his friends visited Jane when she was alone in her house and asked for water so they could take some pills. Then they presented her with three of the same pills, told her to take one at that moment, and to take one other in two days. The third pill, they said, was for her to have analyzed to assure herself it was harmless. They undoubtedly knew that she would turn it over to me.

Two hours after she took the first pill she came down with a blinding headache, her eyes became bloodshot, and the vision in her right eye was affected. When her parents came home they expressed concern because her eyes were glassy and her right eye seemed to have a cast.

The sample pill proved to be a sulfa drug normally prescribed for infections of the urinary tract.

Two days later she obligingly took the second pill and her phone rang shortly afterward. A man with "a crude Brooklyn accent" told her he was Col. John Dalton of the air force and wanted to talk to her about "Mitchell Field." She told him, honestly, that she didn't know anything about Mitchell Field. He insisted that he wanted to talk to her. Would she come to his office? She asked where his office was and he hesitated for a moment, then said he would interview her at her house. He didn't ask for her address and since she hadn't reported anything to the air force, she wondered how he had gotten her phone number.

At 7:45 P.M. the next evening Jane's parents left the house for a few hours and as soon as they were gone Colonel Dalton and his partner, a young lieutenant, rang her bell. Both men seemed normal and were polite and well-spoken. Colonel Dalton was in civilian clothes . . . a black suit, naturally. He was about five feet eight inches tall, had brown hair, brown eyes, and "a very pointed nose." The lieutenant was two or three inches taller, in an air force uniform, with "whitish blond hair that looked dyed" cut very short, "like a crewcut growing back in." They flashed identification cards with their photographs affixed.

The colonel asked her what she knew about a local saucer landing and saucer occupants in the area. Jane laughed and said she didn't believe in flying saucers.

"We know all about the shenanigans in this building," Dalton told her curtly. "A lot of funny people have been going in and out."

"Well, maybe some of my relatives are a little strange," Jane smiled.

Dalton opened his briefcase and brought out a sheaf of printed forms. He handed her a long, complicated form and asked her to fill it out. She took it, read it over, then handed it back.

"If you don't want to fill it out," he said, handing her a pen, "you can just sign it."

"Now that would be pretty stupid, wouldn't it?" Jane said.

Later she recalled that the form did not ask any questions about UFOs but was solely concerned with personal history, education, medical background, and family history. "It even asked when my grandmother died and what she died of," Jane told me.

Finally the two men gave up trying to browbeat her and left. She saw them drive away in a blue station wagon.

Around this same time two young men visited Mary Hyre at her home in Point Pleasant. Both were wearing black clothes, and both had short white hair. "It looked so unnatural," she exclaimed. "I wondered why such young men would dye their hair such an odd color."

At first she assumed they were just more in the endless stream of UFO buffs, but they seemed to know very little about flying saucers. They were mainly concerned with asking questions about me, which she hedged.

"Did they use any unusual words or expressions?" I asked Mary on the phone.

"Not really. Just when they went out the door . . . one of them turned and said something like, "We'll see you in time' or 'sometime.' It sounded odd the way he said it, like it was meant to mean something."

Tom's meeting with Vadig was still six months away so the phrase meant nothing to me.

III.

On June 19 Mr. Apol gave Jane a message to pass along to me. It was a prediction: "Things will become more serious in the Middle East. The pope will go there soon on a peace mission. He will be martyred there in a horrible way . . . knifed to death in a bloody manner. Then the Antichrist will rise up out of Israel."

I was shocked. But here was a statement that could be checked against future events. Apol also said the Vatican was planning to send food and materiel to Arab refugees. There had been no announcement in the press about this.

Two days later Miss Paro had an unnerving experience. A black Cadillac pulled alongside her as she was out walking at 8 P.M. and a well-dressed man in the back seat ordered her into the car. He named a friend of hers and she foolishly obeyed him. The car headed for Mount Misery.

"There was a funny smell inside," she reported. "Antiseptic . . . like a hospital. And there were flashing lights on the dashboard. I couldn't take my eyes off them. I felt like they were hypnotizing me."

The car traveled isolated back roads until it reached a crossroads where another vehicle was waiting. A man holding something like a doctor's bag was standing there. He got into the Cadillac and waved a small object in Jaye's face, like a bottle of smelling salts. She felt her will power drain away and sat there helplessly while the men asked her questions which didn't make any sense to her. Finally they returned her to the spot where they had picked her up. The whole episode had terrified her and she called me immediately.

Was Jaye's experience merely an updated version of the

Mattoon "gasser" and old Springheeled Jack?* Months later when I interviewed Tom in Washington I remembered this seemingly meaningless incident. Had Tom also been gassed or hypnotized the moment he stepped into Vadig's old Buick?

On October 23, 1971, the *Washington Post* published a strange "gas" story involving President Nixon's maid. The story contains some of the elements we have been discussing here.

NIXON MAID STOLE IN TRANCE, SHE SAYS

Miami, Oct. 22 (AP)—A part-time housekeeper at President Nixon's Key Biscayne retreat has testified she was put in a hypnotic daze by a stranger who told her to shoplift four dresses.

Shirley Cromartie, 32, and a mother of three, pleaded no contest Thursday and was given a suspended sentence after law enforcement officers and a psychiatrist testified they believed she was telling the truth.

Mrs. Cromartie holds a security clearance to work in the Florida White House, according to testimony. She said a woman met her in a parking lot and asked the time, then ordered her to take the items and bring them to her.

Mrs. Cromartie testified she fell into a daze when the young woman released a jasminelike scent from her left hand. "I just sort of lost my will . . . it was a terrifying experience," she testified.

Mrs. Cromartie joined the Key Biscayne White House housekeeping staff about a year ago, according to FBI Agent Leo Mc Clairen. He testified her background was impeccable.

Dr. Albert Jaslow, a psychiatrist, said he examined her and

---

*Springheeled Jack was a tall, caped phantom with a bright light on his chest who appeared in England in the 1830s. He was able to leap great distances and he spewed a nauseous gas into the faces of surprised witnesses. Although he was the subject of a massive manhunt, he was never caught or identified. A black-garbed phantom terrorized Mattoon, Illinois, in the 1940s, spraying a noxious gas into bedroom windows.

found she could be hypnotized "quickly and easily" and believed she was telling the truth.

"But it wasn't the same when he hypnotized me," Mrs. Cromartie said. "I couldn't remember anything afterwards. Whatever that young woman did to me, it was like being in a sleepwalk, only awake."

There was no further comment on this strange incident. At the time I wondered if perhaps this was not some small demonstration for the benefit of President Nixon, similar to the power failures that seemed to follow President Johnson in 1967. (The lights failed wherever he went . . . from Washington to Johnson City, Texas, to Hawaii.)

IV.

Woodrow Derenberger found a new world with Cold, Klinnel, Ardo, and company. Now Jane was moving among twilight presences; Mr. Apol, Lia (the name of his female companion), and several others who mischievously adopted names from my obscure (damn it) novels! They amplified their dire prophesy for Pope Paul. He would be attacked in a crowd at an airport, they said, by a man dressed in a black suit and wielding a black knife. After his assassination there would be three days of darkness and worldwide power failures.

On June 28 the Vatican announced that a personal envoy of Pope Paul VI, Monsignor Abramo Frescht, was being dispatched to Cairo to discuss "Vatican assistance to war victims and refugees." On June 30 it was announced that the wooden throne said to have been used by Saint Peter was going to be dug out of the Vatican basement and placed on display for the first time since 1867.

I went out to Mount Misery and hypnotized Jane. She was a good subject and after performing various tests to assure myself that she was really in a deep trance, I began to ask her subtle questions about Apol and his friends. To my utter amazement, the impossible happened. The control was taken away from me. I couldn't direct the session. Instead, I found myself talking directly to Apol through Jane. He wanted to talk about Marilyn Monroe and Robert Kennedy. I didn't want to gossip, I insisted, but wanted some hard facts on the overall situation. Apol persisted, warning me that Kennedy was in grave danger. Where was he talking from? He said he was parked nearby in his Cadillac. He made some specific predictions about pending plane crashes, then returned to Marilyn and Kennedy.

All the while we were conducting this insane conversation, Jane's telephone was ringing madly. Each time I picked it up there was no one on the line. Finally I just left it off the hook.

The session ended abruptly when Jane woke up by herself. Another impossibility. She would have required a suggestion from me before she could awake.*

The predicted plane crashes occurred right on schedule. I was slowly convincing myself that the entities were somehow tuned to the future.

I was making other startling discoveries. I had only to *think* of a serious question and my phone would ring and Jane would deliver a message from Apol answering it.

Other ufologists were also getting predictions from contactees. When Gray Barker arrived in New York for the convention at the Hotel Commodore he told me that he'd received a prediction that "a famous newsman in the Midwest" would die very soon. Two days later, on the evening of June 23, Frank Edwards died suddenly of a heart attack in Indiana. Edwards was a newscaster and author of the 1966 bestseller *Flying Saucers—Serious Business*.

---

*In comparing notes with psychic investigator-author Brad Steiger, he told me he had similar experiences with hypnosis; that is, the control was taken out of his hands by some other intelligence.

The year of the Garuda—1966–7—was only half over and I was talking to half-a-dozen entities through contactees scattered throughout the Northeast. Scores of new games were going on at once, each one designed to prove something to me, not to the contactees. The latter would never quite figure out what was happening to them or what it all meant. Like the UFO enthusiasts themselves, the contactees would be manipulated, used as robots to propagate beliefs and false frames of reference, and then be discarded to sit in the darkness and wonder why the world was not as they had imagined it, why the wonderful space people had abandoned them.

On Long Island, a dozen eccentrics still sit by their phones waiting for Princess Moon Owl to call again and restore their waning faith.

16:

Paranoiacs Are Made, Not Born

I.

"The U.S. government is being taken over by the space people!"

This rumor spread throughout the country in 1967, an updated version of the old devil theory. Actually it got its start in 1949 when James V. Forrestal, the brilliant secretary of defense in the Truman cabinet, went bananas and raced through the corridors of the Pentagon screaming, "We're being invaded and we can't stop them!" He was convinced that his phones were being tapped and some enormous conspiracy was underway. Soon after he was placed in a hospital he leaped out a window to his death. While the press blamed his paranoia on the tensions of the cold war, the UFO enthusiasts knew better. Air force Intelligence had compiled a *Top Secret Estimate of the Situation* following their UFO investigations in 1947–48. Their conclusion, according to the late Capt. Edward Ruppelt, was that flying saucers were extraterrestrial. Forrestal, so the story went, was one of the few to read that report before Air Force

Chief of Staff Hoyt Vandenberg ordered all copies destroyed, and it blew his mind.

Two other top military men, Gen. George C. Marshall and Gen. Douglas MacArthur were obsessed with the flying saucer phenomenon. MacArthur made several public statements declaring that the next war would be fought against "evil beings from outer space." A fabled "think tank," the Rand Corporation, was assigned to feed UFO data into a computer and fight an imaginary war with those evil beings. Since we wouldn't know where they were from, what their technology was, or how to attack their bases, the computer advised us to surrender.

Contactees adrift in the hallucinatory worlds were convinced the space people were walking among us unnoticed. Los Angeles alone had a space population of ten thousand. Actually this was just a tiresome repetition of the earlier beliefs that devils and angels were everywhere in human guise. Early in the Age of the Flying Saucers (1947–69), air force and CIA agents undoubtedly came across MIB cases similar to the ones outlined here and, being human, some of those early investigators leapfrogged to UFO cultistlike conclusions. Paranoia gripped the upper echelons of government. Millions of tax dollars were sunk into UFO research. (In 1952, Captain Ruppelt said the air force was spending one million dollars a year on the subject. Gen. Nathan Twining declared "the best brains" in science and the military were trying to solve the mystery.) Cold war hysteria added to the atmosphere of fear and loathing. A 1953 CIA document, kept classified for over twenty years, noted that the Aerial Phenomena Research Organization (APRO) "should be watched" as a potential propaganda menace. APRO had been founded the year before by a Wisconsin housewife and circulated a mimeographed UFO newsletter to a few dozen scattered buffs. Apparently more thousands of tax dollars were expended in "watching" APRO's Coral Lorenzen over the years, according to evidence she published in a series of paperback books in the 1960s. The only propaganda she ever distrubuted was anti-air force, and she never sold any of our flying saucer secrets to the Soviet Union.

Military men—and the UFO enthusiasts—had no knowledge of or interest in psychic phenomena. Their materialistic, pseudo-scientific approach to the sightings and attendent manifestations merely increased the lore and intensified the mystery. The age-old changeling concept, for example, must have caused many gray hairs in official circles when it was introduced into the UFO lore. Were the space people really switching human beings? Many of the contactees and their open-mouthed followers believed this was the case. Were humans being dragged aboard spaceships and examined like cattle? The contactees' tales indicated this and their stories gave impetus to the expanded devil theory; that government officials were being kidnapped and replaced by clever androids obeying the dictates of the sinister leaders of some other planet. Idiocy was piled upon idiocy over the past twenty-eight years. The paranoia once isolated to the very small lunatic fringe grew until it swallowed up a large part of the world's population.

I was concerned not with the sincere but falsified memories of the contactees, but with a more worrisome question. What, I wondered, happened to the bodies of these people while their minds were taking trips? Trips that often lasted for hours, even for days. A young college professor in New York State was haunted by the same question in 1967. After investigating a UFO-related poltergeist case he suffered possession and was led to believe that he had committed a daring jewel robbery while he was in a trance or possessed state. He abandoned ufology and nearly suffered a total nervous breakdown in the aftermath.

Were our contactees being used by exterior intelligences to carry out crimes, even murder? The answer is a disturbing yes. If you review the history of political assassinations you will find that many were performed by so-called religious fanatics who were obeying the "voice of God" or were in an obvious state of possession when they committed their crime. Even the ten co-conspirators in the assassination of President Lincoln were in this category. And the soldier who shot and killed John Wilkes Booth against the orders of his superiors claimed he pulled the trigger because a voice told him to do so.

The madness that grips crowds and produces violent riots, some of which have changed history, seems little different from the madness that produced the widespread dancing mania of the Middle Ages when thousands of people danced in the streets until they dropped dead from exhaustion. The mania spread from Italy to Turkey. Survivors claimed they believed they were knee-deep in blood and were prancing to get out of it. This was a collective or mass hallucination. Even today there are annual incidents in which whole towns are seized by hallucinations, usually in obscure parts of South America and Asia. Such events are traditionally explained as being caused by tainted bread despite the fact that people who have not eaten the local bread are also affected.

In contactee parlance, persons who perform involuntary acts are said to be "used." Apparently a relatively small part of the population have auras or biological radiations which attract elements of the superspectrum. Such people are prone to controlled hallucinations and possession. Since the entities probably exist as energy in a field outside our space-time continuum they can only see, and be seen, by these special people. (In innumerable UFO reports the ufonauts apparently could not see the witnesses.) Derenberger's Cold identified himself as "a searcher." Searching for what? For biological oddities like Woody, no doubt.

A contactee may feel a sudden impulse to go for a pointless late-night walk or drive. During that drive he encounters, he thinks, the space people and has a fine visit with them. Actually his body proceeds on to, say, Point A where he picks up a letter or object left there by another contactee. He carries the letter or object to Point B and deposits it. Later he has no memory of these actions. Meanwhile some poor slob with the wrong aura, like myself, receives a phone call advising him to proceed to Point B where he will find something left for him by the space people. In short, all physical evidence and manifestations are produced by human beings. They dig holes in fields, rifle mailboxes, and who knows what else.

These games have been going on since ever.

I have received thousands of letters from contactees since 1967, many of them filled with glowing praise for their contacters, others pathetic and touched with terror. One of the first letters arrived unexpectedly in the summer of 1967 from an elderly man in New England.

"I found your name and address on a slip of paper dropped onto my kitchen floor by an 'Indian-like' friend," he wrote. "If this letter is not returned to me I will no [sic] you received it . . . I wish I could tell you how my life has been taken over & what condition our country & government are in. If you have been through the 'misery' you no [sic] you are not alone. I am not a nut. I am sincere. I am concerned for you. . . .

"P.S. I have been 'used'!"

This letter, and others like them, helped to convince me that my own investigations could be manipulated. I was being led to people and cases to support whatever theory I was working on at the time. I tested this by inventing some rather outlandish ideas. Within days I would receive phone calls, reports, and mail describing elements of those ideas. This was the feedback or reflective effect. Other investigators concerned with solving problems such as how flying saucers are propelled have automatically been fed, or led into, cases in which the witnesses supposedly viewed the interiors of the objects and saw things which confirmed the investigators' theories.

If the phenomenon can produce any effect through hallucination, it can easily support any theory. It took me a long time to realize that many of my Men in Black reports were just feedback. It is even possible that affairs like Tiny's visit to the Christiansens were somehow arranged for my benefit, even though I didn't know them at the time. I came across the Christiansens during an investigation far from Cape May. They were almost dumped in my lap, just as the letter from the man in Massachussetts came at a time when I was involved in cases with "Indian-like" entities on Mount Misery. (Note he put "misery" in quotes.)

My thoroughness led to the discovery of coincidences that seemed significant at the time. Two of my silent contactees shared the same birth date—September 6. As soon as I realized this, circumstances added several new contactees to my stable—all women and all born on September 6!

During one of her almost-daily conversations with Apol and Lia, Jane was told that a number of women were being selected for artificial insemination! They would be bearing very special children for the space people. This led to a whole new game in which I found myself trying to cope with pregnant women, though I eventually figured out they were victims of pseudocyesis—false or "hysterical" pregnancies. This was probably feedback from my concern over Derenberger's statement that if the truth were known, women the world over would panic, throw their babies out the window, and commit suicide.

By mid-July I was in indirect contact with the entities through three different systems. First, contactees would relay my questions to them and relay their answers back to me. I was still extremely skeptical, so many of my questions were complicated and beyond the abilities of the individual contactees to answer . . . even if they spent hours in a library trying to research the answers. Second, I was able to communicate *by mail* by sending letters through the U.S. Post Office to addresses which I later discovered were nonexistent. I would receive replies by mail, often the very next day, written in block letters. Some of these replies covered several pages. Third, I was sometimes able to speak to the entities by telephone! A contactee would call me and inform me that an entity was present in his or her house and wished to speak to me. Sometimes I just asked questions and the alleged entity whispered the answer to the contactee who relayed it to me. Sometimes a strange voice would come on the line and speak to me directly. In some, if not all, of these instances the contactee probably entered a trance state and the voice came from their own vocal chords just as "spirits" speak through mediums at séances.

As soon as I entered this communication phase my problems with the mails and telephone intenstified. Important letters of a non-UFO nature went astray . . . or arrived days late and had obviously been opened by someone en route. My telephone rang at all hours of the day and night with beeping calls, eerie electronic sounds, and, most interesting of all, frantic calls from people who were superb actors and who described UFO incidents containing those secret details in cases I was working on, but when I tried to check out these people I found the addresses they had given me were nonexistent and the phone numbers they gave were false.

Someone somewhere was just trying to prove that they knew every move I was making, listened to all my phone calls, and could even control my mail! And they were succeeding.

II.

On July 20, 1967, the Vatican announced that the pope was planning a trip to Turkey. He would be flying to Istanbul where he would be greeted by a huge mob at the airport. Several of my contactees had been gravely concerned with the prediction of the pope's impending death and the three days of darkness that would follow. The accuracy of earlier predictions led me to take this one seriously. Very seriously.

The assassination was supposed to take place on July 26. It would be preceded by a violent earthquake.

On July 22 more than one thousand people were killed in an earthquake in Adapazari, Turkey, one hundred miles southeast of Istanbul. The news really shook me up. The whole prophesied scenario was being carried out to the letter!

The night before the quake, there were a rash of telephone hoaxes throughout the Northeast. These calls consisted of two people talking indistinctly for the most part, but certain names were clearly audible. Ivan Sanderson received such a call on his unlisted phone in the mountains of New Jersey at midnight. My call came through at 11:40. A UFO buff on Long Island received one at 1 A.M. He heard, "Hang up, John . . . and I'll turn off the recorder." On my call the name "Jim" was used.

These calls were part of a broader nationwide pattern which had successfully disrupted, even destroyed, many local UFO groups. The receiver heard the name of a fellow UFO enthusiast and regarded it as proof that the other person was responsible for all the hoax calls he or she was receiving. The very same ploy was used against the civilians quietly investigating the Kennedy assassination! Penn Jones, a Texas newspaper editor who has been investigating the death of JFK for years, received similar calls, including the playing of a tape of his phone conversations with other investigators . . . proof positive that his phone was being tapped by someone and they wanted him to know it. This playback of taped conversations also happened on my phone. The object of such gimmicks is clearly to incite paranoia. Since many of the UFO enthusiasts are very unstable to begin with, the device has been very effective.

I was now receiving many messages phrased in biblical terms. Some came from unknown elderly ladies who phoned me late at night claiming to be from Western Union. Then they would read long bible quotations that were supposedly telegrams. But Western Union disavowed any knowledge of these messages. I had hooked up a tape recorder to my own phone so I could keep track of all these things.

"If it is the days of darkness," said a message received on July 23, "behold there will be voices, thunder and earthquakes and disturbances upon the earth. And at their cry all nations shall fight one against the other. And fear shall fall upon the earth and the sky shall be darkened except for the illuminating round lights that will be the only sparks of light. And rain shall come at the end of the happening.

"John: Do not trouble yourself over trivial matters such as strange calls. We're in greater danger than you can imagine. Not only is your world involved, but many others too."

I am an amateur herpetologist and once kept three-fanged cobras in my New York apartment . . . until my concerned neighbors squealed to the Board of Health. Some of the descriptions of the entities impressed me as resembling some kind of reptile rather than human mammals. I didn't mention this reptile notion to anyone. But on July 24, Lia visited Jane and refused to talk about anything but eggs. She took some eggs from Jane's refrigerator and sucked out the contents like a reptile! Jane was perplexed by this exhibition and called me soon afterward.

That evening I received a phone call from Harold Salkin, a Washington, D.C., UFO researcher. He wanted to tell me that people all over Washington had been receiving strange phone calls during the past week. We had a perfect connection until I started to ask him if he had heard any rumors about Pope Paul. We were instantly drowned out by heavy static. As soon as I changed the subject, the static went away. Later in the conversation I tried again. The moment I named the pope the static resumed. When I again dropped the subject, the line cleared instantly.

Now they were even controlling my phone conversations!

Convinced that Pope Paul was about to be knifed to death at the Istanbul airport, I rented a car, loaded it with flashlights, candles, food, and bottled water, and drove out to the Mount Misery area to await the blackout. On the way I stopped to see one of my contactees and he informed me that a spaceman had just been to see him and had left a silly message.

"Tell John we'll meet with him later and help him drink all that water."

The contactee had no idea that I had several quarts of spring water in the trunk of the car.

Near Mount Misery I picked out a motel at random (I thought). The motel clerk asked to see my identification (very unusual).

"We've got a lot of messages here for you, Mr. Keel," she said, pulling out a sheaf of message slips. I started to protest since I had not even known I was going to stay at that motel until minutes before. The messages were all nonsensical, meant only to prove once more that my movements were being anticipated.

The pope landed in Istanbul safely. There was no three-day blackout. The whole episode served no purpose other than to demonstrate to me how and why so many contactees and prophets go and sit on hilltops to await the end of the world.

Three years later, on November 27, 1970, Pope Paul VI arrived at the Manila International Airport in the Phillipines and the scene described to me in 1967 suddenly became a reality. A man dressed in the black garments of a priest came out of the crowd and sprang at the pope with a long black knife in his hands. Fortunately, security guards wrestled him to the ground and the pontiff was unhurt. The would-be assassin was a Bolivian painter named Benjamin Mendoza who allegedly practiced black magic and witchcraft. Witnesses said that he had glassy eyes and seemed to be in some kind of trance during the attack.

The entities had correctly described the general circumstances of the attempt, but their dates were all wrong, and it took place in the Far East rather than the Middle East.

(In January 1968, I received a phone call informing me that the Reverend Martin Luther King would be murdered on February 4. He would be shot in the throat, I was told, while standing on a balcony in Memphis. I took the prediction seriously and spent some frantic hours trying to contact King by phone to warn him. I never got through. He was not assassinated on February 4, but on April 4, exactly as described to me four months earlier.)

III.

August 3, 1967. Jaye P. Paro was awakened at 3 A.M. by the sound of a baby crying. There were no babies in her house. She got out of bed and searched for the source of the sound without success.

Reports of telephone hoaxes, beeping and electronic sounds, tapes being played back, etc., reached me from as far away as Seattle, Washington. Flying saucer enthusiasts from coast to coast were suddenly having identical problems. Obviously this was not the work of a few random pranksters. It was more like a well-organized, well-financed campaign. On the night of July 21 between the hours of 10 P.M. and 1 A.M. hoax calls were received in Florida, Illinois, Michigan, Ohio, Massachussetts, California, New Jersey, Pennsylvania, Washington, and probably many other places that I never learned about. Unlisted phones were no protection. Were these calls the work of the CIA, as so many of the UFO enthusiasts believed? They seemed too pointless and expensive to be the work of the government.

After the UFO convention in June, Princess Moon Owl faded away, just as I had suspected she would. Aside from the single interview on WBAB, she had not been given any publicity. But in late August she was phoning UFO enthusiasts again, showering them with predictions . . . all largely silly. Then, unexpectedly, she became respectable. She traveled around Long Island handing out money, usually less than twenty-five dollars, to people in need. The entertainment editor of the Long Island newspaper *Newsday*, Bob Nickland, told me he received "over twenty-five phone calls" in September describing the Princess's good deeds. Long John Nebel phoned me to see if I knew how I could get in touch with her so he could interview her on his radio show. I told both men that I smelled a large rat . . . a blatant bid for publicity.

The noble princess was the least of my worries. I was like a general advising a dozen deeply troubled contactees and trying to guide them through the games they were caught up in. One woman in Brooklyn was searching for a mysterious crucifix that seemed to have special meaning to the entities. It was like the search for the Holy Grail. A man on Long Island was frantically making preparations for the big evacuation. He even traveled to a secret underground flying saucer base, in a black Cadillac with a dashboard festooned with flashing colored lights, where he participated in a "dry run." Other normal human beings were present, he said, and manned various kinds of equipment to communicate with the rescue spaceships somewhere overhead. "Funny thing, John," he mused, "all the equipment was manufactured by Western Electric, Hallicrafters, and other U.S. companies."

One woman told me she had been flown to another planet where she was placed in a huge glass hospital and examined by a great eyelike machine. Her hosts told her they were "copying" her insides.

I knew from my lengthy interviews and examinations that none of these people were run-of-the-mill kooks or schizophrenics. And I was impressed that many of their experiences were interrelated even though they were scattered geographically and not one of them knew any of the others. The entities adopted a system of code names, giving each contactee a biblical name. I was the only one who knew which name applied to which contactee. They would tell Contactee A in New Jersey to give me a message or piece of advice about Contactee B who lived in Connecticut. Contactee A wouldn't have the faintest notion of what they were talking about.

Another trick was to use certain key phrases. When a contactee whispered to me, "Do you know that cancer is contagious?," I knew he or she had been talking to this one set of entities.

Then there were those damned synchronized events.

The contactees stopped talking about the pope's fate. They were concerned now about an "EM effect" scheduled for sometime in December. All of them said it would happen in the middle of the month and would affect a large part of the United States. It was going to be a massive power failure.

On September 24, Jaye P. Paro received a phone call from a man claiming to be on the city desk at *Newsday*. He told her that Princess Moon Owl was going to visit WBAB that afternoon and he was sending a photographer to get a picture of the two of them together. Miss Paro went to the radio station and waited all afternoon but neither the princess nor the photographer showed up.

But, curiously, a photographer did turn up in Point Pleasant, West Virginia, at the home of Linda Scarberry. He was very tall, wore a black suit, had a heavy "sunburn," and wanted to take pictures of Linda's "family." She and Roger had no children but she was very pregnant at the time. She refused his offer and phoned her mother in a panic after he left. Something about the man just hadn't seemed right . . .

The next morning Linda woke up to find one of her eyes was swollen shut.

All of the madness of this period came together in a single case revolving around a young woman whom I shall call Shirley. She lived in Seaford, Long Island, a town that enjoyed a brief moment of fame several years ago when it became the center of a widely publicized poltergeist case. Shirley and her husband were separated and she lived alone with her small child.

At 3 P.M. on the afternoon of September 26, she heard a loud humming sound outside her house, which was in an isolated, wooded area. She looked out the window and saw a silver disc-shaped object hovering about one hundred feet in the air. It seemed to be perfectly smooth with no visible windows or doors. While she was staring at it her doorbell rang. When she answered she found "an Indian woman" standing there. This woman was about five foot nine inches, dark-skinned "but not Negro," dressed in a long gray gown that reached her feet and was made from some shimmering material.

"Hello, Pat," the woman said.

"You must have the wrong house, my name isn't Pat," Shirley replied. Unknown to Shirley, Pat was another of my long list of silent contactees.

"I'm sorry . . . I meant Shirley," the woman corrected herself, a reassuring grin fixed on her dark, pointed face. "Could I have some salt? I must take a pill."

Shirley thought this was very peculiar. She had no idea that another contactee was involved in a game which required her to buy large quantities of salt, transport it to Mount Misery, and leave it in a field for the space people in the belief that salt was an essential part of their diet.

She went and got a box of salt and handed it to the

woman who took a large handful and swallowed it. Then she thanked Shirley and walked away into the bushes. There was a loud humming sound, louder than before, and Shirley saw the silver disc rise up and shoot off into the sky. An hour or so later Shirley had an attack of nausea.

When I interviewed her I found her to be a sweet, if somewhat homely, young lady, not very bright, and certainly not imaginative enough to manufacture the things that were to happen later.

A lonely woman living in a lonely place, separated from her husband, perfect fodder for the games the nonpeople loved to play.

Her birthday was September 6.

Following that first visit, Shirley repeatedly heard a baby crying when her own child was sleeping peacefully. The woman returned on September 30, asking for more salt. She identified herself as Cloe (the name of a character in one of my uncelebrated novels) and warned Shirley to lock all her doors and windows that night. This time no UFO was visible.

Later that evening, Jaye P. Paro phoned me to tell me that she had just had a narrow escape. While she was walking along a road near Mount Misery, a black Cadillac had roared out of the darkness and come within inches of running her down. All its lights were out and it disappeared quickly into the darkness. She was very upset.

Shortly after Jaye hung up, Shirley called in a very nervous state. A large black car was parked outside her house, she said, and two men completely dressed in black, with broad-brimmed black hats and turtleneck sweaters, were setting up a camera. At first she thought they were priests.

"They're taking pictures of my house!" she exclaimed. "Now why would anyone want to do that? At night yet!"

The camera they were using had a large bright red light attached to it.

"Don't look at that light," I advised sternly.

"Do you think I should call the police?"

"I'm afraid taking a picture is no crime. They'd probably laugh at you."

"They're getting back in the car. You know, its headlights are out. I don't know how they can see. They're driving off."

While I was talking to Shirley, Mary Hyre was trying to call me from West Virginia. She finally called Dan Drasin and asked him to get in touch with me as soon as my line was free. I called her back and she told me she had just had a frightening encounter with a black Cadillac. While she was walking down the deserted Main Street (the sidewalks roll up about 7 P.M.), a car driven "by a very large man" pulled away from the curb and slowly followed her. She walked to her own car and the Cadillac slowly went around a corner. She got into her car and went looking for the stranger.

"I was heading out to Route 62 when I saw it again," she said. "It headed straight for me. I pulled over as far as I could and it almost ran right into me. It was the same car . . . but now there were three men in it. I could see that one of them was wearing glasses . . . like those sunglasses that wrap around your head. I've never seen any of them in Point Pleasant before. What do you suppose they were trying to prove?"

"I think they were trying to prove something to me, Mary," I answered slowly. "I'm sure they didn't mean you any harm."

As I replaced the receiver I thought to myself: they're doing it, they're turning this old boy into a raving paranoiac.

The phone rang again. I picked it up wearily.

Beep, beep, beep, beep.

17:

"Even the Bedouins Hate Their Telephone Company"*

I.

Every phone call from Ivan Sanderson in New Jersey was an adventure in electronic lunacy. Weird whistles, static, beeps, and loud clicks like an extension being slammed down, haunted his line. Often we were cut off suddenly in the middle of a conversation. Sanderson's involvement in UFOs was strictly periphery. He was primarily a biologist and zoologist and earned a good part of his living writing animal encyclopedias. A tall, thin, handsome Britisher in his mid-fifties, Ivan was an electrifying personality. In his younger days he was familiar to television viewers as the animal expert on the old Garry Moore show, and even had his own program on NBC for a number of years.

In 1967, Ivan was under a great strain. Alma, his wife of thirty years, was terminally ill. Like all authors, he had con-

* *"Everybody* hates the telephone company. Even the Bedouins hate their telephone company." Line from the 1967 movie *The President's Analyst.*

stant financial problems. That summer he was feeling ill. Once he took to his bed and sweated profusely for forty-eight hours. And he confided to me that he had suffered a two-day siege with the cosmic clap,* the symptoms disappearing as suddenly and mysteriously as they began.

One day Jane called me with a message for "the man with skinny arms who wears dresses." Very few people knew that Ivan lounged around his farm in a skirtlike garment popular in Indonesia. The message suggested that he should take a certain kind of vitamin supplement. I passed this on to him and a few days later he called to tell me that he felt "100 percent better" as soon as he started the vitamin regimen.

That fall a woman connected with the air force and the Colorado University UFO project arranged to spend a weekend on Ivan's farm to go through his UFO files, which extended all the way back to the 1940s. She drove up from Washington, D.C., and when she arrived at his out-of-the-way farm on a narrow back road she was excited and nervous. While driving up the New Jersey turnpike she became aware of a panel truck following her. When she turned off the turnpike onto the country roads that would take her to Ivan's, the truck turned off and continued to follow her.

She stopped at a gas station and the truck pulled in behind her. The driver got out and approached her. He appeared very normal, she said, but his coveralls were very neatly pressed and his shoes were highly shined.

"I've been watching your tires," he told her. "I think there's a bad lump on one of your rear tires."

She looked but could see nothing wrong. The gas station attendant came out and the man got back into his truck and drove off. The lady continued her drive, following Ivan's complicated instructions—his farm was not easy to find—until she came to a small restaurant and decided to stop for

---

*Male UFO witnesses sometimes develop a temporary set of symptoms resembling gonorrhea.

a snack. The moment she stepped out of her car the man in coveralls reappeared.

"I'd really better have a look at that tire," he announced. Before she could protest, he crawled under the rear of her car. After fussing underneath the vehicle for two or three minutes he crawled back out.

"I guess it will be okay," he told her. "Where are you going?"

"Not far from here," she answered. Unnerved, she decided to forego the snack, jumped back into her car, and continued on to Ivan's.

As soon as Ivan heard the story he picked up his phone and called me. I snapped on my tape recorder and suggested that he should go out and look under the woman's car while I talked to her about the incident. She outlined the story to me, then Ivan came back on the line very excited.

"Listen, Keel," he began breathlessly. "There's some stuff on the bottom of her gas tank. Three big globs of it, placed in a very neat triangle, all equal distances apart."

When he described the "globs" to me a chill ran down my spine. He seemed to be describing a material I had handled in basic training when the army was hopelessly trying to turn me into a trained killer.

"It sounds like plastic explosive to me, Ivan," I declared. "Maybe you'd better call the police."

Ivan did just that. The police came out and carried away the substance. It proved to be an ordinary, harmless, putty-like material. The woman, who had a phenomenal memory, was able to recall the sign on the side of the truck which named an appliance company and a nearby town. But a police check failed to find any such company in that town.

The strangest part of this episode was my tape recording of our conversation that afternoon. We had an excellent connection with none of the usual interference. Ivan's voice on the tape came through loud and clear. But each time the woman spoke to me on the same phone and same line there was heavy static on the tape drowning out her voice completely! Yet we did not hear any static at all while we were talking.

Later Ivan theorized that the putty had been used to hold wires forming the antenna to a small electronic homing device. The man in the panel truck had gone to elaborate lengths to remove the device, Ivan speculated.

After this incident I began to have more problems with recording phone conversations. Whenever a contactee or mystery voice would call, the tape would just contain static. I switched to another, better recorder but the problem persisted. Even portions of conversations with Mary Hyre were drowned in static when she was discussing some of the more mysterious events in Point Pleasant. Somebody was not only able to manipulate my phone but also my tape recorder!*

II.

After many freakish phone conversations and exchanges of letters to nonexistent addresses, I had a definite date for the big December "EM effect." It was scheduled for December 15. By this time Mr. Apol had assumed a definite personality. He was as real to me as Cold was to Derenberger, although I would never meet him. I studied his psychology, his quick temper, his mischievous sense of humor. I argued with him on the phone, sometimes for two or three hours at a stretch. And I felt sorry for him. It became apparent that he really did not know who or what he was. He was a prisoner of our time frame. He often confused the past with the future. I gathered that he and all his fellow entities found themselves transported backward and forward in time involuntarily, playing out their little games because they

---

* Dr. Berthold Schwarz, a deputy police officer in Pennsylvania, and several other serious investigators have had similar problems with their tape recorders. Even former President Nixon had trouble with his tape recorder.

were programed to do so, living—or existing—only so long as they could feed off the energy and minds of mediums and contactees. I could ask him any kind of obscure question and receive an instant and accurate answer, perhaps because my own mind was being tapped just like my telephone. Where was my mother's father born? Cameron Mills, New York, of course. Where had I misplaced my stopwatch? Look in the shoebox in the upper right-hand corner of the bedroom closet (it was there).

On the weekend of October 7–8, 1967, my phone stopped ringing. My contactees and their friends did not call. The sudden silence was unnerving. But on Monday the ninth, they all began to check in, and they all told me identical stories. They recalled nothing except brief glimpses of some kind of hospital. Shirley said she went to sleep Thursday night and did not wake up again until Monday morning. Her baby was in his crib, happy and well cared for. Nothing in her house was disturbed. She mentioned that her feet were sore and her legs ached as if she had done a lot of walking. All she could remember was visiting a large structure made of red glass. Jane, too, remembered a red-glass building filled with strange beings in white coats, like doctors, who were examining lines of earth people, all of whom moved like robots apparently in a drugged state.

Beneath all the hallucinatory nonsense I could now perceive the roots of many of the ufological legends. A surprising number of contactees were orphans and through them the whole "hybrid" concept was launched. They were told that their parentage was a cross between terrestrial and extraterrestrial, that slowly more and more earthly women were being impregnated by spacemen and eventually the whole planet would be populated with a hybrid race. Some of the games I was involved in were obviously designed to convince me of the reality of this crossbreeding experiment. But I knew it was just an updated version of the biblical begatting theme when the "sons of God went into the daughters of men."

I noted that as soon as my attitude toward a game changed, the entities switched to a new game. My pregnant contactees suddenly became unpregnant.

I was more concerned with squeezing accurate predictions for the future out of my mysterious friends. The dollar, I was told, would soon be devalued. (It wasn't devalued until years later.) Red China would be admitted to the United Nations (correct, but it seemed very unlikely in 1967). Robert Kennedy should "stay out of hotels"(?). Man should not attempt to go to the moon (they were apoplectic over our space program). I would soon be moving to a new apartment on the ground floor of a building north of the United Nations. (This also seemed very unlikely in 1967, but a year later I did find a ground-floor apartment in upper Manhattan and moved.)

In addition to the continuing warnings about the December power blackout, the entities now began to tell me about a terrible forthcoming disaster on the Ohio River. Many people would die, they said. They implied that one of the factories along the Ohio would blow up. On November 3, 1967, I wrote to Mary Hyre and told her: "I have reason to suspect there may soon be a disaster in the Point Pleasant area which will not be related to the UFO mystery. A plant along the river may either blow up or burn down. Possibly the navy installation in Pt. Pleasant will be the center of such a disaster. A lot of people may be hurt. . . . Don't even hint to anybody anything about this."

(The naval installation was a fenced-in area in Point Pleasant, facing the river and tightly guarded. The men who worked there were sworn to secrecy, but during my first visit it only took me a few days to find out what was going on there. I am not going to reveal any national secrets here, but my private conclusion was that some admiral in the Pentagon should get his ass kicked for wasting the taxpayers' money . . . and for putting this type of installation in a populated area.)

Meanwhile the Public Broadcasting Laboratories was having second thoughts about Dan Drasin's UFO special. After nearly a year of work, and several trips to UFO flap areas, the program was suddenly canceled. History repeated itself in 1973 when Fred Freed, an award-winning producer, began work on a white paper documentary for NBC News. Ralph Blum and a team of technicians were in Mississippi interviewing Hickson and Parker when they suddenly received word that the program was being canceled because NBC needed the money and personnel to cover the Arab-Israeli War.

I had other problems. I was going through one of my broke periods and owed the staggering sum of four hundred dollars in back taxes. The IRS sent a representative around to see me every single week. Once, two different IRS men turned up in the same week. (They were not MIB . . . but were definitely from the IRS.) One seedy little character was so obnoxious and insulting that I actually grabbed him by the collar and physically threw him out of the apartment. Another let slip a remark about a movie deal I was working on (it eventually fell through) which no one, not even my friends, knew about. The only way he could have known about it was through listening to my telephone conversations.

Was the IRS tapping my phone for a lousy four hundred dollars? Was I on somebody's "Enemies" list?

I was complaining to the telephone company about my many crank calls and telephone interference, so I asked them to run a check and see if my phone was being tapped. A few days later my friendly telephone representative called me back.

"You were right, Mr. Keel," she said. "Somebody *is* definitely tapped into your phone."

I switched on my tape recorder and asked her to repeat the statement, which she did. Then I asked her to put it in writing, but she hedged there.

"Do you have any idea who's tapping it?" I asked.

"We can't tell that. All we know is there's a drop in the voltage that indicates that someone is hooked up to it."

She promised to turn the matter over to a "Special Agent" for investigation. Nothing ever came of that, either.

When I woke up on July 3, 1967, my line was dead. I went down to the basement of my apartment building to call the phone company on a pay phone. As I walked along the basement corridor I saw the door to the telephone room, which was normally locked, was wide open and a man in coveralls was there surrounded by the jumble of wires from the hundreds of phones in the building. I told him my phone was dead and he only shrugged.

"You'll have to call the main office," was his not very helpful advice.

My service did not resume for another twenty-four hours.

Although all my contactee calls were incoming, my phone bills started to skyrocket that summer. I was out of the city and away from my phone for two or three weeks at a time, but when I returned I would find a phone bill for $150–$200 waiting.

And that was just the beginning.

III.

A reporter on the *Daily American* in West Frankfort, Illinois, picked up his phone on February 17, 1967, and heard a weird echo chamber voice which instructed him to be at a certain pond at 3:15 A.M. the following Sunday. The reporter motioned to his co-workers and they picked up extensions to listen in. The voice immediately said, "Tell them to put down their phones." Electronic sounds beeped and whistled behind the hollow speaker. "Bring no one with you."

The newsmen decided it was all a joke but that it "was a first-rate performance . . . whoever that was had talent and electronic equipment to work with."

In my travels I found that newspaper offices all over the country have received these calls, usually hollow voices that sound "like they're in the bottom of a well," with background sounds like electronic music or Teletypes. The purpose of the background is simple enough . . . it makes it impossible to tape the voices. I've tried and found that the background completely smothered the voice on the tape.

I kept a careful log of the crank calls I received and eventually cataloged the various tactics of the mysterious pranksters. Some of these tactics are so elaborate they could not be the work of a solitary nut harassing UFO believers in his spare time. Rather, it all appears to be the work of either paranormal forces or a large and well-financed organization with motives that evade me.

From my years in show business I know that talented mimics are rare and that some voices are almost impossible to imitate. Nevertheless, our hypothetical Organization is able to mimic almost anyone—including myself. And I have a flat, colorless voice somewhat like former Vice-President Spiro Agnew's. Professional mimics like Rich Little and David Frye were never able to get Agnew's voice down pat.

At 1 A.M. on the morning of Friday, July 14, 1967, I received a call from a man who identified himself as Gray Barker from West Virginia. The voice sounded exactly like Gray's softly accented mellifluous own, but he addressed me as if I were a total stranger and carefully called me "Mr. Keel." At first I wondered if maybe he hadn't been out celebrating. The quiet, familiar drawl told me that he knew I wrote for newspapers and he had just heard about a case which he thought I should look into. It was, he said, similar to the Deren*stein* case. Gray and I had visited Woodrow

Derenberger together so I knew this was not the kind of mistake he would make.

Around that time I had received a number of reports from people in the New York area who had been receiving nuisance calls from a woman who identified herself as "Mrs. Gray Barker." I knew that Gray was not married but when I mentioned these calls to this "Gray Barker" he paused for a moment and then said, "No, Mrs. Barker hasn't been calling anybody up there." He returned to his recital of an absurdly insignificant UFO sighting near West Mifflin, Pennsylvania. It was not the kind of incident that would have inspired a long-distance call. Later I did try to check it out and found all the information he gave me was false.

We talked for about ten minutes and throughout that period "Gray" sounded like a man under duress . . . as though someone was holding a gun to his head. I tricked him several times with different meaningless references and by the time I hung up I was definitely convinced that this man was not the real Gray Barker.

An hour later my phone rang again and a young man said, "Gray *Baker* has been trying to reach you . . . he asked us to give you this number and to please call him." He recited a number that was identical to my own except for the last digit.

There were more calls from strangers that night, and more pointless messages from Gray *Baker*.

The next day I called Gray long distance and he denied having placed the call, naturally.

Soon after that I discovered that another "John Keel" had been phoning people around the country, imitating my voice and mannerisms exactly. Mary Hyre received one such call. I phoned her a few days afterward and she said, "I'm glad you're feeling better . . . you sounded sick or drunk the other night."

"What other night?"

"When you called a couple of nights ago. Remember we

talked about your letter and what you thought was going to happen on the river."

I had not called her and discussed the letter. Nor had I discussed the disaster prediction with anyone other than the contactees who were told about it.

Jaye P. Paro called me one morning to complain.

"You must think I'm crazy. I wouldn't go up to Mount Misery alone at midnight."

"What are you talking about?" I demanded.

"Last night. You called and told me to meet you on Mount Misery."

"I didn't call you last night, Jaye, and I certainly wouldn't ask you to do such a thing anyway."

"You're putting me on. It sounded exactly like you."

I spent most of March 1968 in Washington, D.C. While I was gone an old army buddy, a serious, quiet man who worked in advertising, stayed in my apartment. He was totally reliable and not a practical joker. When I returned I found a stack of messages from phone calls he had received while I was gone. One was from George Clark, a UFO enthusiast in New Jersey. He had called on March 23 and asked for me to call him back. I never got around to it. So a few days later he called again and I apologized for not returning his previous call. There was a stunned silence on the other end and then he slowly told me that I *had* called him back around 10 P.M. on March 27. A voice that sounded exactly like mine had talked to him at length, using my pet expressions and noncommittal statements such as, "Well, we'll just have to wait and see what happens next."

Two days later George said he called my number again around 8 P.M. and a "hippie" answered. "No, man, Mr. Keel ain't here right now . . . but he ought to be back soon. Would you like to leave a message, man?" George left a message with him.

That particular evening I was back in New York and sitting next to my phone.

Three months earlier, on January 18, 1968, my phone went dead again. The main office of my exchange could find nothing wrong, so a repairman was dispatched to my apartment. He examined my telephone but it seemed okay. I accompanied him to the basement where he unlocked the telephone room and began examining the maze of wires. The multitude of connections are coded in such a vague way that only a real expert can pick out an individual line.

"This is where your line is connected," he explained to me. "And you see ... " He stopped and stared at the wires. "Look at this. This wire has been cut." He waved a neatly snipped wire. Someone had managed to single out my telephone line in that maze and cut it with a pair of pliers!

As soon as the wire was spliced and my phone was working again I called my friendly telephone representative.

"*This* I must have in writing," I snapped.

A few days later I received a letter from her stating that my phone had become disconnected on January 18 because *a piece of solder in the main office had loosened.* I knew there was only one piece of solder on my line in the main exchange and I had examined it personally only the month before.

Between the IRS, the phone company, Apol and his gang, and flying saucers I was rapidly becoming a candidate for the funny farm.

18:

"Something Awful Is Going to Happen ..."

I.

Mrs. Virginia Thomas was working in her kitchen deep inside the TNT area when she heard a loud squeaking sound unlike anything she had ever heard before in her years there.

"The best way I can describe it," she told Mrs. Hyre and me, "is that it was like a bad fan belt . . . but much louder. I stepped outside. It seemed to be coming from one of the igloos. Then I saw a huge shadow spreading across the grass. It was just after noon so there shouldn't have been any shadow like that. Then this figure appeared. It walked erect like a man, but it was all gray, and it was much bigger than any man I ever saw. It moved very fast across the field and disappeared into the trees. It didn't seem to be walking exactly. It was almost gliding . . . faster than any man could run.

"It was the hunting season so I knew it wasn't a hunter. No hunter in his right mind would dress in gray. Around here they all wear red coats and red caps. And it wasn't a bear or anything like that. It really scared me."

Since that sighting on November 2, 1967, Mrs. Thomas had been plagued by bad dreams.

"I see a lot of strange people around the river," she explained. "It's like some kind of invasion or something. They come over the bridge in trucks and they pour into the TNT area. We grab the kids and run. I can't figure out what it means."

I had flown to West Virginia after a trip to Atlanta and a quick tour through the Carolinas investigating some UFO landings. Mrs. Hyre had picked me up at the Charleston airport, and as we drove to Point Pleasant she told me about her own dreams.

"Just before I got your letter," she said, "I had a terrible nightmare. There were a lot of people drowning in the river and Christmas packages were floating everywhere in the water."

"Maybe you were just picking up my thoughts somehow," I suggested.

"Maybe. But I've covered a lot of drownings on that river, but never anything like this dream. There were so many people. I've been feeling uneasy ever since. And everybody else feels the same way. You can't really put your finger on it . . . but it's like something awful is about to happen."

Perhaps it was only suggestion and an emotional hangover from all I had been going through, but when we reached Point Pleasant I could feel a heavy atmosphere of foreboding. I wandered around the village under an oppressive cloud. One by one, old friends confided in me. "You know, Keel, something is wrong here. I don't know what. Ever since all that flying saucer business last spring things just haven't seemed right."

"We don't get many UFO reports anymore," Mary told me. "And except for that thing Mrs. Thomas saw, Mothman seems to be laying low. Everything is quiet. Too quiet."

Toward midnight on November 19, Mary and I were cruising through the TNT area. The sky was heavily overcast. It had been raining earlier and no stars were visible. The cloud ceiling was probably below five thousand feet.

"Don't look now, Mary," I said lightly. "But there's one of our friends straight ahead."

A brilliant light was bouncing around in the blackened sky over a row of hills far to the east. Mary stopped the car and we watched it silently for about ten minutes. It dropped down, then shot upward again. It slid from side to side, moving several degrees and then returning to its original position. Finally, Mary started her car again and drove slowly along the dirt road, hoping to find a better vantage point. We passed through a wooded section and when we reached another clearing the object was gone.

"Well, what do you think?" she asked laconically.

"It definitely wasn't a star or a plane," I observed. "It was so low somebody else was bound to have seen it. Let's wait and see if we get any reports."

We didn't have to wait long. At 12:45 that morning Mr. Albert Brown, a shift superintendent at a mine near Elmwood, West Virginia, was driving home from work when he, too, noticed an unusual light weaving around the sky. He stopped his car and watched.

"It seemed to turn colors," he told us later. "First it was white, then blue, then orange. It looked like it was going down on top of a hill."

Mr. Brown was northeast of the TNT area on Route 35, approximately twenty miles from our position in a direct line. After watching the object for a few minutes, he tried to find a road that might lead him into the hills where the object seemed to be "playing." But he couldn't find such a road, so he simply parked and watched, enthralled. Finally he went home and called the Civil Defense in Charleston. They told him to call the state police. A police car was sent to the area but the thing was gone by the time they arrived.

Who or what was on that remote hilltop, I wondered? Was some little cabin being bathed in an eerie light? Was some lonely person there staring fixedly, paralyzed, into the night?

II.

From West Virginia I went to Washington, D.C. Al Johnson, an old army friend, was working for Voice of America and he had been doing a series of broadcasts on flying saucers, covering every aspect. (VOA is our official propaganda outlet and Johnson's pro-UFO programs were heard around the world.) In the VOA studios we taped an hour-long discussion on the subject, covering everything from purple blobs to contactees.

Finally I returned to my New York apartment at 2 A.M. in early December, nursing a heavy cold, a souvenir of the freezing West Virginia rains, exhausted. Before I even had a chance to take off my coat the telephone jangled.

Dan Drasin was on the line and I had never heard him in such a state. His normally calm voice dripped with terror.

"How can I stop all this, Keel?" he cried.

"Stop what?"

"All the things that have been happening. I want to quit. I want out!"

"Look, I just got in. What's wrong? What's been happening?"

"Everything. I can't take it anymore."

I knew Dan didn't drink or take drugs, and I certainly never expected him to go to pieces.

"There's only one way 'out,' Dan. This damned thing becomes an obsession . . . a fixation. The only way to stop all the nonsense it to stop thinking about UFOs. Get rid of all your files. Take up stamp collecting or chasing women. The UFO business is emotional quicksand. The more you struggle with it, the deeper you sink."

I finally calmed him. A few days later he gave me part of

his files and destroyed the rest. I returned his files to him a year or so later. I asked him many times about what prompted that frantic phone call but he would never discuss it.

The day after I returned, Al Johnson called. The tape of our interview had been accidentally erased, he said. He wanted me to come to Washington and do another one, which I finally did several months later. An engineer had accidentally placed the first tape on a pile to be erased. Such errors were becoming routine to me. On one occasion, a German reporter came to my apartment with a camera crew to interview me for German television. Originally he planned to shoot about fifteen minutes of film, but I was so brilliant, charming and informative that we ended up doing a full half-hour. A few days later he phoned me.

"We can't understand it, Mr. Keel," he began, with dismay in his voice. "But the footage we shot in your apartment isn't usable. Parts of it are overexposed and sections of the sound track are filled with static."

The same reporter, incidently, had visited Derenberger in West Virginia and was present when Woody announced, "Cold is over the house right now." They went outside, and, sure enough, a large luminous blob was soaring casually overhead.

Strange things happened to the written word, too. I was at Ivan's farm one afternoon when a New York editor called and demanded to know what had become of a UFO story Ivan had promised him.

"I sent it to you a week ago," Ivan protested.

When we went into town to pick up the mail there was a large manila envelope with a Florida postmark. Ivan opened it and threw the contents down in disgust. It was the UFO story which he had mailed to New York the week before! Somehow it had gone to Florida instead and someone had remailed it back to him.

My own problems were equally bizarre. The editor of a

short-lived occult magazine asked me to contribute an article, "anything . . . it can just be something from your trunk." I dug out a short, unpublished piece from my files and mailed it to him. There was a deafening silence. A couple of weeks later I met him for lunch and he pulled out a sheaf of papers.

"I'm afraid we really can't use this, John," he said. He handed me a dog-eared manuscript, single-spaced in elite type. I have always used pica type and automatically double-space my manuscripts. My name and address were at the top of this masterpiece and it had arrived at his office in one of my envelopes. As I read it I could see that it was a real piece of garbage. To this day I don't know what happened to my manuscript, or how the trashy substitute was switched with it.

When I returned to New York in December I found that my entire stable of contactees was mourning my passing. Apol, Lia, Cloe, and their band of poseurs had convinced them all that I had come to an untimely end in a mine cave-in. This marked the beginning of a new phase. It was no more Mr. Nice Guy. The entities spread vicious rumors, turned against the contactees, and terrified them. Jane woke up one night to find all the gas jets on her kitchen stove were turned on and the house was filling with fumes. The same thing happened to Shirley, and on the same night. Fred Miller, an elderly Long Island farmer who entertained men in shiny spacesuits in his kitchen, suffered a rash of mysterious fires.

Even the old devil and Daniel Webster theme was dusted off. Harassed contactees were ordered to sign an impressive-looking piece of parchment, allegedly a contract for their beleaguered souls. I was caught up in the game, playing old Daniel's role, arguing with demons to save the contactees. They let me win, of course, having proved their point. Good and evil were synonomous in their phantasmagorical world.

When Linda Scarberry gave birth to a baby girl that

month she decided to name her Daniella Lia. No one other than a couple of contactees knew of the Indian-like entity named Lia. Linda had just picked the name from left field because she liked it. Later Dan Drasin told me his mother's name was Lia . . . a fact I had not known. Neither had Linda.

Synchronocity all over the place!

On my way to see an editor of *True* magazine one afternoon, the elevator in the Fawcett building stopped inexplicably between floors and the lights went out for several seconds. That night a contactee called to tell me she had met Mr. Apol and he was chuckling over how I had been "stuck in an elevator."

The big "EM effect" slated for December 15 was now more clearly defined. The space people were timing it so it would coincide with the annual Christmas tree ceremony on the White House lawn, I was told. At the very moment when President Lyndon Johnson threw the switch to light up the tree, the power all over the country would fail. Knowing the entities' perverse sense of humor, and impressed by the accuracy of many of their previous predictions, I bought this lock, stock, and barrel.

My biggest concern, however, was my telephone. My bills were now astronomical. I was constantly being cut off in the middle of conversations, or foreign sounds were injected into my line. Somebody would strum a one-stringed guitar or blow a shrill whistle while I was talking. Like Ivan, I often heard the distinct sound of an extension being picked up or put down. Electronic beeps, eerie music, hollow metallic voices, all became common on the blasted instrument. My gentle protests to the telephone company turned into howls of rage. I demanded the privilege to personally examine my telephone line from one end to the other. And the telephone company granted permission.

On December 13 I visited the main office of my telephone exchange a few blocks from my apartment building. A technician and a young "Special Agent" met me at the door and escorted me through the entire building. The security measures were impressive. Every floor consisted of a series of locked rooms. My escorts were constantly fiddling with keys.

My line passed through the walls of my apartment building to the telephone room in the basement. The lines were built into the walls when the building was constructed so there was no way they could be tapped in the house itself. The basement room was always locked. There my line was hooked to a line which traveled in a tube under the city streets to the exchange building. Here again, a tap was impossible. If any tap existed, it had to be in the basement telephone room or in the exchange building.

Inside the exchange, the tube came out in a locked room and my line was separated from the others and soldered to a set of terminals which were connected to wires leading to the dialing mechanism. I had studied books on the telephone system and I knew exactly how all this machinery worked. The only thing that impressed me was the age of all the equipment. Most of it had been built and installed in the 1920s. It would be a compliment to call it junk. It was all antique. Some rooms contained apparatus so old it looked like young Tom Edison's laboratory. There were coils, meters, switches, and rheostats that were outdated when Marconi was sending his first signals across the Atlantic.

However, all this rickety debris appeared to be in good working condition.

In another locked room a group of people were working with a device called a "pen register." This was a gadget that could be patched into any telephone line to record every number dialed on that phone. A moving pen wrote the number on a strip of paper. Thus the telephone company could obtain a record of every local call made on a given phone (long-distance calls are automatically recorded on another, more elaborate device).

If anyone was tapping my phone, they had to do it from

the two terminals at the tube outlet. Or a connection had to be made at that point and the wires strung to another room. The locked doors and tight security meant that only authorized snoops could connect such a tap. And, as I learned later, the New York Telephone Company was very uncooperative; even the FBI was refused access. Police tappers usually had to figure out a way to do it themselves without the help of the phone company.

I must admit I was impressed by the tour. It seemed impossible for anyone to tap my phone.

Three months later, however, I accidentally discovered what was probably the answer to many of my problems. A friend dialed my number and her finger slipped. Instead of dialing the last two digits—four eight—correctly, she dialed four zero. She realized instantly what she had done and was about to hang up and redial when I answered the phone! She told me what she had done and I suggested we hang up and try four zero again. Again my phone rang. I had two phone numbers and never knew it! I asked other friends to try the four zero number. Sometimes my phone would ring and I would answer. Other times my phone would remain silent but someone else would answer and would offer to "take a message for Mr. Keel." I called the four zero number from a pay phone and someone picked it up.

"Hi, this is John Keel," I said cheerily. "Any messages for me?"

There was an audible gasp on the other end and they slammed the receiver down.

Obviously I was getting four zero's phone bills. I asked my friendly telephone representative to track down the owner of that other phone. But, of course, she could not "give out that information."

So I went to the FBI to lodge a formal complaint. When you visit the New York FBI office you are ushered into one of several small cubicles where a polite young man hears you out sympathetically. You can imagine the loonies and weirdos who must pester the FBI day after day. But after hearing a summary of my story, my man escorted me to another room where I was interviewed by a group of older agents who were obviously extremely interested in my problems. They expressed surprise that I had been given a tour of the exchange building. This was unheard of. The FBI and CIA hate each other, and they both hate the telephone company. The telephone company, in turn, seems to hate everybody.

In April 1968, my outrageous phone bills were unpaid so my service was cut off, both incoming and outgoing. I simply told everyone to use the four zero number. Although my line was supposedly disconnected at the main exchange, I continued to receive phone calls. The line should have been totally dead . . . but there was power coming through on it from somewhere. Technically this should have been impossible unless—unless the New York Telephone Company was the one who was tapping my phone!

Phones in the country are much easier to tap. Lines strung across the countryside offer easy access. It is even possible to mount a small induction coil next to the telephone box on the subject's house. Modern technology is so sophisticated that a physical tap is not necessary. A panel truck containing the necessary equipment can simply park near the telephone line and pick up all the conversations like a radio signal.

In the 1960s there were many mysterious panel trucks cruising around flap areas and sometimes they went to great pains to focus attention on telephones and telephone lines. One tactic was what I call the "silver tape gambit." Lengths of silver tape are strung rather meaninglessly on the telephone poles close to the subject's home. I came across this several times and collected some samples of the tape. It was not electrical tape such as might be used by telephone repairmen but was a common weather insulating tape available in almost any hardware store.

"There was also evidence at this time that [the witnesses's] phone had been tampered with," Jennifer Stevens reported from Albany, New York, in 1968. "She observed two 'light Negroid types' with completely expressionless faces, stringing 'silver tape' on the wires near her home. Since they did not have an official telephone company car, she called the police. The men left before the officers arrived and the only comment made by police was: 'Oh, the silver tape *again*.'"

In March 1968, a large four-engined plane with no visible markings skirted the treetops over Henderson, West Virginia, just south of Point Pleasant, and discharged a large quantity of silver tape over the trees in the area. Sheriff George Johnson collected some of it and passed samples on to me. Matching samples I had collected from Ohio, Florida, and several other places, it was identical to the stuff being used by our mystery men. Since the tapes are extremely sticky (the glue is about equal to the glue on contac paper) one wonders how a fast-moving plane was able to discharge it in a stream and what was the point of the exercise?

III.

The U.S. Air Force had lied to me. The telephone company lied to me. The UFO entities lied to me. My own senses had, on occasion, lied to me. As December 15 drew closer I kept my mouth shut and told no one that I expected a major blackout. After all, Pope Paul had escaped assassination in Turkey. None of the chemical factories along the Ohio had exploded. Maybe this was just another mischievous error of prophecy, or a description of something in the past or far in the future.

A security officer for the Transit Authority and an old friend of mine, Joe Woodvine, happened to drop by my apartment late on the afternoon of the fifteenth. I hadn't seen him in a long time and he knew nothing about UFOs and my capers. I didn't mention the blackout until Dan Drasin stopped in. Joe listened in open-mouthed amazement as I explained to Dan that I expected the nation to blow a fuse the moment President Johnson pulled that switch. Dan was as far gone as I was. He glanced nervously at his watch and decided that if there was going to be a blackout he preferred to be in his own apartment. Joe became very silent, probably wondering if we were dangerous.

Dan left about 5 P.M. I switched on the television. At 5:45 the brief White House ceremony began. I broke out my candles and flashlights. Joe watched me worriedly. President Johnson delivered the customary little speech to the crowd on the White House lawn, reached for the switch, and the Christmas tree blazed with light. The crowd oooed and ahhed as if they had never seen a Christmas tree before. My lights did not go out. Joe studied me silently.

Suddenly an announcer's voice came over the crowd noises.

"We interrupt this program," he announced flatly," for a special bulletin. A bridge laden with rush-hour traffic has just collapsed at Gallipolis, Ohio. Further details as soon as they are available."

I fell back in my chair. There was no bridge at Gallipolis, Ohio. The only bridge on that stretch of the river was the seven hundred-foot Silver Bridge at Point Pleasant. The bridge I had crossed a thousand times.

"They've done it again," I finally muttered softly. "Those lousy bastards have done it again. They knew this was going to happen . . . and when. And they gave me all that bilge about a power failure. They knew. They just didn't want me to be able to warn anyone."

"They . . . who's 'they,' John?" Joe asked gently.

The phone rang. It was Dan.

"Did you hear?"

"I heard. I guess that's what it was all about, Dan. That's what it was all about."

19:

"Where
the Birds Gather . . ."*

I.

Thirteen months to the day (November 15, 1966–December 15, 1967) the year of the Garuda came to an end. Like some evil specter of death, Mothman and the UFOs had focused national attention on quiet little Point Pleasant and lured scores of reporters and investigators like myself to the Ohio River valley. When the Silver Bridge died of old age many of these same reporters returned once again to the village to revisit old friends and to share the pain of that tragic Christmas. Wherever you were, you watched the agonized aftermath on national television and read about Point Pleasant on the front pages of your local newspapers.

The Silver Bridge was constructed in 1928 and was an engineering marvel in its day. It became a main artery from West Virginia to Ohio, but had not been designed for the

---

* On June 16, 1967, Mrs. Gladys Fusaro of Huntington, New York, received a phone call from a woman claiming to be Princess Moon Owl. The princess gave her this statement to pass on to me: "The pebbles on the beach are washed under the bridge where the birds gather and where rays of light show through."

heavy traffic of the 1960s. Huge trucks lumbered across it continuously. People on both sides of the river crossed it daily to shop, go to work, visit friends. The next nearest bridge was almost fifty miles upriver.

On the Ohio side of the river, at the little cluster of shops and dwellings called Kanauga, the stoplight at the mouth of the bridge was malfunctioning that afternoon. It was stuck on green and the rush-hour traffic along Route 7 was creeping past in confusion. Traffic was backing up in both directions and at 5 P.M. the bridge was laden with slow-moving lines of cars and trucks in both directions. The light on the Point Pleasant side had always been recalcitrant, remaining red for so long that many regular bridge users had learned to ignore it. Running the light was a common practice.

Frank Wamsley, a twenty-eight-year-old truck driver, was on his way home to Point Pleasant, riding in a gravel truck with a friend. They found the traffic backed up on the Ohio side. It was to be a black day for the Wamsley family.

On the West Virginia side, Frank's cousin Barbara and her husband, Paul Hayman, were starting across the bridge in their 1955 Pontiac. And his uncle, Marvin Wamsley, was also on the bridge with two friends in a 1956 Ford convertible.

Bill Needham, twenty-seven, of Ashboro, North Carolina, was muttering under his breath because he had been caught in the 5 o'clock rush hour. He inched his loaded tractor-trailer forward in a low gear. His partner, R. E. Towe, sat beside him in patient silence.

"The old bridge is sure bouncing around today," Howard Boggs, twenty-four, commented to his wife, Marjorie, nineteen. She was holding their eighteen-month-old daughter, Christie. There were several small children on the bridge, riding with their Christmas-shopping mothers.

"The bridge was shaking, but then it always shook," William Edmondson, thirty-eight, of King, North Carolina, said later. His partner, Harold Cundiff, was sound asleep in their tractor-trailer.

The traffic jam worsened. The streams of cars and trucks ground to a halt. The old bridge shuddered and squirmed under the weight.

Frank Wamsley spotted his cousin Barbara and her husband and waved to them. Just ahead, he saw Marvin and his two friends. Suddenly the whole bridge convulsed.

The time was 5:04 P.M.

Steel screamed. The seven hundred-foot suspension bridge twisted and the main span split from its moorings at either end. Electric cables strung across the bridge snapped in a blaze of sparks. Fifty vehicles crashed into the black waters of the Ohio, tons of steel smashing down on top of them.

"It sounded like someone moving furniture upstairs, and then the lights went out," State Trooper R. E. O'Dell said. He was in an insurance office a block from the bridge. "When the lights went out, I guess they really just flickered for a minute, I knew something was wrong. I thought maybe it was a wreck, so I ran outside."

Mrs. Mary Hyre was in a drugstore on the Main Street, waiting for the traffic to ease so she could cross the bridge and pick up the daily notes from the Gallipolis Hospital.

"There was a sound like a jet plane or a plane going through the sound barrier," she said afterward. "A rumbling roar that hurt your eardrums. Then the lights flickered. My first thought was that something had blown up. I thought, 'My God, John was right! Something is exploding!' I ran outside and someone yelled, 'The bridge went down!'"

A Christmas tree salesman in Kanauga, H. L. Whobrey, dropped the tree he was holding. "The bridge just keeled over, starting slowly on the Ohio side, then following like a deck of cards to the West Virginia side. It was fantastic.

There was a big flash and a puff of smoke when the last of the bridge caved in, I guess the power line snapped.

"I saw three or four people swimming around in the water screaming. I couldn't do anything. I just stood there and watched. Then I saw a City Ice and Fuel boat come and pick them up."

Frank Wamsley saw the bridge in front of him tilt sharply and suddenly there was water all around him. "I went all the way to the bottom with the truck. For a minute I didn't think I was going to get out. Finally I got out and came to the surface and I caught hold of something and held on and was soon picked up." When a boat pulled alongside he found he could not move his legs and had to be helped aboard. His back was fractured.

Howard Boggs found himself on the bottom of the river, outside his car. "I don't know how I got out of the car, or how I got to the surface. But all at once I was on top and caught hold of something, like a big cotton ball."

His wife and child didn't make it.

Bill Needham's truck also sank to the bottom but he somehow managed to force a window and reach the surface.

"You could see and hear people screaming for help," Mary Hyre described the scene. "I saw a tractor-trailer that floated a little before it sank, and a car and merchandise floating on the water. People on the West Virginia side of the river were so upset they could hardly realize what was going on.

"You could hear people saying, 'This can't be true . . . you read about things like this in the papers, but it can't be happening here . . .'"

Like Howard Boggs, William Edmundson suddenly found himself on the surface of the water, clinging to a truck seat. He had no idea how he'd escaped from his vehicle. His partner didn't surface.

"When I got there I could see this truck floating in the

water," Trooper O'Dell explained. "There was a fellow hanging on the side of it. Then they sank. I don't know if he got out."

People came running from all directions, silent, ashened-faced, knowing their friends and relatives could be out there in the icy water now covered with debris and soggy, gaily wrapped Christmas packages. Boats of all kinds crisscrossed the river picking up survivors.

On both sides of the river people who had been waiting in the lines to drive over the bridge were crying. Some had to be treated for shock.

Night was closing in quickly. Boats with searchlights turned their beams onto the bridge and the surrounding water. A horrible silence fell over Point Pleasant. Sheriff Johnson's tall, spare figure stood on the water's edge.

"Put out a general call for rescue units," he told a deputy softly. "And get everyone here. Block all the roads. Don't let anyone but rescue units into town."

Mary Hyre pulled her coat around her pudgy frame and walked slowly to her office, tears running down her face, her years of experience overriding her emotions. She pushed open the door and walked to her phones. They were dead. She switched on the Teletype machine and started to peck away with two fingers.

"At 5:04 P.M. this afternoon . . ."

Sirens wailed outside and the crowds grew. A girl was screaming hysterically in front of the office. "I almost got killed . . . I could have been on there . . . all those people dead . . . I could have been killed."

II.

Two miles north of the bridge, Mrs. Jackie Lilly was in a grocery store waiting for her teen-aged children. They were planning to go bowling in the alleys on the other side of the river that night. Her husband, Jim, was away, working on his boat.

At 5:20 Gary and Johnny Lilly rushed breathlessly into the store.

"The bridge just fell in the river," Johnny declared.

"That's not very funny," his mother replied.

"It's true. The old bridge just collapsed," Gary said grimly. "And it was full of cars."

Johnny, who was married, drove them home to their little house on Camp Conley Road. Mrs. Lilly headed for a phone. It was dead. As Johnny drove off, dashing back to Point Pleasant to be with his wife, Gary, eighteen, turned on the television set and searched for a news program.

A few minutes later Gary glanced out of the picture window in the living room and gasped.

"There's something out there!" he exclaimed.

Mrs. Lilly looked out and saw a flashing red light disappearing over the trees.

"Do you think those things are back?" Gary asked.

"It was probably an airplane," she answered. But she turned off the lights in the living room so they could see better into the darkness outside.

A few minutes later a second light appeared, moving in the same direction as the first. It was one of those glaringly bright prismatic lights so familiar to the residents of Camp Conley Road. They went outside to watch it.

"It wasn't an airplane," Mrs. Lilly assured me later. "It was one of those things, bobbing up and down like they do. There wasn't any sound."

For the next hour, Mrs. Lilly, Gary, and daughter Linda divided their attention between the TV set and the eerie aerial activity outside. "We counted twelve of them," Mrs. Lilly reported. "Most of them were just above the treetops. They seemed to be coming down from up around the TNT area and moved south toward the town."

The hundreds of people milling around the streets of Point Pleasant did not see anything in the skies that night, however. Perhaps the objects followed their old route, dipping into the ravine behind North Park and cutting eastward to the hills.

"I was getting scared," Mrs. Lilly recalled. "We'd never seen so many of these things in one night. I kept trying the phone, wanting to get somebody to drive out and pick us up and take us out of there."

Finally around 9 P.M. she got a dial tone and was able to place a call to a neighbor who drove over, picked them up, and took them to the home of Mrs. Lilly's mother in Point Pleasant.

A few months later James Lilly moved his family away from Camp Conley Road.

III.

Around 2 A.M. I finally got a line through to Point Pleasant and was very much relieved when Mary Hyre picked up her phone. She spoke very slowly, obviously exhausted.

"It's the most terrible thing I've ever seen," she told me. "But I was kind of prepared for it. You know those dreams I had . . . well, it was exactly like that. The packages floating in the water. The people crying for help. Those dreams came true."

"Is everyone all right?" I asked anxiously. "The McDaniels, Connie, the others."

"I think so. It'll be awhile before we know who was on the bridge. There could have been as many as one hundred people. Some of them were rescued. But an awful lot of them are trapped under all that metal."

After a month of brutally hard work, divers and rescue teams recovered thirty-eight bodies. Several other people in Ohio and West Virginia were never heard from again and it was assumed they also went down with the bridge. A number of UFO witnesses were among the dead.

"I talked to one woman who lives right by the bridge," Mary continued. "She says that two days ago she saw two men climbing on the bridge."

"*Climbing* on it?"

"Yes. They weren't walking across. They were climbing around the sides of it."

"Was she able to describe them."

"They were wearing checkered coats and black trousers. She couldn't see their faces too well because they were so far away. But she did notice their shoes. They weren't wearing boots, just ordinary shoes. She thought that was odd because of the weather we'd been having."

"You'd better have the police talk with her, Mary," I said.

"I will. There's just so much to do. People are coming from all over. And as soon as my phone was working again I started getting calls from newspapers and radio stations all over the country."

"You'd better try to get some sleep."

"I know, but I just can't leave the office now. Ambulances and rescue trucks are coming in from all over. They'll be working all night. I've got to be there."

Later the bridge was lifted from the water piece by piece and reconstructed in a field near Henderson. Engineers finally determined the collapse was due to metal fatigue and structural failure.

"John," Mary began hesitantly, "do you think this had anything to do with UFOs and the 'Bird'?"

"There's no answer to that, Mary. Maybe there were people on the bridge that could have told us something. I knew the condition of the bridge. And I'd had warnings about something terrible that was going to happen. If I could have put things together sooner, maybe we could have saved all those lives."

"It's not your fault. Some things are just meant to be. You

can't change the future . . . even when you know what is going to happen."

I heard the sound of a woman weeping in the background.

"A woman just came in. Her husband is missing," Mary whispered.

After we hung up I sat for a long time by my big glass windows, looking out over the lights of Manhattan Island. For one long year my life had been intertwined with the lives of the people of Point Pleasant. I had been led into relationships and events that seemed to follow a structured pattern beyond my control. Even beyond my understanding. I had stood on those distant hills and watched those wretched bouncing lights mock me. In the months ahead there would be many changes in the lives of those who had been touched by the Garuda. Roger and Linda Scarberry would divorce, as would Woodrow Derenberger who, in what has become a tradition among contactees, would remarry . . . this time to a beautiful young woman who was also a contactee. They would slip away together to obscurity in another state. Others would eventually suffer nervous breakdowns and undergo long periods of hospitalization. A few would even commit suicide.

Death would claim too many of the participants in the dramas of 1967. Mrs. Mary Hyre passed away in 1970. Ivan T. Sanderson left us in 1973. Dr. Edward U. Condon, Fred Freed, and many others would be gone long before the tenth anniversary of the appearance of the winged thing in front of the old power plant. Some of the people who viewed the tall, hairy red-eyed monsters died within six months. Even Mr. Apol staged an odd departure, acting out a charade with the Men in Black that left him broken in spirit. He wasted away like a human suffering from a stroke until there was nothing left but his Cheshire smile.

Out there in the night those puzzling spheres of light still ply their ancient routes in the Mississippi and Ohio valleys. A new generation of young people stand on the hilltops, expectantly scanning the skies. Their elders, jaded by nearly thirty years of signs and wonders, no longer scoff. Believers in extraterrestrial visitants and saviors from outer space are now welcomed on the most respectable television shows to broadcast their propaganda for that imaginary world with its superior technology and its marvelously stupid representatives who adopt the names of ancient gods and moan they are prisoners of time.

People ask me still if I know what the future holds. But, just as I used Socratic irony in my investigations, I can only admit like Socrates that the more I learn the less I know. My glimpses of the future were all secondhand and were frequently garbled by accident or design.

All of the generations before ours were infested with false prophets, workers of wonders, and signs in the sky. In a sense, each generation is truly the Last Generation from their microscopic viewpoint. But our modern electronic Communications and sophisticated press agentry have given present-day prophets tools the ancients lacked. Ideas, no matter how bizarre or fallacious, can span the world in a flash. And there are always people ready to rally to any banner, no matter how absurd. In recent years we have seen a worldwide revival of interest in psychic phenomena and the supernatural. Stern no-nonsense scientists now drag their beards to Loch Ness to search for the monster, while others comb the woods of the Northwest seeking the Sasquatch, and still others soberly discuss robots from outer space with Mississippi fishermen. But gradually all these men are being drawn closer and closer to ontology; to an examination of the question that lies beyond the simplistic, "Can these things be?" The real question is, "Why are there these things?"

Like Mr. Apol and his merry crew of mischief-makers, we do not know who we are or what we are doing here. But we are slowly learning. Once we begin looking beyond the mere manifestations we will finally glimpse the real truth. Belief has always been the enemy of truth; yet, ironically, if our minds are supple enough, belief can sometimes open the door.

After spending a lifetime in Egyptian tombs, among the crumbling temples of India and the lamaseries of the Himalayas, endless nights in cemeteries, gravel pits, and hilltops everywhere, I have seen much and my childish sense of wonder remains unshaken. But Charles Fort's question always haunts me: "If there is a universal mind, must it be sane?"

Afterword

We had begun the 1900s with an unlimited number of beliefs about ourselves and our universe. The world seemed to be a bright and wonderful place. Famed astronomers assured us that Mars was also bustling with life along beautifully engineered canals. Automobiles and flying machines were being perfected. The 20th century was going to be terrific. But, by the end, we were embittered cynics, exhausted by wars and suspicious of mysteries and those who promoted them. The century had become a bloody scam.

For one hundred years, no matter where you lived on this ball of nitrogen, oxygen and cosmic spit, someone within two hundred miles of your home had personally seen a monster with big red eyes and, often, a penetrating stench. They were everywhere, along with the maddened dictators, publicity hungry generals and warlords, and wild-eyed scientists who kept mumbling incomprehensible formulae for manipulating things we could not see. Everyone was clearly nuts and very few of us were left alone to stumble through the forests, swamps and deserts, grimly determined to prove somehow that sanity would ultimately triumph.

We failed. Technology took over and our machines were nuttier than all of us. Our millionaires, who were multiplying like cockroaches, filtered their loot through TV networks, liquor companies, computer whizzes and assorted military contractors to try to capture dinosaurs in the Belgian Congo, giant sea serpents in the lochs of Ireland and Scotland, and tall, hairy humanoids in the Pacific Northwest, China, and Russia, along with kangaroos in the midwest and ghostly demons that mutilated cows and drank blood wherever they could find it. The end result was millions of bucks down the toilet while hundreds of bad movies and even worse TV shows were churned out, along with gigantic stacks of bad books that are still used to prop up tables in poorer communities.

Fortunately, I am a classier type. Let others chase little green men. No millionaire came knocking on my door with an offer to finance a search for the giant worms of Australia. But I must admit I once went to Norway and Sweden where unidentified submarines were causing an uproar. It turned out that American and Soviet subs were playing Cold War games with each other. The last really big UFO flap took place in Russia in the 1980s and that too proved to be a Cold War swindle.

Hoaxes, frauds and blatant chicanery have always been an important element of what really can be described as the carnival trade. For years, a huckster traveled the U.S. with a tent show of a stuffed Bigfoot in a tank of ice. People may still be paying admission to view that Hollywood creation. The Wright-Patterson Air Force Base has a public museum displaying things that supposedly came from flying saucers, including a couple of pancakes. Each year Nessie draws thousands of summer tourists to Loch Ness. Often Nessie is obligingly sighted just before the season starts. UFOs tend to appear in obscure places around the time of the solstices. Mothman—or "The Bird"—has been appearing almost constantly since the 1960s. He reportedly flapped around South Dakota in July, 2001. Judging from the endless mail and clippings that have poured in on me for over thirty years, Mothman seems to follow regular routes in several parts of the country. Red-eyed flying dragons also circle the globe periodically. Earlier, in the 1950s, we seemed inundated by them worldwide; but we eventually learned that the famous U-2 spy plane had one serious flaw. It glowed bright red while traveling at high speed through the upper stratosphere.

When I first visited Point Pleasant in the 1960s and talked to scores of witnesses, I was convinced I was on the track of a very big bird of spectacular size. I have no idea what I would have done if I caught it . . . or it had caught me. In later misadventures, I had experiences with numerous demonic forces and in my dotage I am very aware that our entire planet is occupied by things we see only by accident. They seem able to boggle our minds and even control our feeble little brains.

UFOmania is no different from demonomania. My forms of religious and political fanaticism are linked directly to these other manias and to paranoia and schizophrenia. We are meant to be crazy. It is an important part of the human condition. Otherwise there would be no wars, no Hitlers or Napoleons, no Woodrow Derenbergers (and his unfortunate psychiatrist). This planet is haunted by us; the other occupants just evade boredom by filling our skies and seas with monsters. I was clearly meant to blunder into that little town in West Virginia, and learn things that some men have known for centuries but were afraid to ask. I warned Sheriff Johnson and Mary Hyre that this was folklore in the making. Gray Barker did try to turn it into a celestial fairy tale, making me decide to write this book and tell the truth as it happened. It has taken three decades for the whole story to get out and this would not have happened without the help of many, many devoted friends such as Knox Burger, the Maxwell Perkins of our era; Ivan T. Sanderson, the zoologist who helped guide me through those frightening days; Martin Singer; David Blakiston; Ronald Bonds; Richard Hatem; Coral Lorenzen and a virtual army of advisors, experts, editors, newspapermen and girlfriends who often got scared out of their wits. Hordes of plagiarists, comic book artists, sideshow lecturers, and mindless exploiters of the little-old-ladies-in-tennis-shoes set have all given it a shot. Now it is Hollywood's turn and they have managed to squeeze the basic truths into their film. Not an easy task. But the truth is always the most difficult thing to sell.

—John A. Keel
New York City
August 2001